MURDER ON THE ROCK

MURDER ON THE ROCK

TRUE CRIME IN NEWFOUNDLAND AND LABRADOR

ROBERT C. PARSONS

FLANKER PRESS LIMITED
ST. JOHN'S

Library and Archives Canada Cataloguing in Publication

Parsons, Robert Charles, 1944-, author
Murder on the Rock : true crime in Newfoundland and Labrador / Robert C. Parsons.

Includes index.
Issued in print and electronic formats.
ISBN 978-1-77117-401-5 (paperback).--ISBN 978-1-77117-402-2 (epub).--
ISBN 978-1-77117-403-9 (kindle).--ISBN 978-1-77117-404-6 (pdf)

1. Murder--Newfoundland and Labrador--History. 2. Crime--Newfoundland and Labrador--History. I. Title.

HV6535.C32N48585 2015 364.152'309718 C2015-903442-6
C2015-903443-4

PRINTED IN CANADA

MIX
Paper from responsible sources
FSC www.fsc.org FSC® C103567

This paper has been certified to meet the environmental and social standards of the Forest Stewardship Council® (FSC®) and comes from responsibly managed forests, and verified recycled sources.

Cover Design by Graham Blair

FLANKER PRESS LTD.
PO BOX 2522, STATION C
ST. JOHN'S, NL
CANADA

TELEPHONE: (709) 739-4477 FAX: (709) 739-4420 TOLL-FREE: 1-866-739-4420
WWW.FLANKERPRESS.COM

9 8 7 6 5 4 3 2 1

Canadä Canada Council for the Arts Conseil des Arts du Canada Newfoundland Labrador

We acknowledge the [financial] support of the Government of Canada. *Nous reconnaissons l'appui [financier] du gouvernement du Canada.* We acknowledge the support of the Canada Council for the Arts, which last year invested $153 million to bring the arts to Canadians throughout the country. *Nous remercions le Conseil des arts du Canada de son soutien. L'an dernier, le Conseil a investi 153 millions de dollars pour mettre de l'art dans la vie des Canadiennes et des Canadiens de tout le pays.* We acknowledge the financial support of the Government of Newfoundland and Labrador, Department of Tourism, Culture and Recreation for our publishing activities.

CONTENTS

INTRODUCTION

THERE'S AN OLD SAYING that crime doesn't pay. Former US president Ronald Reagan once stated, "One way to make sure crime doesn't pay would be to let the government run it." In countries and cultures past and present, crime, from petty theft to murder, is with us and the government has not decided—yet—to run it.

Despite harsher and longer sentences, crime flourishes and prisons are overcrowded. Why? According to expert analysts, most wrongdoers feel they won't get caught, so they do the deed. But most are caught.

To that end, good reader, I offer tales of Newfoundlanders and Labradorians who thought they would not be caught. *Murder on the Rock: True Crime in Newfoundland and Labrador* has fifty-nine short takes of unusual events from the shady side of life. Locales vary, as do the timelines, eras, years, and dates of the curious or tragic events.

Again, as in *Courting Disaster* (Flanker Press, 2008), I have not arranged the tales by category or by type of unlawful activity, nor geographically or chronologically. Rather, the chapters are arranged to length. That is, longer accounts are usually followed by shorter ones, all done arbitrarily as to the way I, personally, would like to read a book such as this.

One common element shows: the sea. In the background of most events covered in *Murder on the Rock*, the Atlantic Ocean predominates. The sea governed our ancestors' travel, economy, livelihood, social life, food, and supplies. It determined where towns and villages were situated and where our people settled. Thus, most stories in this work are of, near, or by the ocean surrounding Newfoundland, the dominion's official title a generation or two ago.

The accounts presented here of seedy characters and dark, illegal, or mysterious events are true. However, all are subject to the vagaries of human memory and the fallibility of newspaper reporting. Wherever possible, I tried to verify or support the crime with facts; thus, accounts from archival newspapers and magazines were cross-referenced with verbal information, family anecdotal stories, and court records where the latter existed or if they could be located. In stories where a full identity would reveal sensitive material, I have omitted the last name, using **** to replace it.

Certain individuals and families helped me with background information. I am grateful for the assistance, but due to the sensitive nature of some stories, I would prefer to keep those sources anonymous. The staff at various libraries usually found what I wanted or steered me in the right direction. Specifically they are the Newfoundland Reference Section at the A.C. Hunter Library and three venues at Memorial University: the Queen Elizabeth II Library; the Maritime History Archives; and the Centre for Newfoundland Studies (CNS). As well, I would like to thank Allan Stoodley of Grand Bank for the use of the cover image, which came from a photograph taken by his father and photographer, Robert W. Stoodley, Grand Bank.

The Internet makes long-distance correspondence quicker and simpler and provides ready access to specific sources of information. Recently, Memorial University has put several archival papers online and this helped speed up my research of certain stories. My homemade simplified dictionary of crime terms and legal terms in the back of this book is an example of this, as adapted from http://dictionary.reference.com.

If any errors appear in the information given—the spelling of names, identities, misrepresentation or misinterpretation of events, or in the citing of sources—please notify me, and efforts to correct them will be made in any subsequent editions or reprints.

Well, that's it. Lets you and I take a walk down a shady lane in Newfoundland or Labrador. No! Wait! You go alone.

Preserving Newfoundland and Labrador's Maritime History, One Tale at a Time

THE TROUBLE A CONCERTINA BRINGS!

OLD PERLICAN, THE LABRADOR COAST

OLD PERLICAN, ONE OF the oldest fishing communities in Newfoundland, served as the major fishing station in Trinity Bay for the migratory English fishermen in the 1600s. It was chosen by Poole merchants because of its proximity to prime fishing grounds. The emerging town had a Justice of the Peace as far back as 1729. The census from 1874 shows a population of nearly 1,000 people, enough to warrant a magistrate, a policeman, a doctor, and a blacksmith, all who served the communities on the south side of Trinity Bay, too. Today, Old Perlican has a population of about 700-800.

In the spring of 1880, another salt fish company began business there. Moses Bursey of Old Perlican had heard of young men making a few dollars on the Labrador with this new enterprise. Moses related in his memoir (as written in 1930), "I decided to look for a chance."

He had to walk fifteen miles to the home of his potential employer, but it was his lucky day. Moses said to the owner, "I hear you want to ship a crew of men and boys for the summer." "Well," said the man, "I have enough boys, but I'll see what the Labrador boss has to say."

After a short conversation, the deal was made and Moses would be hired from May until October 31 for the sum of £16. It was good money. Moses was glad to accept and signed the shipping papers right away.

On May 10, he, along with twelve men and five women cooks, left for Labrador. The voyage north as tedious, but they finally arrived. There was much to do before the fishing voyages were to commence. Soon all were working willingly and, before long, the little cove was looking like a seaport.

The crew of twelve took charge of twelve cod seines. Before long they had landed 1,000 quintals. This was salted away and it represented the cost or expenses of the expedition. Bursey says, "Next, work was to begin making our voyage [wages] and as we were all shipped men our skipper was determined to have everything cleared up. We would be home by October 20."

The skipper was not far off. By October 25, all were landed in St. John's and were paid off and each was sent on his way home. Bursey, who travelled to Old Perlican probably by train, was delighted:

> I was a happy boy! I never felt so rich, going home with £16 in my pocket after serving six months. And all mine! It was late in the evening when I reached Old Perlican. After taking a rest I went out to meet my chums.
>
> Now, while I was away, a friend of mine had presented, or sold, me a concertina and, being fond of music, I soon learned to play a few lively tunes.

In Old Perlican, however, it was a different tune, as Bursey says with tongue in cheek. "It was the first concertina ever seen in the town, and when I started up at one of our old tunes, which all the boys knew, it soon brought a crowd."

Someone suggested they all take a walk down the harbour, and this they did, singing and playing an old favourite and lively tune—a version of "John Brown's Body."

"John Brown's body lies a-mouldering in the grave
Glory, glory, hallelujah."

As they went down to the main part of Old Perlican a crowd soon gathered, some with tin pans, some with old kettles. "No doubt," Bursey recalls, "as we went through the harbour some of the people did not know what was coming to pass."

After marching down about the centre of the harbour they stopped and Bursey left for home. Everyone else went his own way as well. Unknown to the young lad, this was the first band that ever played in the place and the first public demonstration ever witnessed. Moses Bursey, being innocent of making any trouble, went home and went to bed.

The next day, about eleven o'clock, a knock came to Bursey's door and "I was told that a policeman wanted to see me." Although the policeman apologized for the bad news, he told young Moses "he was in for it."

Handed a piece of paper, Moses read it over to see that it was a summons stating that he had to appear before the court the next day at eleven o'clock. The charge was "marching through the harbour and being the ringleader of a mob."

"I knew," says Bursey, "it meant no less than two or three years in the penitentiary. I almost fainted, as I knew I had to suffer, being in the hands of law."

> The next day I was present to give my evidence and stand for my trial. There never was such a large crowd attending a case in Old Perlican before. I was called up and told my story.
>
> Several of my witnesses were called up, but instead of speaking in my favour they all went against me. Also, my own evidence went against me.
>
> After the whole evidence was summed up and read out, I was found guilty of collecting a crowd and being a ringleader. I was sentenced to serve a long term in the Harbour Grace penitentiary or to pay a large sum of money.

Bursey realized all his hard-earned wages for a summer's work would evaporate if he paid the fine. Perhaps even his wages wouldn't cover it, so he chose to serve his time and stated to the court he would go to jail.

The lad was carried down to the magistrate's office to await the arrival of a conveyance to take him to the local jail, in time to be taken by vessel to Harbour Grace. During the wait, several of his friends arrived and offered to sign their hands, or pledge, to pay the money. No one had intended for him, they said, to go to prison for such a long while over such a trifle. One of the group of men was Moses Bursey's uncle. Moses recalled:

> I said to my uncle and others that if I broke the law I would go to jail and serve the time. But I said, sir, I have to go to jail innocent. The tears rolled down my cheeks.
>
> One of my friends spoke up and said, "If this boy goes to jail it will cause more trouble in Old Perlican than was ever known here before." The law said they all had to go home and leave me. I stood there, with the old magistrate and the policeman with the

driver to take me to jail, waiting for my little package of clothing to arrive.

Moses said it was the most solemn time of his life. Everything was silent. After a while the magistrate spoke with tears trickling down his cheeks. He said, "Officer, send home the driver. He can't go. I have known this boy for many years. This is his first offence and I have never heard anything bad about him. I will chastise him and let him go."

The magistrate then offered some advice: Go home and be a good boy. Keep off the streets after night. Revere your superiors. Be honest.

"He then presented me with a bundle of books to read in the winter," recalled Bursey. "He wished me goodbye and told me to go home and take his advice. I have listened to lots of sermons since that time, but never a one took such an effect as the one I got from the dear old magistrate of about fifty years ago."

Bursey concluded his memoir, saying he still had the bundle of books, which he prized more than silver or gold. The story reminded him of his many dear old friends who had passed on, and Bursey quoted the words of a poet:

"Our life is as a dream. Our time, like a dream, passes swiftly away."

THE PAINTER WHO WISHED TO BE A FORGER

HEART'S CONTENT, ST. JOHN'S

ON JUNE 17, 1880, the Newfoundland newspaper the *Carbonear Herald* reported on the conviction of Alexander Pindikowsky, a young artist and fresco painter originally from Poland. He had been sentenced two days previously to fifteen months at Her Majesty's Penitentiary, St. John's.

In addition to his prison term, during his sentencing Pindikowsky was also ordered to leave the country of Newfoundland within five days of his release. If he defaulted on this or if he returned to the country at any time, he was to receive further imprisonment of two years.

Pindikowsky arrived in Newfoundland the year before as a professional artist and fresco painter. He had been hired by the Anglo-American Telegraph Company (AAT installed the first successful transatlantic telegraph cable between Ireland and Newfoundland) to give art instructions to interested employees and their wives at the Heart's Content Cable Office.

On March 10, 1880, not long after his arrival in Newfoundland, he was arrested and charged with attempting to forge two cheques signed with the name of Ezra Weedon, the chief of staff of the AAT Company in Heart's Content. Pindikowsky had apparently run short of money while visiting some drinking establishments or other places of dubious distinction.

Mr. Cooke, the clerk at the Commercial Bank, became suspicious of a £232 cheque and called Police Inspector Carty, who sent Sergeant Sullivan to arrest Pindikowsky. He appeared before Supreme Court in May 1880 and was duly sentenced.

Once he began serving his time, the Polish artist's talents as a fresco painter were brought to the attention of the authorities at the penitentiary and his skills were soon put to official use. In return the young man would get a reduction of five weeks on his sentence. He was set to work designing and painting frescoes to relieve the drabness of the staterooms of Government House.

Pindikowsky's artwork on the ceiling of the Colonial Building

Governor John Hawley Glover (1876-1885) was so delighted with the frescoes he suggested to Prime Minister William Whiteway that the prisoner Pindikowsky also decorate the ceilings of the two legislative chambers of the Colonial Building.

The Presentation Sisters at Cathedral Square in St. John's also saw an opportunity for some free design artwork. While in the process of redesigning their chapel and drawing room, they invited the young artist to display his talents there. Pindikowsky also painted several attractive murals on the interior walls of the Athenaeum, a public theatre with 1,000 seats. Unfortunately, this structure, along with the artist's work, was destroyed by the Great Fire of 1892.

Each day Pindikowsky was brought from the penitentiary to his place of work until the frescoes were complete. Outgoing and congenial as ever, Pindikowsky soon had many friends and acquaintances in St. John's, including government officials and socialites.

In time they succeeded in obtaining for Pindikowsky an early release from prison. Also freed from his sentence of banishment, the Polish artist set up a short-lived fresco painting business in St. John's. In November 1882, he filed for bankruptcy and left Newfoundland shortly after, never to return.

One local observer said that the artist's work for the government was one of the first documented cases of a successful prison rehabilitation venture in Newfoundland.

Advertising in local papers in late February-March 1882 for Pindikowsky's fresco painting and artwork

MANSLAUGHTER AT HORSE COVE

HORSE COVE, BROAD COVE

HORSE COVE—renamed St. Thomas in 1922—lies a few kilometres outside St. John's. At the end of the fishing season of 1883, several seamen were heading home from St. John's to Horse Cove and nearby Broad Cove. Before they reached there, at the intersection of Broad Cove Road and Portugal Cove Road, a vicious argument broke out which led to murder.

Levi King and George Squires, both of Broad Cove, and Michael Whelan, of Horse Cove, were fishing with Captain Joy in the Strait of Belle Isle in the fall of 1883. When the season ended and the vessel landed in St. John's on Saturday, October 6, all three made their way home from St. John's. Michael Whelan's people were among the first settlers of Horse Cove, a community now amalgamated with St. Thomas into the town of Paradise in 1992.

Squires travelled with Whelan and his wife in a cart. On the way, Whelan and Squires had a long and violent argument—what was described after as "a wordy battle." Squires jumped out and proceeded on foot. At the junction of Broad Cove and Portugal Cove roads he caught up with fellow fishermen Levi King, Stephen Squires, and Richard Tucker.

On Broad Cove Road, Whelan again began arguing with George Squires and Levi King, but there was no physical violence yet. Just before King reached his home, Whelan attempted to pull him from his cart but did not succeed. This incensed Whelan. King went into his house and embraced his wife. George Squires followed King and went into King's house for a friendly visit, perhaps a cup of tea before continuing his journey home.

Angry and frustrated, Whelan brought his own cart opposite King's gate and called out to King and Squires, taunting them to come out and saying he would fight either of them or both. King went out to the gate and exchanged blows with Whelan. Snatching up a hatchet handle from Whelan's cart, King struck him once with the stick.

King ran into his house with Whelan in pursuit. George Squires attempted to stop Whelan but couldn't. Whelan pulled a sharp object from somewhere on his person, stabbed King near the door, and slashed Squires. King staggered into his house, leaving a trail of blood along the hallway and on the floor.

King's wife followed him into their home and caught him as he staggered across the floor. He said to her, "I am gone. I am killed." He never spoke again, dying four or five minutes later in his wife's arms. Levi King had received two wounds, the fatal one in the lower part of the stomach. Both were made with a sharp instrument.

Squires was stabbed in the side with a similar object. He was rushed to a St. John's hospital, where he slowly recovered from his near-fatal wound.

At 10:30 p.m. Saturday, Police Inspector Paul Carty received news of the stabbing. Carty, a tireless and meticulous investigator, had been a member of the Royal Irish Constabulary. In 1873, he emigrated with his family to Newfoundland when Newfoundland's justice system asked him to come. He was then appointed Chief Inspector of the Newfoundland Constabulary. As soon as word of King's violent death came to his office, he and constables Alfred Rees, Squires, Noseworthy, and Murray travelled along Topsail Road for Horse Cove.

When they arrived at Whelan's house, Carty knocked on the door and asked Mrs. Whelan for admittance but was refused. The door was forced and the accused was found in bed. He was arrested. Carty searched for the murder weapon and found a jackknife with blood on it. One of Carty's police escorted Michael Whelan back to St. John's for incarceration.

After Inspector Carty left for Horse Cove, Judge Daniel Woodley Prowse, accompanied by Head Constable Sullivan, left for Broad Cove to examine the area of the assault and to take statements of the wounded Mr. Squires and the victim's wife, Mrs. King.

When Prowse arrived at Levi King's house, he found that King had already succumbed to his injuries. He immediately proceeded to the house of Richard Squires, the father of the wounded man. Doctors Shea and Howley came from St. John's, examined Squires's wounds, and held a post-mortem examination of the deceased man.

On November 21, a grand jury of eighteen men met in St. John's under the direction of Chief Justice Sir Frederick B. T. Carter to determine if there was enough evidence to try Michael Whelan for homicide. If so, he would be tried for either murder—planned and with malice—or manslaughter. The latter, a less serious crime, is committed without forethought and is considered a crime of passion.

Grand Jury for the Trial of Michael Whelan

Edwin B. McDougall	James Murray, foreman
Thomas H. Walters	James Baird
James Whelan	Thomas Grant
Richard Hillery	Alex Parsons
Dennis Golway	Alex F. Shirran
Michael Lynch	Aubin Pierce
Robert L. Sclater	William Cambell
John Lindberg	Levi Garland
James Goodfellow	Michael Tobin

After instructions and guidance on the nature of the Broad Cove murder, the jury returned in a short while and determined Whelan would be tried for homicide. The Supreme Court trial began on the morning of November 28, 1883. Chief Justice Carter, assisted by Justice Robert John Pinsent and Justice Joseph I. Little, presided for the Crown. Lawyer Robert John Kent defended the accused, Whelan. The jury was selected from a pool of twenty-seven St. John's men (above).

By November 30, the trial ended and the jury deliberated for an hour and fifteen minutes, finding Whelan guilty of "manslaughter, without mercy" and sentencing him to life with hard labour in the St. John's Penitentiary.

THE DISAPPEARANCE OF THE HORSE COVE KILLER

ST. THOMAS, ST. JOHN'S, PLACENTIA

EXACTLY WHERE HE WENT and how he slipped into oblivion became one of Newfoundland's unsolved mysteries. Michael Whelan (in the preceding story) escaped from the penitentiary almost exactly four years after he was lawfully confined. Despite an intensive manhunt and a large reward offered for his capture or information leading to his apprehension, Whelan was never caught. Nor did anyone figure out how he left the island, if indeed he did.

It was a mystery that persisted for more than twenty years, until the story finally faded into obscurity. A fisherman from Horse Cove, Whelan was charged with the wilful murder of Levi King of Broad Cove and was tried in late November 1883. On a verdict of "manslaughter, without mercy," he was sentenced to a life of hard labour in Her Majesty's Penitentiary, St. John's—the "Pen."

Whelan had pleaded not guilty and fully believed he was meant to live a life outside of prison walls. Thus, he planned his escape. As a reward for good behaviour he was allowed to join a work contingent outside the Pen. He and six other prisoners left to work on a ditch being dug from the General Hospital on Forest Road to Quidi Vidi Lake. On that morning, November 25, 1887, two prison officials went with them.

Around 8:00 a.m. he asked if he could step aside for a moment to "use the bathroom" in the great outdoors. He was permitted, but at that moment the two warders were drawn to break up a fight between other prisoners. When Whelan saw this, he made the dash for freedom.

He was a tall, strong man, described by the media of the day as "a stalwart typical Newfoundland fisherman" and also a fast runner. Whelan followed the margin of the lake toward the eastern end and the village of Quidi Vidi.

One of the officer wardens gave chase and, as he was armed, could have fired at him, but didn't for fear of injuring or killing another person. He kept up the pursuit, but Whelan outdistanced him and disappeared over the White Hills. That was the last any official lawmaker ever saw of the convict.

Inspector General John Roche McCowen, an Irish-born policeman and then governor of the penitentiary, immediately sent other prison wardens to search for the fugitive. The superintendent of the Constabulary dispatched two mounted police officers. No doubt had they foreseen Whelan would be so illusive, a more sizable posse would have been sent out. Whelan was nowhere to be seen.

The next day, Maurice Fenelon, Newfoundland's Colonial Secretary, put notices in the local papers and also posted them about St. John's, offering a $200 reward for information leading to Whelan's whereabouts. Police kept a surveillance on his home and questioned his friends and neighbours, but to no avail.

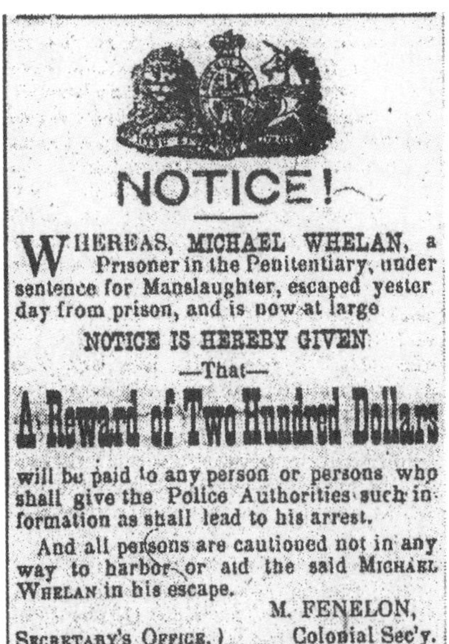

NOTICE!

WHEREAS, MICHAEL WHELAN, a Prisoner in the Penitentiary, under sentence for Manslaughter, escaped yester day from prison, and is now at large

NOTICE IS HEREBY GIVEN

—That—

A Reward of Two Hundred Dollars

will be paid to any person or persons who shall give the Police Authorities such information as shall lead to his arrest.

And all persons are cautioned not in any way to harbor or aid the said MICHAEL WHELAN in his escape.

M. FENELON, Colonial Sec'y.

SECRETARY'S OFFICE, Nov. 26th, 1887.

The notice which appeared publicly asking for information of the escapee Michael Whelan. Despite a $200 reward and an intense search by lawmen, Whelan was never found.

In its day it was quite a reward, but it failed to produce the desired outcome. An intensive manhunt with full police resources followed, but Whelan had melted away.

It was a planned escape, as determined by an inquiry set up to investigate the prisoner's actions. A prison guard stated he should have known something was up because Whelan had taken his rosary beads with him on a ditch-digging job. According to a short piece on the "enigma of Whelan's whereabouts" issued by archivists at The Rooms

Provincial Archives, usually he went to work sites without his beads, leaving them hanging in his prison cell.

Nevertheless, rumours flew. Whelan was last seen, it was said, on the first day of his escape on King's Bridge Road near Honourable John Harvey's residence, heading toward the St. John's waterfront, presumably. Some said he drowned trying to swim across the harbour. Others speculated he travelled to Placentia (where he had relatives and friends), joined an American fishing banker, and found a working passage to America.

The most substantial and frequent rumours put Michael Whelan in the "Boston States," somewhere in Massachusetts. It is known his wife left Newfoundland some years after and immigrated to Boston, lending credence to the belief Whelan was alive and well. Even up to 1906, twenty years after his escape—according to the *Evening Telegram* of November 27 that year—Michael, his wife, and children were still living in the USA.

Fuel for that story came after a native of St. John's was arrested in Boston by local detectives. That man was mistaken for Whelan. The strongest clue the police followed was that the arrested one had a finger missing on one hand; Whelan also had a finger missing. That man was freed after it was conclusively proven detectives had caught the wrong man.

Michael Whelan made good on his own belief that he should never be found guilty—he slipped into obscurity, freed from confinement. The final chapter of his life is still debated to this day.

THE FIRST TRAIN FATALITIES

SALMON COVE (AVONDALE), CONCEPTION HARBOUR, HARBOUR GRACE

CONSTRUCTION AND MOVEMENT of trains on Newfoundland's railway line began in 1881. The first short run of a locomotive on the island went from St. John's to Donovans in January 1882. By that summer there were regular excursions across the Avalon Peninsula, and by the fall the line had reached Holyrood. Each year thereafter, the Newfoundland Railway Company constructed the line across Newfoundland until it reached the western terminus, Port aux Basques, in 1893.

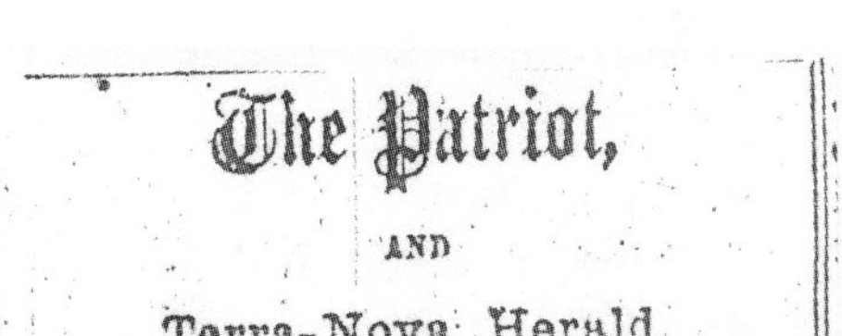

The Patriot,

AND

Terra-Nova Herald.

Be just and fear not. Let all the ends thou aim'st at be thy God's, thy Country's and Truths.

ST. JOHN'S, MONDAY, DECEMBER 5, 1881.

ARRIVAL OF THE FIRST IRON HORSE!

The Ss. *Merlin* arrived to-day with a LOCOMOTIVE and other materials for the RAILWAY!!!

Carmen are keeping the roads lively

The St. John's paper *Patriot and Terra-Nova Herald* announces the arrival of the first "iron horse," saying "The SS *Merlin* arrived today (December 5, 1881) with a locomotive and other materials for the RAILWAY!! . . ."

The first railway fatality occurred between Lance Cove and Upper Gullies on July 17, 1882, when Mrs. Ryan, a widow woman from Colliers, asked if she could hitch a ride on a flatcar with labourers returning to St. John's. Her request was denied, but she attempted to board the moving train anyway. She was killed as she lost her footing, slipped, and fell between two cars.

Some independent witnesses testified in a brief investigation, but no one could be pinpointed as responsible. One of the labourers, in his efforts to reach the woman to save her, almost shared her fate.

Some anti-government critics commented that the Newfoundland Railway Company didn't mind putting "jokes" in the newspaper of the killing of cats on the railway line or crushing hardtack on the track. It was amusing to report on the iron horse's steam whistle scaring flesh-and-blood Torbay horses. But the Company didn't comment on or publicly chastise reckless foreign engineers and employees, nor did they offer an excuse or an apology for negligent deaths on the track.

As the railway progressed on the Avalon, handcars, or muscle-propelled "pump" cars—railway trolleys—became a common sight as they carried materials and workmen along the line.

Early in 1887, the first life-threatening incident centring around a hand carriage happened five miles from Brigus Junction. Two men, William Burke and William James, both of Brigus, placed an obstruction—a log or stick—on the track. Before the regular train roared through, four railway men on a trolley travelled along the line at a rapid rate. The carriage struck the obstacle and the men were thrown into a ditch; two received serious injuries.

On January 27, the two Brigus men appeared before Judge Conroy in St. John's. The case against them was clearly proven and Conroy sentenced them to three months hard labour in the St. John's penitentiary. The judge, in passing sentence, spoke strongly against this type of crime, saying it was a serious matter that could have resulted in death and a much more severe sentence.

With the trolleys becoming more commonplace, it was probably inevitable that a trolley and a locomotive would collide sometime, somewhere in Newfoundland.

That first collision between the train and trolley happened eleven months after the "Brigus" incident. On December 5, 1887, two young people were killed on a trolley car not far from Harbour Grace. The line to that Conception Bay town had been completed two years previously.

Two men, Frank Haley and his helper, a Mr. Martin, both employees of the Newfoundland Railway Company, were propelling the handcar. Also aboard were two "passengers"—a young man, William Kennedy, and a girl, Mary Connors. The machine was going down the north slope of Cat Hill, somewhere between Harbour Grace and Salmon Cove (today's Avondale), at a speed estimated to be about fifteen miles per hour.

Suddenly, around a curve, Haley and Martin saw a train coming toward them. They jumped off with little difficulty and no injury. However, Kennedy and Connors, who were on the back of the trolley, either did not see or hear the train or, presumably, hear any warning shouts by the two men.

A hand-propelled push trolley on the Newfoundland line with a work section crew in 1905. A passenger sits on the back as Kennedy and Connors did a few years previously. Photo courtesy *The Book of Newfoundland Volume III*.

Going at a speed estimated at twenty-two miles per hour, the locomotive hit the trolley, sending the young man and the girl and the trolley several feet in the air. The trolley was smashed to splinters and the two passengers struck the ground. Both received traumatic injuries to their heads.

When they were picked up, both were unconscious and were hastily carried to a Mr. Kelley's house in Salmon Cove. Dr. Fitzsimmons from Harbour Main arrived and advised the railwaymen to rush the two to St. John's, yet the men waited until 6:00 p.m., three hours after the accident, for a Dr. Duncan of Brigus and Father O'Donnell to arrive and attend to the victims. Shortly after, they were brought on to St. John's.

Kennedy, of Salmon Cove and aged nineteen, died before he reached St. John's. Mary Connors lived to reach the St. John's Hospital but died from her injuries the next morning. The sixteen-year-old belonged to Conception Harbour.

The next day, a magisterial enquiry opened before Judge D. W. Prowse. Mr. E. H. Saville, manager of the railway, gave a lengthy statement, as did the engine driver, Thomas Brien. However, in the end no charges of manslaughter or criminal negligence were laid.

Yet the rules of the line clearly stated, "No section men are allowed to carry outsiders on the trolleys." As well, all trolleys were to be kept off the track unless work was being done on the rail line. At the enquiry it was stated that Haley had distinctly disobeyed orders on both counts. The railway company, through Saville's assertion, absolved themselves and also cleared the employees of any blame.

NEGLIGENCE OR ACCIDENT? NEWFOUNDLAND'S WORST TRAIN WRECK

BENTON, CARBONEAR, POUND COVE, KINGWELL, NEW CHELSEA, AND OTHERS

IN THE EARLY MORNING of February 5, 1917, a news flash of a train disaster with fatalities came in to St. John's telegraph operators. Details were scanty, but it was known there was more than one fatality and several people had been injured. It happened between Benton and Glenwood when a section of a six-car passenger train left the track while westbound. A trickle of information seemed to indicate only four deaths at first as some bodies were readily identified. Later, the names of four more victims were released. It became known as the worst train accident in the short history of the Newfoundland railway.

THE WRECK

The Reid Newfoundland Company's No. 1 Express, pulled by Engine No. 115 with driver Arnold Webber, left Clarenville on Sunday. Conductor Lush, as was the custom or general rule, had charge of the rest of the train. At 3:30 a.m., the tender or coal/wood car, the baggage car, and the second-class car left the track ten miles east of Glenwood, near Benton at a place called Kennedy's Cut, or "Walls Grade." At the time the town of Gander, now situated between these two points, did not exist.

Derailed cars went down over a steep embankment. The engine and two or three cars at the rear stayed on the track.

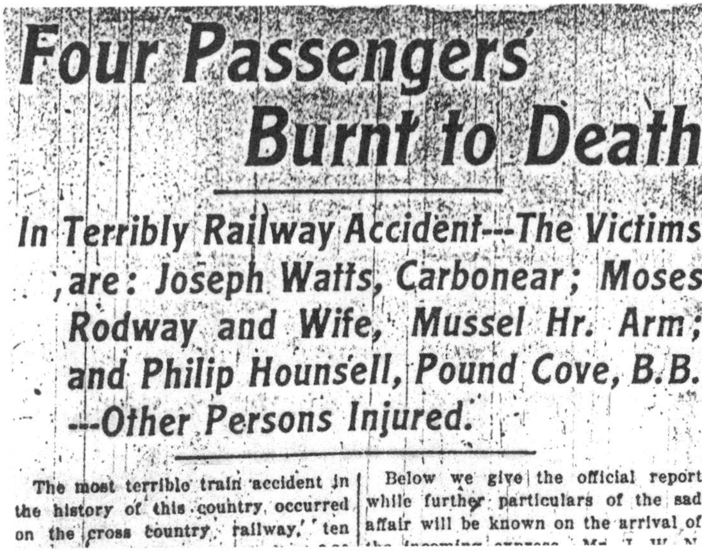

Four Passengers Burnt to Death

In Terribly Railway Accident---The Victims are: Joseph Watts, Carbonear; Moses Rodway and Wife, Mussel Hr. Arm; and Philip Hounsell, Pound Cove, B.B. ---Other Persons Injured.

The most terrible train accident in the history of this country occurred on the cross country railway, ten

Below we give the official report while further particulars of the sad affair will be known on the arrival of

Leading news of February 5, 1917, was Newfoundland's worst train disaster, in which eight people died. For several days only the names of four victims were known and published. Another four were burnt beyond recognition.

The second-class car tumbled down the incline, caught fire, and was completely destroyed. The majority of passengers were in this car sleeping when it hurtled from the track and burst into flames. Trapped inside, several people could not be rescued and met their deaths. The names of four were made public almost immediately: Joseph Watts, Carbonear; Philip Hounsell, Pound Cove, near Wesleyville; and Moses Rodway and his wife, Mildred.

The latter two belonged to Mussel Harbour, located at the north end of Long Island, Placentia Bay. In later years, the north side of Mussel Harbour Arm was exclusively a Church of England community (later renamed Kingwell), while Mussel Harbour Arm South was Roman Catholic and came to be known as Port Royal.

The tragic tale of the Rodways is recounted on the website "All Aboard: Exploring the Newfoundland Railway":

> Mildred (Coombs) and Moses Rodway, just married, were travelling through Newfoundland by train. The young couple was heading to Port aux Basques, where they intended to catch the ferry for their honeymoon in Nova Scotia.
>
> As was customary in those days, men and women, even married couples, slept in separate train cars. In the early morning hours, the

Rodways were in their berths when their happy journey took a tragic turn. Moses Rodway's car was unaffected by the blaze, but Mildred was not as fortunate. Aware of the danger, Moses rushed aboard the burning car to save his bride. Both died in this accident.

When his car toppled over, Mr. Rodway was the first to escape, intending to make the way clear for his wife to follow. However, the unfortunate woman had collapsed and did not hear the cries of her husband directing her to the only way of escape, which was through a window near the door.

Receiving no answer, he plunged into the flaming car and reached the side of his poor wife, never to return.

Surviving Passengers Aboard No. 1 Express, February 5, 1917

R. G. Reid, his wife and Miss Lois Reid
Dan Whelan, heading for Grand Falls
Thomas Downey (of Colinet), for Millertown Junction
James Russell, for North Sydney
William Russell, for North Sydney
Albert and Hubert Burden, for Boston
Douglas Nichol, for Boston
Thomas Howell, for Boston
Benjamin Basha (of Bell Island), for Curling
Mrs. George, for Grand Falls
Francis Newell, for Sydney
Edward Button, for Curling
John Harris, for Niagara Falls
James Noseworthy, for Sydney
George G. Spracklin, for Lewisporte
Joseph A. Young (of Twillingate), for Lewisporte
Eugene Wells, for Curling
Levi Davis, for Badger
J. C. Cashin, for Grand Falls
William F. Horwood (of St. John's), for Lewisporte
Miss Lindsay, for Lewisporte
G. Halls, for Glasgow
G. H. Phillips, for Grand Falls
Dr. Jones, for New York
Mrs. M. Bailey, for Everett, MA
W. S. Todd, for Durham, England
J. C. Sapp, for New York
W. Ackliss, for Durham, England
S. C. Mifflin, for St. George's
W. Baird, for Lewisporte

When their remains were recovered, they were found lying close to each other. Their bodies were brought to Placentia Junction to be shipped to Mussel Harbour.

On February 6, two survivors arrived in St. John's: John Harris and Edward (or Elihu) Button of New Chelsea, Trinity Bay. Local papers were anxious for news of the wreck and both men obliged and gave their versions, although they did not know the names of four others who were known to have died.

Harris, the last one to be rescued, said there were thirty-five people in the second-class car, commonly called the Colonist. When the car rolled, the lamps exploded, flames filled the air, and in a second most passengers' clothes were afire as the coach tumbled down the embankment. The scenes of horror were too graphic for Harris to describe fully, although he said some of the passengers were women who, when they recovered from the shock of what had happened, rendered what assistance they could to the injured. One poor fellow lost a roll of money amounting to about $400, which he had beneath his pillow.

Also aboard was Robert Gillespie Reid Jr., the son of the man who financed, built, and managed the railway. Robert, now manager and vice-president of the Company, was with his wife and his daughter, Lois. En route to mainland Canada, they were in the first-class car. Mr. Reid, said Harris, did everything possible to rescue and care for the unfortunate passengers. Fortunately for the severely injured, Dr. Jones of Avondale was aboard as he was en route to New York.

The two mail clerks, William Thistle and Leonard Knight, were in the mail car, which was immediately behind the Colonist car. As was their custom on leaving Gambo, which was forty miles east of Glenwood, mail clerk Thistle lay down for a few hours' rest while the other man kept watch.

Knight was standing watch at the time of the accident and sorting his mail in preparation for Glenwood, the next station. He then extinguished one of the kerosene lamps and turned the other one down low. The turning down of the lamps saved the lives of both men in the baggage mail car. When it was thrown from the track, the lit lamp went out, but oil from both was sprayed all over the car and mail and saturated their clothing.

Knight and Thistle were thrown across the bags of mail, which saved them from receiving severe injury. After extricating themselves from beneath the mail, they grabbed the loose registered letters and climbed out through the top of the car, which was badly broken up. Both were slightly injured but continued the journey to Port aux Basques late Monday evening.

A plea for information from the general public hastened the identification of the remaining four. Learning just who they were was delayed as the bodies had been burned beyond identification.

It was not until February 10, five days after the wreck, that the names of the four were published through the media: Thomas Stapleton, aged seventy, St. John's; John Jacobson, living in St. John's but believed to be from Norway; Ambrose Rodgers and Simon Rodgers were from St. Jones Within, Trinity Bay.

The Reid Newfoundland Railway Company said nothing publicly about the cause. The railway men, in hushed voices, figured among themselves that the coupling, or joining mechanism, connecting the tender to the engine snapped at a time when the train gave a heavy jolt. Without the weight of the locomotive to keep them stable, the tender and the two foremost cars—the baggage car and the second-class car—were forced over the side of the track. But nothing was official until an inquiry to the wreck was convened.

THE INQUIRY

On February 14, 1917, Mr. Francis J. Morris, King's Counsel, presided over the official inquiry into the wreck and fatalities on No. 1 Express. For the Crown were Government Engineer Thomas Henry Hall and Deputy Minister of Justice Charles Henry Hutchings. Lawyer William John Higgins represented the Reid Newfoundland Company.

Conductor Lush, the first to take the stand, explained the makeup of the train when it left St. John's, then reached Clarenville, and what he felt or noticed when the train stopped near Benton.

When asked about the burning second-class car, Lush said he and the baggage man kicked the door open on the east end while the brakeman went to the west end to do the same thing there.

As soon as Lush had the door breached, passengers streamed out for three or four minutes, then all was quiet. He knew whoever was left inside had suffocated with smoke or had burned to death. He discovered, through the course of the day, eight passengers had died and two were injured, but none of the train personnel were hurt.

He stayed at the site until 5:00 p.m. Monday, when railway workers had repaired the rail. He, with other trainmen, took the three cars that were intact to Bishop's Falls and the train continued on to Port aux Basques, its original destination.

Regarding the cause of the fire, Lush stated that in the second-class car there were three lamps with two branches each, making six lamps in all, and three of those were lit when the accident happened. It was not possible for the surviving passengers to have gotten out in any other way except through the door at the east end. Lush thought the windows would open sufficiently for people to squeeze through, but they were double windows with a wooden screen.

After two and a half days of testimony during which time he was cross-examined by Hall and Higgins, Lush stepped down and Engine Driver Arnold Webber took the stand.

Webber said that, as a driver, he kept a close look out for the condition of the rail and roadbed, stating that in the section where the accident occurred the road was very good, but in some places a little rough. He continued (in summary):

> My attention was attracted by the tender going off the track. I felt the jolt and looked behind. As I looked I saw the tender was jumping and going off the track to the left. The others, as far as I could see, were all on the track. I immediately put on my emergency brake, reversed my engine, and brought it to a standstill. I walked back and saw the other cars over the bank. . . .
>
> . . . I found the baggage car off the track on its side; the second-class car off the track and on its side and the diner partly on her side and partly off the track. The second-class car was all on fire. What passengers that could get out were out before I got there. . . .
>
> I believe that particular part of the road near Benton is as good as we can get it for this time of the year, but I have no idea how it is the tender went off the track. . . . I have nothing to do with the passenger cars. I know they are heated by steam and lit by kerosene lamps. . . .

Upon cross-examination by Engineer Hall, Webber said that night the weather was clear, the moon was full, and there was not enough frost to affect the condition of the track. "At the time of the accident he was running about ten to twelve miles an hour. . . . The tender was fastened to the baggage car by a patent coupler and not a link and pin. . . . I examined the track and found a broken rail just ahead of where the tender left the track. I did not come to a conclusion as to whether the rail was broken before or after the accident.

"The dogs, or the large logs for fire," he said, "are carried in back of the tender and would not have fallen off until the tender turned over. I never saw or heard that there was anything found on the track that would cause the derailment. . . . I am perfectly satisfied I did not put on the emergency brake before the tender came off the track."

During cross-examination by lawyer Higgins, Driver Webber stated he believed that the motive (forward force) of the rear cars would probably not have forced the other cars off the track. When he came back to the rear after the accident, he noticed the rail, which was broken, was spread apart some three or four feet.

In his opinion the baggage car, second-class car, and diner all went out through this gap.

In the evening of February 16, the magisterial inquiry ended with the evidence of Alexander Graham, road master, whose duty was to keep the rail and bed in good condition and to repair and get derailed cars back on track. He was stationed at Bishop's Falls and, when he heard of the accident, went to the scene with a wrecking crew. Graham stated he was sure the rail was broken when the first truck (wheel) of the tender left the track. However, he said, broken rails were not very common in the winter.

When asked by Mr. Hall, Graham stated the train wheels were good and practically new. The grade and elevation of the track near Benton was correct and, from the position of the cars, the train was not running too fast. Finally, he stated, he formed his examinations without consultation or suggestion from anyone, and in his opinion the accident was due to a broken rail.

With the witness of other trainmen employed by the Reid Newfoundland Company, the statements of employees wound down. Two were on the train that night: Fireman Berishel Strong of Clarenville and Mail Clerk William Thistle. Engineer Alfred Hartery and Edward P. Hughes, in charge of the air brake department, and two of Reid's road masters, Thomas P. Conners and Daniel Ferguson, ended that part of the inquiry.

WHAT THE PASSENGERS SAID

George G. Spracklin, a teacher at Lewisporte, took the stand on February 20. After reviewing events leading up to 3:00 a.m. Monday morning, he stated he saw burning oil from the lamps running down the roof of his overturned car. In his car there were bunks that could be pulled down or opened for sleeping. One of the top bunks, with a man lying asleep in it, had closed up when the car tipped over.

Typical train wreck similar to the derailment of February 1917 in which several passenger cars flipped over, causing the deaths of eight Newfoundlanders. Photo courtesy of Maritime History Archives, MUN.

Spracklin was told after that this man, a Norwegian, was trapped in the bunk and perished in the smoke and flames. Upon cross-examination by Higgins, passenger Spracklin said the fire started from oil in the burning lamps. The varnish on the walls would have helped spread the fire.

Joseph A. Young from Twillingate testified (after explaining where he was sitting and the recollections of the train leaving the track) that the smoke inside the car was very dense.

When the car went on its side, he grabbed his two coats and hat. Some passengers said they couldn't get out the west end. Young worked his way to the other end, stepping on the bars of the windows holding onto the seats. He reached the east door in the smoke just as a shutter fell, reducing the hole he had to squeeze through. He put his clothes out first and crawled out. All the sleepers on the left side were shut in a locked position when the train went over. Young knew people were in them.

Passenger Ben Basha, of Bell Island and travelling to Curling, stated he was in a top fold-up bunk in the rear of the car. When the car tumbled, he fell onto the berth on the other side, which had closed up. His arm got caught in the closing-up and, worse, he said, burning oil from the lamp got on his sleeve. A man came along and tried to put out the fire with a coat. The man told Basha to get out, but Basha told him he couldn't as his arm was caught. Someone pulled the fixture down and freed the trapped passenger.

He heard someone breaking glass in the easternmost door and crawled out. He survived the cold and trauma of the next day without his two coats, cap, and boots. About noon, someone loaned him a coat and cap.

On February 23, Elihu (also identified as Edward) Button testified he was a travelling sales agent who had been on the second-class car that night. He described how he realized someone had broken the glass in the door and he was the second man out. He saw Philip Hounsell in his last minutes alive as Hounsell's clothes were all afire. He saw five bodies in the west end of the car all piled up.

Responding to King's Counsel Morris, Button said that in his opinion, if it had not been for the lamps catching the car on fire, all would have gotten out without serious injury.

William Frederick Horwood, a lumberman who was born in Carbonear but lived in St. John's, described under oath the conditions leading up to the derailment. The sleeper car he was in did not go completely off the track. He looked out the window and saw the second-class car afire. Horwood's knee was injured and he could not help in rescue. The second-class car was completely ablaze by the time he walked up to it.

He did organize passengers in an attempt to push the private car and sleeper back on the track. When that effort proved unsuccessful, he convinced a group it would be to their advantage to save the diner car from the fire. This they did with snow and buckets of water. Upon cross-examination, Horwood said he did not think the speed of the train prior to the wreck was excessive.

Detective John Byrne, who gave witness next, described the condition of the track when he arrived with Mr. Hall at eleven o'clock the next day. Byrne was followed by Mail Clerk Leonard Knight. Knight explained how he and Thistle saved the mail from fire. The month of February concluded with the statements of Samuel Gough, the Reid Company blacksmith and car repairer, Section Foreman Samuel Pardy, and finally a Mr. Davis, who had officially examined the condition of the track.

FINDINGS, IN CONCLUSION

On June 13, 1917, the inquiry finished up its investigation. The recommendations for greater safety in the passenger cars and of the track itself were not available in the *Evening Telegram*. Families of the victims sought no compensation, nor did they pursue a civil lawsuit. No criminal charges were laid against the owner-operators of the railway system, indicating perhaps the powerful influence of the Reid conglomerate in keeping reports of the catastrophe in low profile.

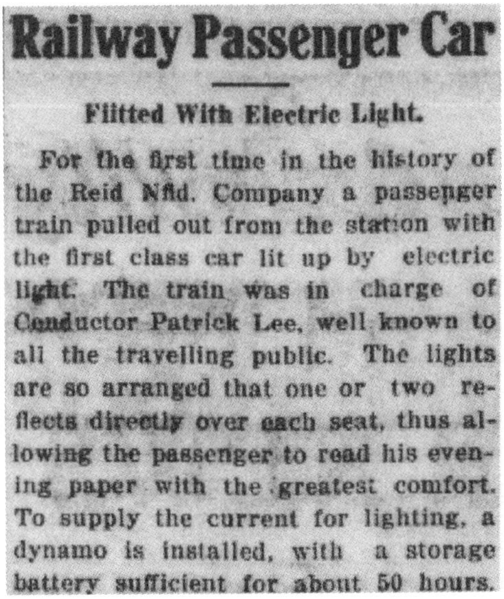

Railway Passenger Car

Fiitted With Electric Light.

For the first time in the history of the Reid Nfld. Company a passenger train pulled out from the station with the first class car lit up by electric light. The train was in charge of Conductor Patrick Lee, well known to all the travelling public. The lights are so arranged that one or two reflects directly over each seat, thus allowing the passenger to read his evening paper with the greatest comfort. To supply the current for lighting, a dynamo is installed, with a storage battery sufficient for about 50 hours.

Eight months after a tragic train wreck, the *Evening Telegram* of October 12, 1917, reported, "For the first time in the history of the Reid Newfoundland Company a passenger train pulled out from the station [St. John's] with the first-class lit up by an electric light." Second-class passenger cars still had to contend with the dangerous oil-filled lanterns.

Six years after the Benton train tragedy, the Reids sold the railway to the Newfoundland Government.

However, in mid-October, eight months after the accident, the local newspaper congratulated the Reids for installing electric lights in its first-class passenger car. A modern innovation, artificial lighting enabled those riding in Conductor Patrick "Paddy" Lee's first-class to "read their evening paper with the greatest comfort."

To supply the power for lighting, a small generator, or dynamo, was connected to the car axle, producing more than enough energy. Access power went to a storage battery sufficient for fifty hours' extra lighting. The public and the papers agreed. Oil lamps were obsolete, stated the media: "The new order of things is a step in the right direction and will be appreciated by the public."

HUNGER IN MARYSTOWN

MARYSTOWN

BY THE EARLY 1930s, the Dominion of Newfoundland was in the midst of a worldwide Depression. International markets for her main product, dried salt fish, had practically disappeared. This era, termed locally "the dirty thirties," lasted roughly from 1929 until the onset of World War II. It was a time of little money and less work. Government handouts, lack of employment and hard cash, and rations and the scarcity of food have etched the years 1929–1939 firmly in the minds of those who lived through it.

Poor times, a euphemism for abject poverty, predominated in many Newfoundland communities. Hungry children had to be fed; some people chose to find food by fair means or foul. They did what was right under the circumstances to care for desperate families and were heroes in their own community. Any person would do as much.

"Food riots" and skirmishes over dole orders erupted in several Newfoundland towns: Carbonear, Bay de Verde, Twillingate, Spaniard's Bay, St. John's. The latter was loud and damaging around the Colonial Building in April 1932. In Twillingate, dole orders were filled on the first day of the month, as they probably were in the rest of Newfoundland as well. December 1935 was a hard winter: homegrown vegetables and wild game were scarce, and people relied on government handouts to survive and to put food on the table, especially for the children.

That year, the first day of December fell on a Sunday. Those people of Twillingate who were on able-bodied relief lined up outside Ashbourne's store, located in Twillingate South, on Sunday to get their "dole" orders filled.

However, William Ashbourne wouldn't open the store to fill the orders because it was the Lord's Day, Sunday. The crowd of hungry people grew longer and angrier. Finally, Ashbourne sent his son Howard, then a young boy, with a note to the north side of Twillingate to ask the other two male employees of the store to come and help protect the store. Otherwise, the frustrated people would have broken into the store with possible criminal repercussions.

According to the tale told many years later, the Ashbournes didn't mind asking the shopkeepers to work at protecting the store on a Sunday but, ironically, wouldn't have them work the same day to serve the people. William Ashbourne opened the store shortly after noon on Monday and the employees filled orders until four o'clock in the morning.

In other locales, hungry and desperate citizens did run afoul of the law. In Marystown, young men clashed physically with the "dole givers" in an incident briefly mentioned in Barbara Walsh's book *August Gale* (Globe Pequot, 2011).

> William Reid was arrested by the Rangers, the government police, for stealing a sack of flour to help feed his family. Angered over the injustice, Jessie [Reid] pelted the officers' boat with wood and rocks as they hauled her son away to serve his time.

Situated in the wide harbour of Mortier Bay, Marystown (in its earlier years called Mortier Bay) in Placentia Bay is today a regional commercial centre for much of the Burin Peninsula. The municipality of Marystown includes several places that were formerly considered separate communities, including Mooring Cove to the north, Little Bay to the east, Creston North, and Creston South.

Like all towns in Newfoundland, Marystown struggled through the hard times of the Great Depression. Local tradition says (although the incident of the illegal taking of flour by the Reids is not part of the following anecdote) that in 1939 young Emile Reid, whose father had been lost at sea in an August gale four years previously, wanted to ask local authorities for extra food.

He rowed from Marystown South across the gut to Marystown North to explain his situation to the town policeman, Newfoundland Ranger Morgan. In addition to enforcing the law, Morgan's duties also included acting as the Relieving Officer responsible for dole orders or able-bodied relief. His office was located on the northeastern end of Queen Street.

Although Reid explained he had no father, but did have hungry siblings and that there was no work or money, he was "turned down" and ordered out of the ranger's office. Back home the story was related to an older brother, William "Bill" Reid.

An angry Bill rowed across the harbour and strode up Queen Street. By this time he had also conscripted the help of some thirty or forty men, equally hungry and angry. Confidence bolstered by the presence of the crowd behind him, Reid barged into the office with no regard to the door or door frame and confronted Morgan.

Again Ranger Morgan explained there were others more needy and that both Emile and Bill were young men who should be working. Though the Reids explained to Morgan that there was no work available, the law, in no uncertain terms, wouldn't take that as an explanation.

According to town lore, Reid grabbed the ranger's typewriter off the desk, threatened to throw it through the window, and ended up tossing it in the wire wastepaper basket. In the scuffle that ensued, the ranger followed the typewriter into the basket. The ranger's gun was hanging on the wall, but the law officer reached it first.

The men outside, sensing a scuffle, began to shout, surrounded the office, and pelted it with whatever objects were close at hand. Eventually, Morgan subdued Reid and marched him along Queen Street to the waterfront. Shouting and taunting the law but otherwise not violent, the crowd of men followed. Reid was taken away by boat amid shouts and the throwing of rocks, sods, and junks of wood.

Several boys walking to school watched in awe as the motley procession passed: the determined police, the frustrated prisoner, the furious, muttering crowd. One of the schoolboys felt more anxious than the others. He knew his father, Captain Paddy Dober, was in charge of the boat that always transported the magistrate (and other government officials) on his justice circuit of Placentia Bay.

However, Reid was carried without incident to Placentia, then St. John's to face incarceration. But the miscreant had already enlisted in the Royal Navy and, since England and Newfoundland needed seamen more than prisoners, he did not serve his sentence, said to be six months.

Although several people present during the skirmish that day appeared before Magistrate Clarence Powell, only Reid was charged with obstruction of justice and creating a disturbance.

Some months after the confrontation with Ranger Morgan at the

Marystown relieving office, other desperate men, mostly from outlying towns of Placentia Bay, broke into William Murley's store in Marystown and demanded food. Murley, powerless to stop the angry, desperate men who wished to feed their hungry families, requested two stipulations: to make a list of all items taken; and not to take any goods other than food and the necessities of life. Items like tobacco, rope, and hardware were not to be touched. In time, the store owner was repaid for his losses by the Newfoundland Government.

Able-bodied relief and the hated six cents a day dole disappeared by the early 1940s when the North American economy strengthened. At that time, too, many South Coast men found ready employment and good wages in the form of "real" cash when the United States Government constructed the Argentia Naval Base. The time of trouble in the dirty thirties became a distant memory in the minds of those who lived through it.

THE TRAGIC DEATH OF RANGER GREENE

LAMALINE, DANTZIC POINT, PLACENTIA

THE NEWFOUNDLAND RANGERS existed from 1935 to 1950 when the police force was disbanded. During those years, 204 men served, but only two tragic deaths touched the force. On March 12, 1936, Ranger Dan Corcoran left his detachment at Harbour Deep on the Great Northern Peninsula en route to Port Saunders. He became lost and wandered through the wilderness for days, frostbitten and half-starved, until he was found by a rescue team on March 28.

Although he reached hospital in St. Anthony, Corcoran died of tetanus coupled with the effects of exposure. Earl Pilgrim's informative book *Will Anyone Search for Danny?* (Flanker Press, 1999) is an account of the journey.

The second tragedy happened almost exactly two years later, but the death of Ranger Corporal Michael Greene is not as well-known as that of Corcoran's. On March 4, 1938, Greene died in the line of duty after falling through the ice with his horse and sled while on a patrol near Lamaline.

On that Friday, Ranger Greene had gone out to the end of his district at Dantzic Point and was returning to headquarters at Lamaline when his horse broke through Broad Pond on the eastern side of Point May. The pond, as the local people say, had a "hot spot," a section of the pond that never froze over no matter how low the temperature dropped. Most likely Greene knew of this phenomenon.

Greene managed to climb out of the hole and crawled across the ice for about 100 yards to the shelter of a fence and a small stand of tuckamore. But in the bitterly cold evening he perished. Searchers found his body—in a sitting position by the fence—on Sunday. To family members it was a strange death. They and other members of the force who knew him well could not explain why he had taken that path, that particular route across a saltwater pond. Michael was known to be a careful and thoughtful young man who had travelled the route several times before.

A photograph of S.S. Ranger taken from the deck of S.S. Imogene by Mr. James Grieve. Picture w taken when the S.S. Imogene was manoeuvring into position to shoot a rocket aboard the disabled Ranger.

Tragic Death Overtakes Member Ranger Force

For the second time since the formation of the Newfoundland Ranger force death under tragic circumstances overtook one of its members when the lifeless body of Corporal Greene was found by searchers a few miles from Lamaline on Saturday night. Mar 4

As far as can be learned Corporal

Clipping taken from the *Evening Telegram* of March 6, 1939. Photo of SS *Ranger* and *Imogene* above the headlines "Tragic Death Overtakes Member Ranger Force."

Ranger Greene, about twenty-four years of age, had been in the force for two and a half years. He belonged to Placentia and had graduated from St. Bon's College. Reverend Father Greene, then stationed at St. George's, and Magistrate Greene at St. Mary's, were his brothers.

CAPTURE OF THE "WRACKERS" OF STEAMER BURGOS

ST. SHOTTS, ST. MARY'S, ST. JOHN'S

IN A DENSE FOG ON THE NIGHT of July 14, 1879, the SS *Burgos* struck the rocks at Mariner's Cove, St. Shotts. During the night, the crew sent up rockets in hopes of obtaining help, but no person or ship answered.

The 1,152-ton *Burgos* under the command of Captain Martin was steaming from Montreal for London. It had a cargo of wheat, peas, and 410 live sheep. The captain and four hands left in a boat to seek some assistance. Shortly after, the rest of the crew and the two passengers left the wreck, assuming it would break up. They reached St. Mary's.

About six o'clock in the morning, the captain and some crew returned with a number of fishermen in their boats. By then the ship was swarming with wrackers. According to a report in PEI's *Examiner* of July 30, 1879: ". . . the cargo was immediately plundered by the half-civilized inhabitants; even the ship's stores and saloon furnishings were stolen."

Once *Burgos*'s captain reached his ship again, he tried to enter into a written agreement with these local fishermen to "render him aid." It could be readily seen the great ship would never steam again, but the cargo could be salvaged.

They all worked well and unmolested with the crew until about 10:00 a.m. At that time, more than forty large boats and several small boats arrived with between 300 and 400 men aboard. Some of the men boarded *Burgos* in spite of pleadings and threats from the captain.

The wrackers began throwing the bagged wheat into their boats. The captain offered them salvage, but this they disregarded and persisted in the illegal work with threats of violence against the captain and crew. These plunderers cleaned the decks of all the materials and gear they could lay their hands on.

Then came the sheep; 400 of them were on board. For the sheep the captain agreed with one wracker to let him have them on the halves. In this forced deal, 200 sheep would be salvaged legally and one of the men hired by the captain would take 200.

As soon as the now-rightful owner began to take possession of them, a number of men rushed forward and grabbed the sheep. In a short time, all the animals were put on board other boats alongside and they left presumably for St. Shotts and surrounding villages. In the end, the stripped *Burgos* was abandoned as a wreck.

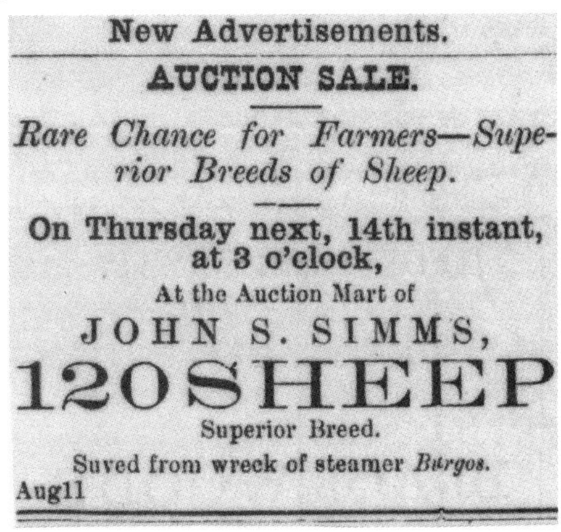
New Advertisements.

AUCTION SALE.

Rare Chance for Farmers—Superior Breeds of Sheep.

On Thursday next, 14th instant, at 3 o'clock,

At the Auction Mart of

JOHN S. SIMMS,

120 SHEEP

Superior Breed.

Saved from wreck of steamer *Burgos.*

Aug11

Clipping taken from the *Evening Telegram* of August 11, 1879, advertising the auctioning of 120 "superior" sheep from the wreck of SS *Burgos*.

But that was not the end of the matter. Judge D. W. Prowse, Police Inspector Paul Carty, and a group of police went to the area between St. Shotts and St. Mary's looking for the materials taken from *Burgos*. On July 25, 1879, a considerable quantity, "two schooner loads" of the wrecked property, had been recovered.

It had not been found in one place or two places, but scattered about in several localities of the district, and only rooted out through much labour and difficulty. Furthermore, some of the wrackers, classified as "marauders" by Prowse, had been identified and arrested. Only the ringleaders, not all of the 300–400 wrackers, were brought to trial.

Prowse and Carty had them brought to St. John's for trial, saying that "no proper means will be unemployed to vindicate the law. The conduct of the offenders in this *Burgos* case is described as unmitigated outlawry. An effective blow must be struck at these barbarous practices if the country is to be rescued from that wreck of character."

On November 21 that year, a jury was called for Supreme Court. One of the cases mentioned was the wreck of *SS Eirene* and the fact that, because of distance and time, no offenders—wrackers—had been apprehended for the criminal activity on that ship.

On the other hand, four men—Edward Walsh, Michael Lundregan (Lundrigan), a Kielly, and a Sullivan—now stood accused for having been leaders in the *Burgos* wreck. On November 26, Edward Walsh was found not guilty; on December 2, Kielly and Sullivan were acquitted. Only Michael Lundregan was found guilty and duly sentenced.

WHAT EVER HAPPENED TO ANN HOPE?

CROQUE, ST. JULIEN'S

ALL OVER NORTH AMERICA there are accounts of many thousands of people who have vanished under mysterious circumstances and never returned. Despite intense searches, the people or their remains are never located.

Some of those are individuals who carefully plan their departure, slipping away to avoid family or social pressures. Others who are declared missing are men, women, and children who have been seized against their will; they are kidnapped and brainwashed or forced not to reveal their whereabouts. A few vanished people have genuine cases of amnesia, having gone through whole or partial loss of memory. Then there are those who are murdered and their remains disposed of, never to be found.

One of the most puzzling vanishing acts in the annals of Newfoundland and Labrador centres around Ann Hope and her two children. When it was all over and the investigation, if it can be called that, ended, the newspaper stated, "The sudden disappearance of Ann Hope and her two children remains therefore enveloped in the greatest mystery."

Quite simply, no one knew what happened to her and her children. Neither Ann nor her babies were ever seen again. There was no evidence, no bodies. The last person to see the Hopes alive, Mr. Cooney, was the best suspect in the disappearance, but no incriminating evidence against him was found.

The tale of mystery begins with fisherman James Hope. He and his wife, Ann, settled in Croque in the early 1830s. Croque, situated south of St. Anthony on the Great Northern Peninsula, was once a principal fishing station on "Le Petit Nord," as the northeast coast of Newfoundland was called by the French. War, conflict, and treaties between England and France allowed French fishermen to fish off of Petit Nord harbours but not to settle there. In 1904, the French relinquished all claims to Newfoundland.

At the height of their occupation, the French employed local people during the winter months to protect their extensive curing, processing, and barrelling premises. Many of these eventually settled permanently in various French harbours. According to the *Newfoundland Encyclopedia*, Patrick Kearney and James Hope, both Irish, had settled in Croque. In summer they did their own fishing; in winter they were employed as the caretakers, or protectors, of the French rooms, premises, and stages in Croque.

By 1833, James and Ann Hope had two children aged six and two (and whose names are obscure). James was a "planter." That is, he fished, farmed, and employed others, mainly fishermen, to work for him. During the summer of 1833, he had two male servants hired—a Power and Thomas Cooney.

By October, before early autumn frost and cold had set in, the French had already gone back to France, and the Hopes, Power, and Cooney were the only inhabitants of Croque. It was early October when James found he had to travel—to sail and/or row—north to St. Julien's, about four miles distant, to obtain some supplies. He would return the same day.

At 7:00 a.m. on October 5, 1833, he took his servant Power with him. He instructed Thomas Cooney to spread some fish on a flake located about one mile from the dwelling house. Ann remained home and James asked her to make some bread bags.

Between noon and 1:00 p.m., James Hope returned to Croque, only to be met by Cooney at the stagehead. Cooney had the news for James that his wife and children were missing. Where were they? Cooney didn't know and claimed he had not seen them all morning.

From that time on, no tidings, no evidence of them whatsoever had been found despite a diligent search and inquiry. Presumably Cooney was the last to know of them.

A short time later, Cooney was arrested by British authorities and carried to St. John's to be brought to trial for the murder of Ann Hope and the two Hope children. He was held in prison for two sessions of the courts, about twelve months. Whether he protested his innocence or not is not recorded, but he was released. Court records of late November 1834 say, "There were no witnesses for the Crown, no legal testimony of the Hopes' death, and Cooney's case had to be disposed of." The jury that had been called to hear that case and others were instructed to ignore the bill of indictment against Cooney, and he was entitled to discharge.

The disappearance and presumed death of these three people remain forever shrouded in mystery.

MUTINEERS, VILLAINS, AND COWARDS

ST. JOHN'S

AN EVENT OCCURRED IN ST. JOHN'S HARBOUR on August 3, 1797, that was totally unprecedented, or repeated thereafter, in any Newfoundland port.

On the English ship *Latona*, thirty-eight guns and newly arrived in St. John's, a mutiny broke out. In that year, England and France were fighting one of their numerous wars. This made a mutiny aboard any of the ships of King George III (reigned from 1760-1820) all the more serious.

Around this time, there was great discontent in the lower ranks of British tars, who numbered around 100,000. Gloom and misery was their lot and rebellion was bubbling just below the surface. These lower-class ordinary seamen wanted, among other things, better pay, improved food or grub, and elimination of forced labour. The latter resulted from dreaded "press gangs," which captured, kidnapped, or shanghaied men, civilians, to forcibly sail on British ships.

Although a long list of complaints had been presented to the Admiralty several times, nothing improved. In the spring of 1797, two renowned mutinies took place. One of these was at Spithead in the English Channel. A more serious mutiny occurred at the Nore, a place in the Thames estuary and a well-used anchorage for any British man-of-war.

The Spithead rebellion did improve the situation for the "lower-deck" men when terms were negotiated between them and the Admiralty. However, at the Nore mutiny the mutineers, under leader Richard Parker, said the terms of the Spithead concessions—also offered to them—were simply not good enough.

The mutiny at the Nore became violent. Gangs of men from the ships attacked a town, looted merchant ships, and practically blockaded London. The Admiralty acted quickly. Marines were summoned, the Nore ringleaders were arrested, and the court martial began. Soon leader Richard Parker swung from a ship's yardarm at the Nore.

Latona, anchored in St. John's harbour, had many disgruntled lower-deck men aboard and, it appears, they had heard of the concessions at Spithead and knew of the Nore discontent. However, *Latona* had sailed to Newfoundland before violence broke out at the Nore.

In St. John's harbour, according to correspondence written by Governor William Waldegrave to the Duke of Portland of the Admiralty, on August 3, 1797, a group of tars of *Latona* refused to go aloft when ordered. The ship's captain isolated the ringleader and ordered out the cat (cat-o'-nine-tails) for a severe flogging. But the men interfered.

At this point *Latona*'s officers drew their swords. Marines on *Latona* affixed their bayonets. In the movement backward, or in the scuffle, some would-be mutineers received cuts or slashes from the bayonets as they retreated.

The ringleader was then punished appropriately with a flogging from the cat. The governor's missive said that the language of the seamen was atrocious. Once *Latona* left port, they said when below deck, there would be "bloody work" dealt out to the marines.

A short time, perhaps a day or so, after the *Latona* mutiny, an English vessel reached St. John's with copies of a London newspaper, reporting the squashing of the Nore mutiny, the court martial of Richard Parker, and his subsequent hanging.

This was a good time to reinforce the gravity of an attempted rebellion by *Latona*'s men. Thus the mutineers were marched ashore and surrounded by marines, soldiers of the Royal Artillery, and a company of the Newfoundland Regiment.

First, according to military records, the governor thanked the marines for their loyalty during the mutiny. He then addressed the mutineers, voicing his desire there might be some among them who had honour for their King and Country. He added:

> But if I am to judge from your conduct, I must think that the majority of you are either villains or cowards. If you refuse to obey your officers, then you are traitors to your King and Country. . . . I maintain

you are a set of dastardly cowards for suffering to be bullied by a few villains who wish nothing better than to see us become the slaves of France.

You are all eager for news and newspapers to see how your great leader, Parker, is getting on. I thank God I have the satisfaction to inform you that he is hanged with many others of his atrocious companions.

Today the most visible reminder of a mutiny in St. John's by British tars is the street sign for British-born Governor William Waldegrave (1753–1825).

One of his reforms was to have the chief justice remain on the Island during the winter. It was Waldegrave's intent to discourage and prevent further trouble among local troops.

Parker and twenty-nine others swung from the yardarm of HMS *Sandwich*, on which the mutiny started.

The governor had a formidable warning for the batch of malcontents. He told them he had given orders to *Latona*'s officers that, in case of any further signs of mutiny, they need not put the ringleaders in irons. They were "to put them to death instantly."

He also told them he had given orders to the officers in command of the batteries (on the hills overlooking the harbour, e.g. the Queen's Battery) to burn *Latona* with red-hot shot. This was "in case you drive me with your mutinous behaviour to that extremity."

In such an event the ship's officers would also die, but the governor said he felt these men were ready to sacrifice themselves for King and Country.

The governor ended his address on a chilling note. He regretted his commission did not allow him to conduct a court martial in Newfoundland. If it did, he said, the ringleaders of the *Latona* mutiny would have been hanged.

Thus ended the one and only Royal Navy mutiny in Newfoundland waters.

COULD THE WITNESS REPEAT THAT?

A COURTHOUSE, SOMEWHERE

A MR. WOOD, SENIOR, called to the witness box, was asked to give his name to the judge. Mr. Wood smiled and said, "Ott. Ott Wood."

"Ott," said the judge. "Is that your full name? If not, what is it?"

"Ottiwell Wood."

The judge, perhaps wishing to write the name down, addressed the distinguished gentleman, saying, "Pray, Mr. Wood, how do you spell your name?"

The man replied:

"O double T, I double U, E double L, Double U, Double O, D."

Whereupon the astonished lawgiver laid down his pen, saying with a smile it was the most extraordinary name he had ever encountered in court and in life. After two or three attempts to write it down as Wood repeated it, he declared he was unable to record the name.

Meanwhile, the court, clerks and audience, were convulsed with laughter.

MANSLAUGHTER ON THE FISHING GROUNDS

BELLEORAM

TWO FISHERMEN OF BELLEORAM were supposedly friends. They were well-known and respected in the south coast community as hard-working, honest toilers of the sea. Both John Fudge and Thomas Savory set their cod traps close to each other in Fortune Bay, not far from Belleoram, located on the east side of the Connaigre Peninsula.

In the summer of 1903, feelings toward each other changed. One day, Fudge accused Savory of putting his mooring for his fishing traps inside or too near his. After all, Fudge shouted, he was there first.

An argument broke out and hot words were spoken. Thomas Savory's skiff was close to Fudge's. Fudge picked up an oar and swung it at Savory, striking him on the left side of the neck. The blow was so hard it broke off the oar. Blood gushed from both ears of the injured man.

Knocked unconscious, he was taken to hospital in St. Jacques and attended by two doctors, but Savory died a few hours later. John Fudge was arrested and taken by the SS *Fiona* to St. John's to prison to be later tried for manslaughter.

It was November 30, 1903, before he was brought before Supreme Court. As the fall session was nearly completed, and due to delays in getting witnesses, Fudge would be arraigned on April 18, 1904, before a grand jury looking for a "true bill"—an indictment endorsed by a jury as being sufficiently supported by evidence to justify a trial—of wrongdoing and hearing the preliminary evidence. This pretrial would determine if there was enough evidence to try the accused. Fudge's pretrial began in the spring session at the newly built courthouse, opened May 2, 1904.

Other than the two doctors, FitzGerald and Giovannetti, who had examined the victim just before death and after he died, very few witnesses were available. Constable Bartlett went to Belleoram to find others who had seen the criminal actions of Fudge. By the second week in May, he was back with hearsay but no physical evidence.

On May 14, the grand jury listened to Constable Bartlett and the two medical men. Dr. Con FitzGerald, born in England, served Harbour Breton and St. Jacques from 1873 to the 1930s. Dr. Louis John Giovannetti was born in Nova Scotia and served with FitzGerald in St. Jacques in the early 1900s. Both could only describe the extent of Savory's injuries but had nothing to say about, much less prove, who inflicted the blow to the head nor why or exactly what instrument had dealt the damage.

Due to a lack of witnesses and physical evidence, the grand jury found no "true bill of manslaughter" for John Fudge. On May 16, he was freed to return home. The violent death of Thomas Savory on the fishing grounds off Belleoram remains unresolved.

Belleoram in 1910, just a few years after the untimely death of Thomas Savory. The SS *Glencoe* backs out of the harbour.

THOSE CHARGED WITH BARRATRY

FORTUNE HARBOUR, POUCH COVE,
ST. BRENDAN'S, SALVAGE

BY THE BEGINNING of the nineteenth century, the occurrences of barratry in one form or another were rampant in Newfoundland. Allowing a ship to go adrift for the purpose of wrecking it, and usually to collect insurance monies after, happened all over the seafaring world. An editorial in the *Evening Telegram*, November 14, 1895, said, "Such a sin can well be laid at the doors of . . . Newfoundlanders. In late years our courts and the Crown prosecutors have rigidly enforced the laws dealing with this offence."

The crime scene in Newfoundland and Labrador was set: isolated and hidden bays and coves, hundreds of schooners, scores and scores not making a profit for owners, erstwhile captains and owners many miles remote from authorities. They had the means, motivation, and opportunity to cause the demise of a schooner. Who would see or know? Was the vessel blown onto a rugged shore or intentionally allowed to drift there? Did the hole in the bottom come from an auger or a jagged rock? How would investigators find out in the vast ocean under sixty fathoms of water?

THE WRECK

The paper referred specifically to the events surrounding the schooner *New Era*. In the beginning it seemed innocent enough, perhaps a vessel lost, like scores of others that year, due to poor navigation or contrary winds. On November 7, 1893, Captain John Lannon of Fortune Harbour sailed toward St. John's near Cape St. Francis. Just before daylight he ran upon the Brandies, rocks that became just awash at low tide, off Cape St. Francis.

The steering apparatus and rudder were damaged, but when some fish was thrown overboard, *New Era* came afloat enough to get in on a beach at Pouch Cove, a few miles away. Lannon anchored *New Era* on Pouch Cove's south side, but dangerously near some rocks and a cliff. The scene was described thus:

> It, in fact, touched the rocks. Soon the schooner was boarded by a band of men, certainly not the best men of the place, eager for booty. It was not long till the spars were cut out, whatever fish and lumber was on board taken out, and much general destruction done, not easily credited by the sober-minded.
>
> Eventually the selling of the vessel was considered the best way out of the difficulties.

Within a day, William Shea bought the wreck at a public auction for $10. He chartered the St. John's harbour tug *Favorite* to tow *New Era* to Bennett's wharf in the city.

Built in Fortune Harbour in 1891, *New Era* was forty-four ton net, fifty-nine feet long, and owned by John Cowan's Shipping Company of St. John's. Cowan, into the fish procuring and sealing business, had fish brought from various outports, chiefly Fortune Harbour, in Notre Dame Bay. It was insured by the Labrador branch of the Montreal Marine Club for $1,120.

THE BARRATRY CHARGE, ONE YEAR LATER

A year later, almost to the day, Inspector Sullivan of the Constabulary went to Fortune Harbour and arrested Captain John Lannon and his four crew for barratry—intentionally causing *New Era* to wreck and often termed "casting away."

On November 28, he arrived back in St. John's on the SS *Virginia Lake* with prisoners Lannon, Michael Byrne, James Byrne, James Crooke, and William Carrol (with spellings as they appeared in official records), all of Fortune Harbour and vicinity. Lawyer Edward Patrick Morris represented Captain Lannon and, since there was no arraignment for the crew, they probably were absolved of wrongdoing and returned home. An additional charge against Lannon was defrauding the insurance company.

On November 24, 1894, Captain John Lannon pleaded "Not guilty of barratry on *New Era*, the property of John Cowan." Capable and eloquent, Morris (later the Right Honourable Sir E. P. Morris and Prime Minister of Newfoundland) would have about five months to prepare his defence. The trial would begin the spring session of Supreme Court. Meanwhile, Morris applied for bail. Lannon was free until May or June of the next year.

TRIAL DAY: MAY 31, 1895, SUPREME COURT

On the first morning of Lannon's barratry case, a number of witnesses were called, all Pouch Cove men. Those covering the trial figured all the men in Pouch Cove had gotten their share of fish taken from *New Era*. Details of the wreck and the amount of dry salt cod that had been aboard came basically from one witness, John Moore, one of the first to go aboard the stranded *New Era*.

The flakes and fishing stages of Pouch Cove, circa 1941, taken from A. C. Shelton's *Newfoundland: Our North Door Neighbor*. Photo courtesy of the Maritime History Archives, MUN, Accession No. pf036_002.

"All the Pouch Cove men," he said, "took dry fish from the after pile. There were men down taking the fish before me. When I jumped down on the fish, my head could not reach the deck. Three men of us took about three and a half quintals each. I saw all the fish taken out of her in about an hour and three-quarters. In my judgment there were about fifteen to twenty boats taking her fish. The dunnage, or covering for the fish, was dry birch rind and I saw no sign of a leak anywhere in the vessel."

Regarding the wrecking of *New Era*, Moore said:

> All the sails were set. From the time I saw her until she struck, she didn't appear to alter her course. I saw the vessel driving off round the Long Point. The foresail was set and I think the foresail was no help to get her off the rocks. When the vessel swung down round the Long Point, her stern was caught.
>
> From the time I boarded her until it came off the rock, the captain asked for no assistance. Nobody was prevented from taking the fish. I know nothing about her sale. I didn't see her rudder when I went aboard.
>
> I gave Sergeant Sparrow about three-quarters of a quintal of fish and he said he was satisfied with that. I didn't tell him how much I had. I don't know how much dry fish he got in Pouch Cove.
>
> I did not give an estimate of the quantity of fish in her. I'm not competent to do so. I saw her coming in with a free wind and I helped to hoist the foresail on her to get her off the sunken rock and when she floated inside into deep water. I don't know who warped her off or who cut her up.

Mr. Daniel Joseph Greene, Queen's Counsel, questioned John Moore on the wrecking, to which Moore responded, "Going in over the rock didn't improve her chances of getting off, as her stern still held on." Moore then described on a chart the course *New Era* took at the time of striking and afterward.

To the questions of defence lawyer Morris, Moore said he helped hoist the foresail. Why? Because the captain gave orders. To the court's questions he responded that hoisting the foresail could only carry her farther onto the mainland.

JOHN ESTERBROOK, WITNESS

"I live on the south side of Pouch Cove. She was partway between our place [Pouch Cove] and the Brandies. I watched it pass Bald Head in a northeast wind. I did not see her strike. After breakfast I went down to her. She was lying head on to the shore, heading about southwest. As she lay on the rocks, she appeared so light that I thought there was nothing in her. I saw the rudder above deck, unshipped. I noticed no water in the hold."

Since Esterbrook was the only one of the Pouch Cove witnesses to mention seeing the rudder, several members of the jury asked Esterbrook about it. To other questions he said he was there at the sale and the schooner was lying by the point when sold to William Shea. "There was no water that I could see when I was on board at 9:00 a.m. The masts were standing when I jumped on board at Long Point."

TRIAL DAY TWO: WITNESSES, THE CREW, AND PATRICK LANNON

Basically, two crew (the others could not be present) of *New Era* testified their vessel struck the Brandies about 5:00 a.m. on the morning of November 7. Half, or about half, the fish then on board was thrown into the sea for the purpose of lightening the vessel. When the vessel came off the Brandies, she was leaking and the captain decided to run for the land.

Patrick Lannon, the brother of defendant John Lannon, testified, saying he recalled seeing *New Era* loaded for the voyage on which she was lost. He stated, "My brother delayed my crew to help him load his vessel. To the best of my knowledge, there was six or seven hundred quintals in her, but I am not sure of the exact amount."

A TALE WITHIN A TALE

E. P. Morris tried to determine from witnesses just how many quintals of fish was in the ship. This would help put a monetary value on the cargo. As well, it would show that *New Era*'s crew threw much of it overboard to lighten the ship. That is, they had no intention of getting the fish to shore to sell it to local people.

Morris followed a line of examination that became a vignette or story within a story, all acted out in the courtroom, much to the delight of the audience. How much Labrador fish could a man yaffle (carry in his arm) and throw overboard in an hour? The witness, a crewman, said a quintal an hour. To satisfy the jury, Morris produced a stopwatch and timed the witness simulating walking across the deck, throwing the fish overboard, and walking back to the hold.

When the minute was up, Morris again put the question to the witness. By this time the witness crewman allowed he could throw more than a quintal over in an hour.

Morris said that, calculated on this basis, the five men on *New Era* might have thrown more than 600 quintals during the two hours that the vessel was caught on the Brandies, thus there wouldn't be much left to sell or give to the Pouch Cove people.

THE DEFENCE RESTS

In the afternoon of June 1, the witness and show of evidence for the defence ended. Mr. Morris, in summing up, said he did not expect to speak at length, except to briefly refer to the facts as presented. He had requested the bench allow Captain John Lannon to testify on his own behalf, but was denied. The law, as explained by Justice Winter, would not allow this because of the tendency toward perjury. Winter said two crew had testified and that would suffice.

Morris, in summary, stated that if the vessel had 800 quintals aboard, there was no motive to losing the vessel. In fact, there was every good reason why Captain Lannon should bring his ship safely to St. John's. "The evidence of owner Cowan tells you, the jury, the vessel was assessed at $1,400 and Lannon had a promise of her for the sum of $1,000." Morris also reviewed the open and normal manner in which *New Era* was beached. The actions of the Pouch Cove men as they swarmed on board and took possession of the wrecked vessel hints at wrongdoing by them.

DAY TWO SUMMING UP: MR. GREENE, Q.C.

Greene, regarding the amount of fish aboard *New Era*, said there was no such quantity as 800 quintals when the vessel left Fortune Harbour. Forty quintals had been sold to Lethbridge at Twillingate for cash. In the attempt to defraud the insurance for the provisions that were supposedly bought at Twillingate and on board the vessel when it was lost, there was no such quantity. The vessel went into Twillingate to get out of the weather.

THE VERDICT AND SENTENCE

With that, on the evening of June 1, the trial ended. The jury deliberated for an hour and returned to the court on July 2, saying, "The prisoner, John Lannon, was guilty of attempting to cast away the vessel and also attempting to cast away the vessel with the intent of defrauding the insurance." Sentencing would come in the fall.

That summer, concerned citizens who knew John Lannon's even disposition, fine character, and basic honesty circulated a petition. Numerous people, including prominent citizens with whom Lannon had close business relations, signed the petition. They fully believed Lannon was unfortunate and was entirely innocent. He had had an excellent reputation and was blameless.

In essence, the public protest had results. In a more or less unprecedented meeting, the island's Chief Justice Winter and Judge Little met on July 11 to consider setting aside John Lannon's verdict. Lawyer Morris spoke all morning. Prosecutor Greene spoke in the afternoon. It became a wait-and-see all fall.

Other tales of Lannon's troubles came to light. In an *Evening Telegram* article about him (July 11, 1895), one person recalled that around 1882 all his household property and a dwelling house were destroyed by a disastrous fire. He and his brother were living in the house at the time, barely escaping with their lives. Both had severe burns about the face and hands.

Two years previously, Lannon had lost a vessel only three years old on which there was no insurance. Lannon and his father always kept property and vessels well-insured, but this one was not covered. The summary of Captain Lannon's life then was:

> He has had several hard rubs. He is a hard-working and frugal man. He certainly has a great deal of sympathy in his present unfortunate position and those who know him best cannot believe him guilty.

It was not until December 19, 1895, when sentencing was passed on Lannon. At the sentencing phase, E. P. Morris spoke favourably on Lannon's behalf: his conduct in the penitentiary was exemplary and Captain Lannon, engaged in business, had many persons dependent upon him. Ultimately the public and private outcry against barratry prevailed. Justice Winter sentenced Lannon to eight months from the date of his incarceration, June 1, 1895. He still had six more months to serve.

IN THE END

After his prison time was up in early February 1896, Lannon continued to be a contributing citizen. In the shipping news for the spring of 1897, it is noted Captain John Lannon still worked for the Cowans. His *Little Lottie*, or *Lottie*, as it was called, arrived from the icefields off the Virgin Rocks and had 1,500 seal pelts on board. As well, the *New Era* lived again. Not long after its near-destruction by the Pouch Cove fishermen, it was reacquired by Cowan and repaired. In 1912, it sank at sea off Western Head, St. Mary's Bay.

THE DIRE DEED OF JOHN O'GORMAN

RIVERHEAD (ST. JOHN'S), THE HIGH SEAS

JOHN O'GORMAN, born at the Riverhead of St. John's, was cook on the fully-rigged ship *Fanny Wright*. The vessel had a crew of eighteen men and all were born in Ireland, except the Newfoundlander O'Gorman. What eventually happened to the unfortunate cook has been told in the poem and song "The Loss of the *Fanny Wright*" and also in a story written in 1951 by Michael P. Murphy.

Sometime in late October in the 1850s, *Fanny Wright* left St. John's, sailing for Ireland with a miscellaneous cargo. It sailed in good weather until fourteen days out of port when a typical mid-Atlantic storm arose.

Fanny Wright, old and probably unseaworthy, was beaten by the heavy seas that pounded the ship mercilessly. At this point it was many hundreds of miles at sea, somewhere between Newfoundland and Ireland. To return to port was just as hazardous and lengthy as to sail on to Ireland.

One of the helmsmen must have been an inexperienced seaman in such weather. A high breaker fell on *Fanny Wright*, causing the wheel to jerk from the man's hands. The ship fell over on her beam ends, that is, on her side with masts and sails parallel, or nearly so, to the surface of the sea.

Quickly, as there was not a second to lose, the crew set about to right the ship. The foremast and mainmast were cut away and, as they were jettisoned, they carried the mizzen-mast overboard with them.

The ship came upright somewhat, but it was next to impossible to get below deck as everything had filled with water. The cabin, forecastle, hold, and storerooms were flooded. There would be no warm food or tea, and in fact no food at all on the deck. The kegs holding drinking water, usually lashed on deck, had been washed away.

On the morning of the November 15, the sailors and officers were in a desperate way. Three men—First Mate Griffis and two sailors—had been swept overboard during the storm and drowned.

The only items taken from below deck were three bottles of port wine. This was rationed. The crew managed to get some rainwater by holding the cover of a pot or tureen under some canvas. *Fanny Wright* had taken on so much water the decks were awash and there was nowhere to lie down on deck.

Yet a ray of sunshine helped cheer spirits. The weather moderated somewhat, enabling the men to find some planks in the cabin. Having been on their feet for nearly ninety-six hours, they took that opportunity to snatch a catnap and to get a little rest lying on those planks.

Gradually, all became weak from lack of food and water. Their legs were covered with saltwater sores and scabs from standing in sea water for hours.

However, most of the crew did not give up hope that some vessel would come along, see their plight, and take them off the sinking ship. All would be well again. Indeed, straining eyes scanning the horizon saw a passing ship or two, but none came near enough to be signalled.

On November 18, nine days after the storm bore down on *Fanny Wright*, the captain called the crew together and made a shocking proposal: one of the men would have to die in order that the rest might live.

It might be days, he said, before a ship came close enough to see them. Someone would have to be sacrificed to save the rest. This suggestion was met with approval by some and with disgust by others. Cannibalism was simply a horrendous and appalling thought.

Despair and gnawing hunger pangs dictated to most. They agreed with the captain. For them it was an open utterance of a thought that had been in their minds for days. In the end, majority ruled, but with one provision—the married men would be exempt. After all, the married men had wives and children to support. John O'Gorman of St. John's was apparently married and was exempt from death by murder.

There were four boys known only by their last names in the ship's complement: Sheehan, Burns, O'Brien, and another lad whose name is not known. They were lined up on deck as one of the crew held four sticks of different lengths in his fist.

The trembling and horrified boys drew out the sticks one by one. The shortest stick, the fatal one, was drawn by O'Brien, a lad from Limerick, Ireland. The captain had ordered all this to be done as quickly as possible.

A bandage was soon tied over O'Brien's eyes and he stood on the deck alone, moaning in fear and despair, tears coursing down his cheeks, and making every appeal to save himself.

The captain looked around for someone to do the killing as no one had volunteered to do this, despite hunger pangs and the prospect of a slow death by starvation. The captain selected O'Gorman, the only Newfoundland sailor on board. Perhaps the captain thought that by not selecting a fellow Irishman he could save his own skin back home, should he survive.

At any rate, O'Gorman was ordered forward and a knife handed to him. The reluctant man was shoved toward the trembling boy. The crew, sensing food and not wanting delay nor to have to do the cruel deed themselves, struck and swore on O'Gorman, trying to hasten him to make the knife thrust. Kill him or be killed yourself, they said.

O'Gorman, shaking uncontrollably, made a swipe, but only succeeded in cutting O'Brien's wrist. He was horrified to see no blood came and saw this as a terrible omen or sign from God. O'Gorman backed away, howling in terror.

Pushed toward the boy with the point of a blade at his back, O'Gorman made a swing and struck O'Brien in the throat. Blood flowed for a few moments and the boy fell onto the deck and soon died.

The crew, starving and desperate, gathered around the dead boy, encouraging the cook O'Gorman to make a fire somewhere and prepare food. Just at that moment, a sailing ship was sighted, bearing down toward the wallowing *Fanny Wright*.

What to do! Someone threw a piece of canvas over O'Brien's remains and the crew, except the murderer O'Gorman, ran over to the rails to hail with happy cries the oncoming vessel.

The ship was the American brig *Angenora*. Soon the survivors of *Fanny Wright* were rescued and brought to port, from which they made their way to Ireland. Presumably the wallowing vessel was abandoned and soon sank.

Likewise, nothing was said of the deed of John O'Gorman, the cook from St. John's. He had been forced to kill a shipmate. It is not known if he returned to St. John's or if he ever had to answer for his actions at sea.

What remains? Is there any truth to this story? At sea, with thousands of ships and tens of thousands of sailors in the era of sail, anything and everything that could happen to a ship and the sailors aboard it most certainly happened. Doubtless the prospect of death by starvation and thirst (not uncommon in the era of sail) drove humans to commit unspeakable deeds on land and sea.

This tale was not reported in any newspaper or personal memoirs. However, there is a booklet that was published in 1902 by James Murphy which includes a song "The Loss of the *Fanny Wright*." In a note on its origins, Murphy says, "This song is so old that the oldest inhabitants of St. John's have but a meagre knowledge of the events recorded in the song. It was given to me by a seaman who has probably the truest version of the sad tale."

The details in the song or folk poem mirror what is outlined in the story. One verse of the song says:

"Then", said the cruel captain,
"This work will never do.
O'Gorman, you must cut his throat,
Or else you'll suffer too."

The trembling cook he took the knife
And did him sore confound,
He cut his throat and drank his blood,
As it flowed from the wound.

ACCUSED OF SHEBEENING

ST. JOHN'S

IN THE SUMMER OF 1898, when the St. John's courthouse was situated on Henry Street, one amusing incident occurred. No doubt many curious and bizarre things happen in Newfoundland's provincial and Supreme Court trials, but this one stemmed from the use of language and terminology that was foreign to the accused.

The first permanent courthouse in St. John's opened in September 1730, housing a wooden jail and courthouse and was located at 309 Duckworth Street, St. John's, on approximately the same site as the courthouse of today.

In 1831, the governor had a second St. John's courthouse and jail built. Fifteen years later, this wooden building was destroyed by one of the great St. John's fires. The replacement, too, was destroyed by fire on July 8, 1892, along with approximately three-quarters of the buildings in St. John's.

As a result, Supreme Court sittings were held in the Colonial Building for several years. Superintendent of Public Buildings John T. Neville prepared plans for a temporary wooden courthouse, which would eventually become the Star of the Sea Hall on Henry Street. Although the structure was built for the Star of the Sea Association, the government rented the premises until May 1904.

It was decided by the government of the day during the summer of 1899 to create plans for a new courthouse in St. John's at an estimated cost of $100,000. On June 18, 1988, the St. John's courthouse was declared a National Historic Site. A plaque on the building commemorates its historic and architectural significance.

However, it was from the Henry Street courthouse that media of the day, the *Evening Herald* of June 7, 1898, reported, "There was quite a scene in the courthouse the other day. . . ." A woman (unnamed) was charged with shebeening. No doubt the word "shebeen," of Scottish-Irish origin and meaning an unlicensed house or tavern where liquor is sold illegally, confused the woman. It was likely even the court reporter had to consult his dictionary.

The woman had been visiting one such illegal establishment, a shebeen, and had been caught, and now a police official was prosecuting her in the Magistrate's Court. Perhaps seeing the woman's confusion or lack of understanding of the term, the official decided to place some other strange words upon her.

He threw in a French term and maybe some Latin as well. The official asked her if she was "on the qui vive" when the constable arrived. In other words, was she on watch, on the lookout for the law? It was a circumstance of denigrating or belittling someone—an embarrassment and surely unacceptable by today's standards.

The woman, not having the slightest clue what "qui vive" meant, took the term to mean a reflection on her morality, hinting at illicit sex. At this point the woman became quite vocal and began to berate and shout at her questioner. No doubt her words suggested such activity or lack of it.

Her lawyer, taking a cue from this, jumped to his feet and demanded an apology. The whole scene caused screams of laughter from the spectators and nods, mild snickers, and giggles from court employees. With that the magistrate threw his arms up in the air, dismissed the case, and left the bench.

SIXTY AGAINST ONE: CONSTABLE REES

FOGO

THERE HAVE BEEN OCCASIONS, especially when the cod fishery was poor or non-existent in Newfoundland and Labrador, when abject poverty predominated in many Newfoundland communities. Families struggled through hard times waiting for the spring and renewed hope with better cod catches. In 1898, such times arose in Notre Dame Bay.

In the face of dire circumstances, some breadwinners chose to find food by any means necessary. They did what they felt was right under the circumstances in order to care for hungry families. In essence, they were considered heroes in their own families and community.

Recently, a letter came to light describing hungry times. The story within also outlines the bravery of a Newfoundland Constable, A. E Rees. The missive, headed Fogo and dated June 6, 1898, was signed anonymously by "Looker On." Given the circumstances of the troubled times, anonymity was probably for the better. No doubt the letter writer did not want to draw attention to himself but wanted to highlight the actions of a policeman rather than the starving conditions of his fellow islanders.

The letter served to honour Rees for his coolness and bravery during a riot that took place at Fogo on Wednesday, June 1, 1898. On that day, a mob of about sixty hungry men arrived in skiffs, including several from Ladle Cove and Rocky Bay (today's Carmanville)—some had travelled forty miles or so to get to Fogo.

They proceeded to march to Dr. Malcolm's residence. Thomas S. Malcolm, born in Scotland, came to Fogo as a physician in 1887. In 1898, about the time of the food riot, he was appointed Stipendiary Magistrate at Fogo. As the chair of the Road Board, perhaps he could appeal to higher authorities or could find some work for the people there.

The men told the good doctor they were destitute. Their families when they left them that morning were starving. There was not a morsel of food in most of the houses. Since the government stopped relief monies (about a month previous), the people had been living on mussels and flatfish. There were no staple foodstuffs, particularly flour.

Sympathetic to their plight, Dr. Malcolm told the men to wait until the next day, Thursday, and he would send a message to St. John's for instructions.

"The poor fellows," said the letter writer Looker On, "decided to wait, declaring that if no news was received by four p.m. the next day, they would enter every store in Fogo until they had flour and bread enough to at least keep them and their families alive for a few days."

The Evening Telegram

RIOT AT FOGO!

Stores Attacked!

Bravery of Police-Constable Rees, Who Stood Alone and Kept in Check a Crowd of Fully Sixty Hungry Men.

(*Editor Evening Telegram.*)

DEAR SIR,—Permit me space in your esteemed paper to give the particulars of the outbreak which took place here the past week, and especially to show to the public the bravery and coolness of Constable A. E. Rees on that occasion. The constable deserves the greatest credit for the valiant way in which he stood alone and checked a mob of about sixty hun-

These poor fellow
Fogo, have been
about in old boats
with what food th
Cannot the Gove
Thanking you for
Yours tru
Fogo, June 6th,

LOCAL H

A WOMAN'S PR
well made, can b
LINO'S for 20 cen
fully cheap.—adv

NEW TOILET S
fumed. Nice va
perfume); "D
O'MARA'S Drug S

NEW PE
"White Lilac," (
Cashmere Bouque
Breath Perfume.
Store.—adv't.j8,tf

THE Tobacco is

Headlines of the riot at Fogo, *Evening Telegram*, June 8, 1898.

They waited until the next day after that, Friday. No orders had come from headquarters and the mob proceeded to the stores owned or managed by H. J. Lind. In fact, Lind's store was the only merchant in Fogo who at that time had a supply of flour and bread in his building. This was probably Henry Lind, the father of Francis Thomas "Mayo" Lind, a soldier and letter writer of World War I fame.

The crowd made an attempt to smash down Lind's door, but Constable Rees was returning from duty at the premises of the local Justice of the Peace and owner of a substantial business on Fogo Island, Henry J. Earle. Rees arrived at the very moment of the break and entry.

Perhaps knowing or hearing rumours of trouble afoot, Rees was in full uniform—belt, baton, and sword. He saw what was happening at a glance and stood gallantly in front of the business, keeping the mob away from Lind's door. Looker On stated that, had the officer not arrived at the moment he did, Lind's store would have been cleaned out by sixty hungry, angry men. Amazingly, "Rees did not have one special to cover his back!" A "special" in those days was a citizen sworn in as a temporary peacekeeper.

When the mob saw Rees's determination, they withdrew, threatening to come back at a later hour. During that reprieve, Rees found the time to hastily wire his Inspector at St. John's for instructions to swear in special constables.

Apparently he received directions, but when Earle and Rees were hunting up men to be sworn in as "specials," the mob made a second attack on Lind's store. However, the ever-alert Rees promptly went to the scene again as the rabble was attempting to force entry to the shop.

The officer at once ordered them to retreat. At first they refused, but when they saw the officer was determined, they gave up. He then ordered them off the property and onto the public road. Amazingly, said Looker On, they complied.

By now other men had joined the original sixty and the gang had swelled to about 100. Nearly all the residents of Fogo had gathered nearby and were witnesses to the whole proceedings. The angry hundred uttered threats, curses, and angry words—in front of them stood one lone man fortified with "coolness and determination."

H. J. Earle arrived soon after. He addressed the men, reasoning with them and asking them to wait until the following day. He would do his utmost to procure food for them. The gang was not satisfied. The leaders—identified by Looker On as "Wests by name"—declared they would wait no longer; their families were starving.

Earle, too, deserves much praise as he was Fogo's Justice of the Peace and the responsibility of law and order fell on him. He knew most of these men by name or was familiar with them. Looker On, the letter writer, said: "On the other hand he stood his post loyally and, at last, the mob yielded. Rees, too, patrolled the street near the scene of the riot until midnight, Thursday."

The next morning, a reprieve came. It was a sight to warm the heart of any onlooker, including the letter writer. A man, addressed as "Esquire," Mr. J. G. Lucas, was surrounded by the same crowd of hungry men. Mr. Lucas, with the aid of the clerk of Lind's store, was measuring out flour and bread to them. Lucas was paying for the same out of his own pocket.

From six in the morning until eleven o'clock he purchased, allotted, and doled out three barrels of flour and much bread. Even then there was not enough to go around and about twenty of the original group had to return home empty-handed, just as they had come.

The tale of hardship ends here. No court action was taken; no further recriminations were issued. For two or three days, the destitute breadwinners had waited in Fogo for better times that never came. As the letter writer concludes:

> These poor fellows, since they came to Fogo, have been living like dogs, lying about in old boats and forced to put up with what food the charity gives them. Cannot the Government do something?
>
> Yours truly,
> LOOKER ON
> Fogo, June 6, 1898

Fogo in an earlier era, looking toward Brimstone Head, centre

THE STAG HARBOUR RUN WRACKERS

HARBOUR GRACE, STAG HARBOUR RUN,
FOGO, CHANGE ISLANDS

FOR VESSELS UNLUCKY ENOUGH to strike the reefs off Newfoundland and Labrador's rocky shore, landsmen in the area do what they can to save lives. That becomes their primary concern. But, historically, when human lives were not in danger, people swarmed to the crippled, stranded vessel, making good use of the spoils of the sea.

When a ship was abandoned, these looters, termed "wreckers" or "wrackers" in some localities, usually took whatever could be lifted and carried away. Food, ship's fittings, sails, gear, equipment, and articles of cargo became particularly desirable. While it is true that many wrackers operated within the legal limits, on permission and obligated to report their bounty, others disregarded the law, taking what they could despite the captain's warnings. The Newfoundland Government had, for many years, tried to control unlawful looting.

One area known for a high volume of sailing ship traffic, a narrow and potentially dangerous passage, was the sheltered Stag Harbour Run, off the southern shore of Fogo Island. It shortened the sailing time between leaving Labrador and arriving in Bonavista Bay or Conception Bay. By using this passage, Captains did not have to sail out into the open stormy seas and around the northern end of Fogo Island. Occasionally, all-sail vessels were lost there. The potential and temptation for wreckers was great.

One well-known case was that of Captain Alcock of Harbour Grace, who had lost the *Stella Maria* in the run in 1886. Scores of wreckers—

many from Eastern Cove on Eastern Indian Island—boarded his stranded vessel before the crew and passengers got a chance to leave the ship. Only for the appearance of other Conception Bay schooners who helped guard and fend off the pack, wreckers would have dismantled *Stella Maria*. For a longer version of this unique tale of the sea, see *Rock and Tempest, Fire and Foe: From the Shipping Files of Robert Parsons* (2010).

Captain W. Taylor of Carbonear had done well in the fall of 1903 on the Labrador fishery with the schooner *Bessie Williams*. Before winter ice set in, he left the coast well laden with 1,200 quintals of cod in the hold. Owners Rorke and Sons of Carbonear would be pleased.

On October 15, while sailing through Stag Harbour Run, he struck a ledge and went aground. Residents of the area boarded the casualty before it had been officially abandoned, taking sails, tackles, and fittings, and making a complete wreck of the vessel. In addition, the fish in the hold was lifted out and distributed or sold to other families in the vicinity.

Once Taylor and crew reached Carbonear (via a passage on another vessel), they filed an official complaint with the law. This resulted in a full investigation. The government steamer *Fiona* left St. John's with Police Superintendent John J. Sullivan and several constables aboard. On the way it stopped at Carbonear to pick up the district judge and Magistrate Alfred Penney (born and living in Carbonear) and some of the crew of *Bessie Williams* who were witnesses to the crime.

The first stop was Stag Harbour, where constables questioned fishermen and residents of several communities, essentially proving the people concerned had boarded and pillaged *Bessie Williams* before the vessel was properly and legally abandoned. Others summoned to appear before the court set up on *Fiona* were those who received "stolen" goods—they bought the fish taken from the schooner.

Once all the summoned men were assembled on *Fiona*, the cases were tried at several localities—Seldom-Come-By, Indian Islands, Rocky Bay (Carmanville), Change Islands, and Dog Bay (today's Horwood)—no doubt to impress upon residents the seriousness of the crime. In total, fifty-seven men had to appear before Magistrate Penney. Superintendent Sullivan conducted the prosecution with efficient, thorough ability and was commended after the affair for his successful handling of the "*Bessie Williams* Case."

First tried were those who had bought or received stolen property. Mark Penny was fined $150 for buying some of the fish; Fred Scott was

$10 and had to give up the received goods he had. Philip Noel passed back his twenty quintals of fish. Sol Roberts of Change Islands was fined $250 and delivered up to the magistrate the value of the fish bought. Of the 1,200 quintals of fish on *Bessie Williams*, about 400 quintals were recovered, as well as its chains and anchors.

Then came the trial of each wrecker. Fines ranged from $1 to $300, and in the end it was determined there were five ringleaders. William Edgar Sheppard, Lemuel Hodnott (Hoddinott), Joseph Gale, and George Sheppard received six months and Leander Perry four months. They were put in chains on *Fiona* and brought to St. John's to serve the time. Others, fined but released, are listed in Appendix A with surname spellings as they appeared in the report.

On December 18, SS *Fiona* left Stag Harbour Run, expecting to arrive in St. John's on December 20 with the five prisoners aboard. Before leaving, the magistrate sent the following message to the Honourable E. P. Morris, Minister of Justice:

> Change Islands
> 18th December, 1903
>
> To Minister of Justice: –
>
> Statements of captain and crew of *Bessie Williams* verified. Fifty-seven wreckers and receivers convicted; five ringleaders six months. Others paid fines ranging from one dollar to three hundred. Probably leave for St. John's tomorrow.
>
> (Signed) A. Penney

THE BONNE BAY HOSTAGES

WOODY POINT, BONNE BAY, CURLING, CORNER BROOK

THE NEWS OF A CURIOUS DRAMA came to Newfoundland's east coast when the passengers of the express train pulled into the St. John's station. It had arrived from the west coast, where people learned of "a regrettable incident" that occurred at Bonne Bay the previous week—August 24, 1938. Apparently, Sir Wilfred Woods had visited that section of the west coast when certain people took exception to his visit.

Woods, born in England, was appointed by Newfoundland's Commission of Government as Commissioner of Public Utilities. In that role he, accompanied by Commissioner for Public Health and Welfare John C. Puddester, visited Bonne Bay. There, he and Puddester would view living conditions of the people, status of roads and bridges, transportation, woods operations, and so on. Sir Wilfred's wife, Lady Ethel Palmer Woods, travelled with him.

They travelled by train to Curling and joined the customs cutter *Shulamite*, Captain J. St. Clair, to proceed north to Bonne Bay. The citizens of Bonne Bay—the loudest and most vocal were of the town of Woody Point—had long been disgruntled by the lack of government attention in their area. They were fed up, disgusted that no road existed between Bonne Bay and Deer Lake.

A road would mean quicker transportation to key and vital jobs during a tough economic time in Newfoundland—the Great Depression, a worldwide downturn in economy, jobs, and cash, resulting in poor living conditions. Many families there, as in other parts of Newfoundland, were on "the dole," or payment of six cents a day, given by the government as relief monies.

In August of 1938, tempers were at a boiling point. And here comes the very man responsible for the road construction (or non-construction, in this instance). Word got around that Woods, reduced now to the derogatory "Sir Wilfred," was coming to Woody Point on the *Shulamite*.

On August 24, a large crowd, estimated to be between 200 and 500 people, gathered at the public meeting, at which Sir Wilfred was asked what the government's intention was regarding public works, i.e. roads, in that locality. "Will we be joined up to Deer Lake so most of us can travel to find work?"

Not getting what they thought was a satisfactory reply, someone at the gathering suggested their only alternative was to stay on the dole: relief, brown flour, six cents a day, handouts.

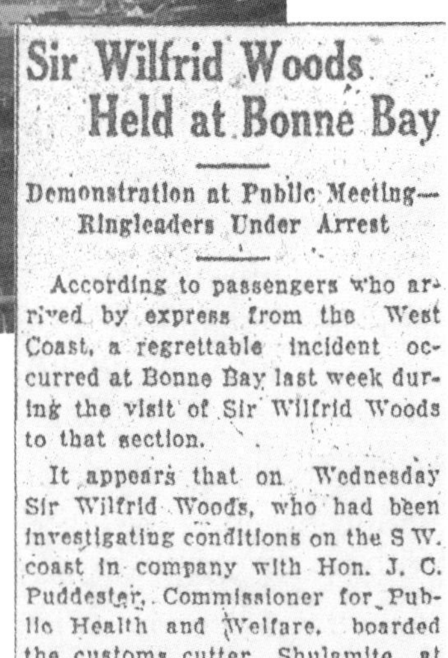

Sir Wilfrid Woods Held at Bonne Bay

Demonstration at Public Meeting—Ringleaders Under Arrest

According to passengers who arrived by express from the West Coast, a regrettable incident occurred at Bonne Bay last week during the visit of Sir Wilfrid Woods to that section.

It appears that on Wednesday Sir Wilfrid Woods, who had been investigating conditions on the S W. coast in company with Hon. J. C. Puddester, Commissioner for Public Health and Welfare, boarded the customs cutter Shulamite at

Right: The *Evening Telegram* of August 29, 1938, says: **DEMONSTRATION AT PUBLIC MEETING – RINGLEADERS UNDER ARREST.** Above: Woody Point, showing the Table Mountains in the background. This quiet Bonne Bay town was the scene of civil disobedience and subsequent arrests in the days of Commission of Government. Photo courtesy of CNS, Memorial University.

"We'll keep Sir Wilfred here for two weeks on the dole to see how he likes it!"

With that, an angry mob numbering about 200 rushed down to the public wharf where the *Shulamite* was moored and attempted to detain the ship by pulling it up on a beach. Sir Wilfred and Lady Woods lagged behind or were intentionally slowed from reaching the wharf.

Six men jumped aboard *Shulamite* while others ran with her mooring ropes along the shore to haul the ship aground. Those now on the vessel illegally were Charlie Snow, Harvey Mudge, Jim Humber, Roy Young, and Jack Ellsworth, all of Woody Point and area. John Barnes, from Norris Point, jumped overboard when *Shulamite* was relatively closer to shore and he swam to land.

Anticipating what might happen, Captain St. Clair put the vessel in "full speed astern," bursting the ropes that held it to the wharf and pulling them from the protesters' hands.

With Sir Wilfred still ashore at Woody Point and a virtual hostage, St. Clair had no choice but to steam out of Bonne Bay and return to Corner Brook. Five of the mob, the most vocal and deemed ringleaders, were still on board.

In essence there were now two sets of hostages: Sir Wilfred and his spouse left alone in Woody Point with disgruntled Bonne Bay folks; and the ship-boarding protesters (now quite contrite and quiet) stranded on *Shulamite*. One source says Woods was at the mercy of an incensed mob—which was true—and that some of them wanted to put him in chains and parade him through the town. The latter may have been implied or thought rather than actually vocalized. At any rate, Commissioner Wilfred Woods was not harmed or threatened in any way.

En route to Corner Brook, St. Clair met the government passenger freight steamer *Argyle*, proceeding to Bonne Bay with court officials. They were headed there on a regular mission without knowledge of the dispute that had just erupted.

St. Clair went aboard, reported the trouble to Chief Justice Higgins, and steamed on to Corner Brook. There the ringleaders were handed over to police.

The next day, Thursday, August 25, District Inspector John Walsh, with twelve to fifteen police, boarded *Shulamite*, travelling at top speed to Woody Point. The protesters were aboard as well, headed back to Woody Point.

Sometime that day, Sir Wilfred and his lady were taken aboard the cutter and brought back to Corner Brook, none the worse for wear.

Some media of the day downplayed the incident, stating in bold headlines: **Teapot Tempest at Bonne Bay**. "Presumably the authorities have viewed the incident as being the prank of irresponsible youth."

However, James E. Candow in his fine and informative book *Lomond: The Life and Death of a Newfoundland Woods Town* (1998), says the protesters spent the night in jail and appeared before a Corner Brook magistrate the following morning. "Although," says Candow, "they were sentenced to seven days in jail pending further discussion, they were released later the next morning and returned to Woody Point on the *Shulamite*."

Government cutter *Shulamite* and smuggling prevention vessel, which also carried justices into outport Newfoundland and brought back the accused. It was later renamed *Norsya* and lost in 1953. Courtesy of Maritime History Archives.

Sir Wilfred, in a standoff peace negotiation, apparently had wired St. John's asking for the release of the prisoners because he felt his own life was in danger.

The fifteen police officers stood tall in Woody Point in a stance to nip in the bud any further trouble, but there was none. Back safely in Corner Brook, Sir Wilfred and Lady Woods took the next train back to St. John's.

According to local sources, the protest had some benefits, as work began on the much-needed road the next year.

On the other hand, Sir Wilfred's stay in Newfoundland as commissioner was rife with other troubles and strains. He tried to negotiate a proposed pulp mill for the Gander River. Bowater, the company involved, later decided to ship the wood to Corner Brook.

During World War II, Woods was also in charge of a controversial wartime wages policy that limited the salaries of people employed on Canadian and American military bases. The policy, designed to keep wages in other areas of the economy from rising, was resented by many employees. There are many, even today, stilling residing in the Stephenville area and in Placentia Bay who recall that policy.

In 1944, Woods left Newfoundland and was replaced by Commissioner George London.

DESECRATION, SACRILEGE, OUTRAGE

ST. MARY'S, PLACENTIA

ON JUNE 27, 1884, a piece of mischief played itself out in St. Mary's. The words used to describe the dire deed, though, were harsher—invariably "despicable" and "outrageous." The desecration to a church was considered so offensive that it made newspaper headlines not only in Newfoundland but internationally and was featured in papers as far away as New Zealand.

On that Saturday night, several crew of the *Lady Elibank* went on a rampage. The 222-ton brigantine had been built in Plymouth, England, in 1880 and eventually sold to the St. John's firm of Thorburn (Sir Robert) and James Carter Tessier. The vessel had sailed into St. Mary's to discharge fishery salt, but five sailors decided they had little else to do but to pillage the Roman Catholic Church.

They demolished the furniture and the appointments for the sanctuary, destroyed the tabernacle (an ornamental cupboard used for the reserved sacrament of the Eucharist), took out the chalice (cup for the Eucharistic wine), and smashed candles, holders, and other sacred vessels. Much of the debris was strewn around the church and some out onto the streets of St. Mary's. In other various and vile ways, they desecrated the church.

Five men from *Lady Elibank* were arrested, but as soon as news of the vandalism spread around the community, citizens of the town manned about 500 small boats with the intention of setting fire to the brigantine and scuttling the vessel. However, the parish priest and supplying merchants, those who shipped or received goods on the vessel, convinced them not to do anything rash. The law would prevail. The *North Otago Times* of New Zealand said, "An outrage was perpetrated . . . five men were arrested."

Soon, news spread around St. Mary's and other southern Newfoundland villages that the five accused sailors were four Germans and a coloured man of African descent. According to the *Newfoundlander*, "This is the first act of scoundrelism of that kind that has taken place in this country of Newfoundland." The paper assumed strong drink was the prime motivator.

On July 7, an investigation by the local magistrate had ended. The lone African man was discharged and the four sailors were committed for trial at Placentia. The Supreme Court on circuit would meet there later that month.

The probe, which would come out in the trial, found they had entered the church through the window, torn off the altar rail, and used it to force open the tabernacle. From there they took away the ciborium (a container for the sacred bread) and other items, then tore down altar furnishings, vases, and candlesticks. In the vestry, or a room off the main structure, they took four articles of priests' clothing, the censer (the container where incense is burned), and the monstrance (a container for the sacred Host).

Word of the latter acts of outrage circulated around the town when the investigation went aboard *Lady Elibank*. Many of the latter articles were brought to the ship and hidden away in various parts of the hold and among the forecastle bedding.

Captain Lee and the mate of *Lady Elibank* did all they could to assist the officer of justice. In fact, the people of St. Mary's knew Lee and, owing to his personal influence and popularity, they were restrained from physically assaulting the accused.

Judge Joseph Ignatius Little presided over the trial in Placentia. A grand jury of Placentia and area citizens found a "true bill" of criminality against two of the four Norwegians: Gustafsen and Kenner. Lawyer George Henry Emerson was assigned to defend them.

When the court sat on Friday, August 22, Kenner, who at first declared he was innocent, confessed his guilt. When Judge Little asked was there any reason or statement to be made as to why sentence should not be passed, Emerson rose to give a long and passionate address.

He told the court the two men came from a barbarous land, thus they were ignorant waifs, basically uncivilized and uninstructed. Emerson's strongest point was a sweeping charge, without giving any names or specifics, against the illegal liquor sellers of St. Mary's. He stated, "St. Mary's is of so deleterious a character that not my unfortunate clients, but the vendors of such poison, should be placed upon the dock to be tried."

Judge Little corrected the defence council, stating that the accused came from Norway, a civilized and Christian land. They were not ignorant, for both could read and write. Furthermore, they were not drunk on the night of the crime.

Nor was the judge paying any attention to Emerson's argument that the wrong group was on trial and that "a sweeping charge should be made against the liquor sellers of St. Mary's." He proceeded to give instructions to the grand jury.

Kenner was sentenced to two years, Gustafsen one year and ten months, both with hard labour in the St. John's Penitentiary. Their terms would begin from the time when they were first placed in jail in July. Furthermore, they had to forfeit any monies or wages due to them by Captain Lee or the owners of *Lady Elibank.*

This incidence of destruction in St. Mary's was not the only one to occur in the summer of 1884. The fact that it happened only a day or so after the two Germans were sentenced may not have had anything to do with a spot of "Church trouble" on the Labrador Coast.

OUTRAGE BY ORANGEMEN.

ST. JOHN'S, Newfoundland, Aug. 25.—Orangemen numbering hundreds attacked the Roman Catholic Church yacht at Henley Harbor, and threatened Missionary Father Lynch with death. They tore down the papal flag and tarred the yacht.

The New York Times

Published: August 26, 1884

Leading newspapers in other lands commented on the outrageous acts of crime and lawlessness, under the guise of religion, in Newfoundland.

On August 25, Orangemen—Protestants loyal to the Royal throne of England, said to number in the hundreds—attacked the Roman Catholic

Church yacht at Henley Harbour. Most were fishermen from the coasts of Newfoundland who threatened Father Lynch with death, tore down the church flag, and threw tar over the yacht.

However, no investigation was held and no one was deemed responsible. As well, no public utterance had been given from the so-called perpetrators to defend or refute the claims. Yet, as with the outrage in St. Mary's, newspapers in another country ran the story, and it appeared thus in the *New York Times* on August 26, 1884.

THE CASE AGAINST ROBERT STRICKLAND

ISLE AUX MORTS, PORT AUX BASQUES

THE CASE OF ROBERT STRICKLAND, charged with manslaughter, was heard before a jury on November 15, 1917. His alleged offence had happened fourteen months previously. On September 13, 1916, Strickland left his home port of Isle aux Morts in a small schooner en route to Port aux Basques.

Close to the land between Snooks Head and East Baldwins, he collided with a small fishing boat. One man, William Ingram from either Hunt's Island or Burgeo, was the lone fisherman in that boat and died at the scene. He was about seventy years old. The day was calm and clear, about seven thirty in the morning.

St. John's Jury Which Heard the Case of Robert Strickland, November 14-15, 1917

Michael J. Donnelly
W. F. Donnelly
Michael Healey
Henry J. Wiseman
William J. Jocelyn
James C. Baird
William H. Jackman
Michael Wadden
Joseph Halfyard
Joseph Stick
William H. Ewing
Andrew Wright

In St. John's on November 14, the jury found a "true bill" against Strickland for manslaughter via the skiff of which he was master. Supposedly he had failed to keep a lookout. Charles Edward Hunt represented the Crown; lawyer McNeily defended Robert Strickland. Justice James Mary Kent presided.

William Knott of Isle aux Morts, a crewman on Strickland's skiff, was the first witness. He stated he left Isle aux Morts at 6:00 a.m. and, about an hour and twenty minutes later, "We ran into a boat. I was sitting on the quarterdeck; the skipper was steering. I did not see the boat until we struck it. We had no boat or dory on the skiff."

McNeily cross-examined Knott: "The skipper usually steers and does the looking out at the same time, except in dull weather, when he has a man stand forward to look ahead. At the time of the accident, the boat was sailing as near the land as possible. We saw no boats on the way from Isle aux Morts. After we struck Strickland's boat, we got into another boat that was coming out of Port aux Basques and pulled the body on board."

John Ryan, examined by lawyer Hunt, said he was on board George Marshall's skiff, of which Robert Strickland was master. "Between Snooks Head and East Baldwins we struck a boat. The first time I saw it was when it was under the bow of our skiff. I could see the Eastern Baldwin as we were about 700 yards from it."

McNeily, for the defence, asked Ryan where the course should be when off the Baldwins and went on to query Ryan about who was supposed to be on the lookout. Ryan said on fine days the steersman did the looking. According to Ryan, they were not on a fishing berth or place—off the Baldwins—where anyone did any fishing.

The doctor who examined William Ingram's body was called to the stand. He said he had been the medical practitioner at Channel for the past twenty-two years. The body was brought to Channel and he viewed it: the nose and one of the legs were broken. Since there was no water in the lungs, he had no hesitation in saying that death had been caused by a blow to the head. The doctor stated Ingram was about seventy, infirm, and should not have been fishing alone.

When asked by the defence about Robert Strickland, the doctor stated he had known him for more than twenty years as a hard-working, prosperous fisherman. The doctor also said, when questioned about the topic, that it was not customary for any particular person except the man at the wheel to keep a lookout.

Llewelyn Walters of Fox Roost stood in the witness box next and was questioned by Hunt. "I belong to Fox Roost and was coming out of Port aux Basques on the morning of September 16. I was signalled by a skiff. I then helped pick up the body of the man. I did not see any marks on the man." McNeily asked him about lookouts. "The man at the tiller is the man that would be on the lookout."

Constable John Squibb of Channel stated from the box that he proceeded to the scene of the tragedy shortly after and made an examination of the boat. Police Sergeant Gray, also of Channel, gave evidence that he examined the body after it was brought to Channel.

Finally, the sole witness for the defence took the stand—Robert Strickland. He was forty-one years old and had been master of a skiff for more than twenty years, mostly as a fisherman out of Isle aux Morts. The fishing grounds were situated, he said, "about seven and a half miles off the land."

"On the morning of the accident there was no fog, the wind was fair, and the water smooth. I was steering but saw no sign of a boat. Because I was keeping close to land, I collided with a boat. I cannot understand how it is I did not see the man or his boat.

"Immediately after we struck Ingram's boat, I signalled to Walters, who was sailing out of Port aux Basques. He came alongside, I jumped into his boat, and I picked up the poor man who was then underneath his boat."

The final questions came from Crown prosecutor Hunt, to which Strickland replied he had known the old man Ingram for a long time.

McNeily's address to the jury lasted fifteen minutes, Hunt's for about twenty. Kent instructed the jury, who deliberated about fifteen minutes. The verdict came back "not guilty."

The case against Robert Strickland was dismissed. He was free to go back to Isle aux Morts.

THE GOLD COAST POLICE

STAG BAY, LABRADOR

GOLD! GOLD IN THE HILLS! Reports of nuggets and flecks of the valuable mineral in the prospector's sluiceway touches off a human tide to fabled hills of riches. The most memorable were the Gold Rushes of California between 1846 and 1849 and the Klondike Rush in the late 1890s. Labrador, with its vast expanses and untapped mineral wealth in the early twentieth century, has not as yet experienced a Gold Rush equal to the Klondike, although in the summer of 1923, island newspapers hinted at gold in the rocks of Stag Bay, south of Makkovik.

The first Newfoundland vessel to leave port for the sole intention of exploiting the gold fields of Labrador was the *Climax*, sailing from St. John's on June 6, 1923. Captain Peter Roberts, a man with much experience in navigating the Labrador Coast, commanded the fifty-four-ton schooner. It was fitted out for mining, provisioned accordingly, and supplied with prospecting apparatus.

The Labrador Gold Deposits Limited hired Robert Henry to go along as supercargo and, as such, he had control over supplies and any subsequent cargo of the shiny yellow stuff of which dreams are made. *Climax* stopped at Hare Bay for lumber and pit props for a mine and sailed on to Stag Bay. Months later, it returned empty and the crew disappointed.

Rumours of gold in the hills of Labrador drew enough interest that explorers and prospectors came from England, but it turned out to be a fool's rush. However, enough searchers and would-be millionaires stumbled into the hills that the Newfoundland Constabulary sent a small contingent of police to Stag Bay—Labrador's first police force, albeit temporary. The twelve so-called "Gold Coast Police," outfitted with brown and khaki uniforms similar in style to traditional Royal Canadian Mounted Police garb, set up headquarters at Black Duck River.

Eventually, when the expected gold failed to materialize, the unit returned to St. John's.

Detachment of "Gold Coast Police" who left St. John's on June 18, 1923, on SS *Watchful*, returning home August 29, 1923

Sergt. Fred Churchill
Graham Trickett
Acting Sergt. F. Bennett
Alfred Cochrane
William G. Pike
Brett Oke
Michael Cahill
Jack Lewis
Gordon Lovett
Cyril Seaward
Hayward Snelgrove
B. Snelgrove

DEATH AT BEAUMONT

BEAUMONT, WARD'S HARBOUR, LONG ISLAND

BEAUMONT, ON LONG ISLAND in western Notre Dame Bay, was once called Ward's Harbour. A short while after 1918, it was renamed Beaumont, after Beaumont Hamel in France, where many of Newfoundland and Labrador's soldiers fought and died in World War I. In fact, a large number of men (per capita) enlisted from Cutwell Arm (or Cove), where Beaumont and other towns are located.

The 1836 census, the earliest reference to permanent settlement on Long Island, recorded fourteen people living at Ward's Harbour. Tradition holds that Joseph Rowsell and Abraham Burton were the first settlers. By the mid-1800s, there were about thirty people living at Ward's Harbour, Cutwell Arm (now Beaumont Central), and Quintons Cove, near Ward's Harbour. Principal family names there in the late 1800s were Burton, Croucher, Heath, Paddock, Rideout, and Rowsell. The population today is about 400.

It was a young man Burton, Lemuel Burton, who discovered an enigma at Ward's Harbour. On August 22, 1883, Lemuel accidentally stumbled upon some bones, seeing the white glistening in the underbrush. Upon closer inspection he found the skeleton of a human whom he thought to be a man.

He lifted the skull and a three-quarter-inch ball dropped out. The ball, or bullet, was flattened about one-third by the impact of striking bone. There was a red substance on the ball which appeared to be blood.

The skeleton was lying exposed somewhat near the beach in the harbour, about seven feet from the high-water mark. Soon all the community and towns around knew of the discovery; it became a puzzle of unanswered questions. It was a wonder it had not been discovered before; it was impossible for the body to have washed ashore.

No person at Ward's Harbour nor on Long Island had gone missing within the recollection of the current generation. The only satisfactory conclusion the people could arrive at was that the skeleton was that of an Indian, a Beothuk. The man must have been shot during one of the Beothuk's frequent quarrels with the white people and left exposed in the place where he was found.

In its commentary on the curious find, the newspaper *Twillingate Sun* said, "Great mystery surrounds the whole thing, however, and conjecture and speculation is in vain."

THE CAUSE OF THE CRASH: UNKNOWN

OUTER COVE, TORBAY

"AT FIRST I THOUGHT IT WAS AN EARTHQUAKE." "We hardly knew what it was, it came so fast," said members of the Richard Stack-Kinsella family in Outer Cove. "I got such a fright, I hardly knew what was happening." Whatever it was sheared off the top storey of their Outer Cove home. The bottom floor was in shambles, devastated by something that struck it. The only room left more or less intact was the kitchen, and that was the very room where four or five members of the family were sitting when something plowed into the top of the home.

The roof was torn off, and two walls of the house were knocked flat. Inside was a twisted confusion of boards and wrecked furniture. Then, to cap it all off, what was left of the dwelling caught fire. A neighbourhood bucket brigade fought the blaze until the St. John's firemen arrived sometime later. Fortunately, no one inside was hurt seriously, except for some bumps and bruises from flying house beams and lumber.

On that morning of January 9, 1956, Mr. Stack was on the road walking back to his house, but slightly out of sight of it, around a bend in the road. "It sounded to me like an earthquake. At first I thought the family had been killed," he said after. The *Daily News* reported:

> Had they [the Stack and Kinsella family] been in any other room of the house but the one in which they were sitting, they would have met instant death. Beds and other fittings were sucked out of the dwelling as if by a tornado. Pieces of the two-storey wooden frame building were carried far out to sea.

Neighbours said a plane—low-flying would be an understatement—had struck the top of the house, ripping it off. The noise when it hit the house was loud—the rip could be heard from as far away as Logy Bay, two miles distant. The aircraft, a jet, as the Stacks and neighbours learned after, had gone on at a downward angle, low over the nearby cliff, and crash-landed a few hundred feet offshore.

Following the devastation, the Stack family went next door to the home of a relative. Meanwhile, three men in Outer Cove went out in dory to view the jet debris and to search for any human remains.

A few hours later, pieces of the who-and-what puzzle began to fall in place. There was one man in the T33 jet trainer: Colonel Carl Payne, a fighter jet pilot with fourteen years experience. He had been born in Columbus, Ohio, served in World War II, and had been on duty on Newfoundland's east coast. On his final mission on that January morning, he took off from Torbay en route to Harmon Air Force Base, Stephenville. His body was recovered.

Public relations statements from Pepperell Air Force Base said Colonel Payne left fog-enshrouded Torbay using a radar beam for ground control approach and takeoff. The beam held Payne until he became "lost in ground clutter. He was too low." It was never explained why he took off in such dense fog, nor why the takeoff trajectory was so low.

His jet burst out of the fog cover four miles beyond Torbay Airport, clipped the chimney off Mr. Roche's house, trimmed the tops off fences and trees, before skimming over the 200-foot cliff edge and plowing into the sea.

Equally curious yet providential was the fact that Mrs. Stack, her two daughters, and one grandchild were all in the kitchen, the only room left intact. As well, the young Stack boy was, fortunately, outside playing and a safe distance from the lifting suction of the jet engines. Mr. Stack was walking up the road toward the doomed structure that was once his house. It was the first fatal air accident connected with Torbay Airport in its fourteen years as an air base.

ARSON

GRAND BANK, ST. JOHN'S

AT MIDNIGHT, MARCH 9, 1898, a fire broke out at a home in Grand Bank. Right away it was suspicious in nature from the intensity and the point of origin when discovered. Nevertheless, the fire alarm spread among the people, and soon the church bell called inhabitants to the scene of the blaze now roaring out of control.

The house was owned and occupied by a Mr. Rose, known in the community as a hard-working, well-mannered man. A strong wind blew that night. Fears spread among all that much of the town would be engulfed, for many other wooden structures stood near the Rose house.

But all went to work with a will—men, women, and children. The people quickly organized the long line of a bucket brigade from the sea to the burning home. Buckets of water were passed from hand to hand, and desperate work brought the fire under control. Although other homes were ten to twelve feet away, it was confined to one dwelling.

The dangerous blaze helped the people realize it would be essential to have a horse-drawn fire engine in the growing town; they knew St. John's had several fire wagons. Providence favoured Grand Bank as well, for that night a gentle but steady rain fell, helping to keep the fire under control.

Once the initial danger was over, the question arose as to how the fire originated. At the time, in Grand Bank there was a conscientious policeman, Sergeant Oldford. It was not long before the constable investigated and had made an arrest for arson. According to popular opinion, it was not the first time Oldford had used his abilities as a detective to solve a crime. He was considered in Grand Bank to be "a worthy and esteemed constable."

Not long after, word got around of the arrest—an announcement that surprised the whole community. It was learned that Oldford was en route to St. John's with his prisoner. The town knew but kept the prisoner's name mum. On May 27, 1898, the *Evening Herald* carried a clip announcing the arrival of Sergeant Oldford in St. John's with his prisoner:

> Sergt. Oldford brought to this city last night a woman from Grand Bank named Griffin, who is charged with arson and whose case will be at once submitted to the Grand Jury so as to admit of its being tried at the present term of Court.

On June 6, the Supreme Court jury assembled and found a "true bill"—sufficient cause for a trial—against the arsonist, ***** Griffin, in a crime committed at Grand Bank. The prisoner, when told she would be arraigned by Supreme Court and brought to trial, decided to plead guilty. There would be no trial.

Without a trial, many hints, innuendoes, and unanswered questions remained. Motivation, method, and opportunity would not be revealed. The woman, however, was remanded to await sentence.

TRIAL OF THE LOOTERS

BAY OF ISLANDS, LARK HARBOUR, BOTTLE COVE

THE GLOUCESTER SCHOONER *FERNWOOD*, which had been to Bay of Islands collecting herring, became jammed by Arctic ice pans on January 19, 1904. Two nights later, when it seemed as if the schooner would be crushed by ice, it was abandoned by Captain Vincent Nelson and his six or seven crew. All were American citizens.

In freezing temperatures and a violent blizzard, they walked over the ice to the tip of the Port au Port Peninsula. There, families of Jesso and McDonald took them in, fed them, and helped them find transportation to a train, thence across the Gulf of St. Lawrence and home to the United States. A longer tale of the arduous trek by Nelson and crew can be found in *Rock and Tempest, Fire and Foe: From the Shipping Files of Robert Parsons* (2010).

The *Fernwood* was not completely destroyed by ice but drifted in close to land at Lark Harbour, a fishing community on the north shore of the Bay of Islands, near its southwestern entrance. The community name originated with Captain James Cook, who, while surveying the area in 1767, named the harbour after one of his ships, HMS *Lark*. By the mid-1800s, English settlement was well-established here. Many families came from Conception Bay, others from Bonne Bay and Placentia Bay, while some came directly from the Channel Islands. Principal family names there in 1935 were Childs, Murrin, Park, Sheppard (thirty-three families), Vincent, and Youden.

THE SUMMONS

That winter, 1904, *Fernwood* was considered by local inhabitants to be an abandoned wreck. Several men had gone out to the derelict and taken goods illegally. By then *Fernwood* had drifted with the ice back northward, closer to land, and finally came to rest three miles off Little Harbour Head.

Word came down to shipping authorities that *Fernwood* had been plundered of everything movable and much that was nailed down. Salvage and wrecking laws of Newfoundland said goods taken from a wreck had to be declared and that salvors could claim a portion of the goods or its value, usually a third to a half.

But *Fernwood*'s material had been carried to shore, not declared, and hidden from prying eyes. Word reached the Minister of Justice in St. John's, who instructed Bay of Islands Wreck Commissioner Angus McEchren to launch an investigation and to look for the alleged looters and their plunder. Sergeant Sheppard went with him to Lark Harbour, where many of the perpetrators were believed to be. There, Customs Collector and Preventative Officer W. A. Gabriel told him who was alleged to have taken and secreted property belonging to *Fernwood.*

Police Superintendent John J. Sullivan was slated to come from St. John's to prosecute and lawyer Michael P. Gibbs to defend. However, mid-winter snow and storms delayed train service. Levi March, born in Old Perlican, had been the magistrate in Bay of Islands since 1898 and knew most of the principal defendants involved. They assembled before him on February 23, 1904.

March asked each defendant if he wished to wait for legal counsel, but each wished the case to be heard at once before him. (They were given advice that the case against them was strong and to hire a lawyer could be money wasted.) George Sheppard was charged with inciting the men of Lark Harbour and other nearby places to loot the abandoned American vessel. Nine or ten others were charged for looting or plundering the vessel.

WEDNESDAY, FIRST DAY OF COURT

The next day, Wednesday, court began. First witness for the Crown and questioned by Mr. McEchren was Henry Norman. On January 28, he said, he and Jonathan Sheppard (of George) and Richard Sheppard were the first out of the abandoned vessel. "It was in A-1 condition. Being the first on board, I claimed the privilege of directing the movements of the ship. About two p.m. the next day, another group reached the ship: William Parks, Ll. Gabriel, Fred Gabriel, John Joyce, John Childs, William Sheppard, and John Snooks.

"When these men heard I was in charge, they left. Then another crowd came—William Sheppard, Jonathan Sheppard, Moses Sheppard, Isaac Sheppard, and others who all left when they knew I was in charge.

"About noon, a third group of men showed up. I recognized George Sheppard Sr., Henry Gallant, Joseph French, John Sheehan, John Sheppard, Leonard Perdy, and James Drugget. They looked over the vessel but understood I was in charge. George Sheppard incited the men to take things and also told his son, Jonathan, to go back to shore.

"George and Jonathan Sheppard left the vessel, but before they did, Jonathan asked if there was anything he could do for us. I replied, 'Yes, send some good men from Lark Harbour,' and gave him the names.

"Others remaining then began to take items from the forecastle: provisions, an axe, bedding, cooking utensils, and so on. I left the vessel about four in the afternoon to go home to Lark Harbour, and Richard Sheppard, one of our men, stayed.

"At home, I wrote a letter to the magistrate at Bay of Islands, telling him of my position and my determination to stand by the vessel. I was prepared to guard the vessel, even if it was for a month or two.

"Richard Sheppard returned to Lark Harbour, bringing with him the riding light and foghorn."

At this point, defendant George Sheppard asked Norman about the condition of *Fernwood*, the ice around it, and if it was safe to go aboard of it. To the latter question Norman stated he was satisfied to risk his life to go aboard.

James L. MacAulay, another witness for the Crown, took the stand. He went on board *Fernwood* alone just when Norman took charge, understanding that Norman and two others were in charge. Everything was intact then. In addition to Norman's group, he saw George Sheppard, John Sheppard, and George Mallow on the ship. He left, went back the next day, and saw a large crowd taking the mainsail ashore from the ship.

Upon questioning, he said he met George Sheppard in the ship's forecastle but heard him used no inciting words, except to tell his son to pack his bag. "I did not hear Norman advise men not to touch anything."

A resident of Bottle Cove (a little north of Lark Harbour), John Sheehan, was up next. He went on *Fernwood* on January 28 with Henry Gallant, James Jesso, Peter French, and John Travers. There was no one aboard then. "The next day, I found Mr. Norman and Jonathan Sheppard in charge, but George Sheppard and others were there, too. George Sheppard advised his son to leave the vessel. I saw Joseph French with something in his possession but don't know what it was. I took a kettle, a shovel, and some old clothes."

George Mallow went to the ship on January 29, he said when up in the witness box. William Joyce was with him. He heard George Sheppard address his son. Mallow did not take anything, as he knew it was illegal. He saw Mr. Jno. Travers Sr. take away some beef.

James Joyce, when called, admitted to being on the *Fernwood*. He learned Norman was in charge and took nothing. Next was John Joyce, who said he was from Lark Harbour. He went out to the ship in company with David Park, Joseph French, and John Childs on January 28. Although he knew Norman was in charge, he saw others taking things ashore, so he took an old baking pot, one sidelight, a flag, a piece of rope, and some plates. "I told Mr. Gabriel, the customs officer, about what I took the next day."

When questioned about George Sheppard being in charge, he said he saw the man talking to his son but didn't think he gave orders to anyone else.

The man who first aligned himself with Henry Norman as self-proclaimed caretaker, Jonathan Sheppard (of George), was sworn in next. He remained all night of January 27 on guard, but other parties came later: William Sheppard, Moses Sheppard, and others. They didn't stay, but Francis Sheppard and Richard Mullins came, too, but didn't take anything.

"My father, George Sheppard, came on board and he requested me to leave. When I was on board, all sails and running gear were intact, also the cooking utensils. Richard Sheppard and myself prevented Mullins and Francis Sheppard from taking things. George Mallow took some old clothes, Francis Sheppard a pair of paddles, John Sheppard some beef. I did not hear my father tell anyone to take anything."

The final person in the witness stand on Wednesday was George Sheppard Sr., who was accused of inciting others to plunder. "I went out with the intention of getting my son to leave. Two men—Henry Gallant and Leonard Perdy—went with me. I went down into the forecastle and told my son to pack his bag, as it appeared to me the vessel was not in fit condition for a man to risk his life on board.

"After half an hour, four or five others came out to the vessel, including John Travers and Joseph French. One of them said he would have a piece of beef. I have had connection with other wrecks and knew it was wrong to take anything from an abandoned vessel. If Norman had told the men not to touch anything, I don't think the vessel would have been stripped."

THURSDAY, SECOND DAY OF COURT

The defendants Henry Gallant, James Jesso, Peter French, Joseph French, Leonard Perdy, John Sheppard, James Drugget, and John Travers pleaded guilty and claimed they took items through ignorance of the law. Jonathan Sheppard (of Isaac) and Richard Sheppard pleaded not guilty.

George Mallow, a Crown witness and a resident of Lark Harbour, said he went on board *Fernwood* on Saturday morning but did not see the sails being taken off. James Joyce, also a witness, was on *Fernwood* on Friday and Saturday. Sails were intact; he didn't see anyone handling sails. "I saw Peter French going ashore with a stove on his back." He also saw others—Martin Sheppard and Richard Sheppard—with goods. He met two slides between Lark Harbour and Little Harbour, both with canvas, and one was owned by Francis Sheppard.

Wreck Commissioner Angus McEchren swore witness next, summarizing his instructions from the Minister of Justice and his investigation with Sergeant Sheppard. He stated on the stand that he visited certain premises in Lark Harbour: James Jesso, Richard Sheppard, Jonathan Sheppard, Joseph and Peter French, John Travers Sr. and Jr., Henry Gallant, Francis Sheppard, John Sheehan, John Childs, Isaac Sheppard (of Isaac), David Park, John Joyce, John Sheppard (of Moses), Frank Sheppard, Richard Mallow, Richard Childs, Leonard Perdy, James Drugget, William Sheppard (of William), George Childs, and Stephen Sheppard.

The goods collected (listed right) were stored in Mr. Norman's premises. Jonathan Sheppard expected salvage for taking the sails ashore and, at first, was unwilling to relinquish his claim on the sails.

Items taken from grounded schooner *Fernwood*

35 fathom rope	paddles
bedding	looking glasses
blocks	gun
foghorn	compass
anchor	four charts
lightstove	flags
clocks	cooking utensils
chairs	axe
lamps	flour
log	provisions
grindstone	kettle
canvas	shovel
beef	clothes

On the stand, Sergeant Sheppard said he interviewed Jonathan Sheppard (who acknowledged having taken the mainsail off the vessel), together with Isaac Sheppard, Henry Sheppard (of Isaac), and Moses Sheppard (of Moses). Richard Sheppard admitted to taking the foresail, riding light, and foghorn. Martin Sheppard and Leonard Vokey had taken doors and halyards.

Preventative Officer W. A. Gabriel testified he heard of *Fernwood*'s position in the ice on January 27. He sent his son on board to look at its condition and then understood Mr. Norman had charge of the vessel:

> When I learned of goods being landed from *Fernwood*, I told the parties concerned to report them to me. Those doing so were David Park, John Joyce, Jonathan Sheppard, Richard Sheppard, Jonathan C. Childs, Francis Sheppard, and John Sheppard (of Moses). When the Wreck Commissioner arrived, I referred these men to him.
>
> Only then did others come forth with quantities of rope, canvas, paddles, and so on: John C. Childs, John Childs, George Childs, John Snooks, William Sheppard (of William), Moses Sheppard (of Moses), and Isaac Sheppard.

Finally, there were short statements by four defendants during which one, Richard Sheppard, said he had taken the foresail off with the intention of giving it to whoever owned it and that it was landed on Mr. Jonathan Travers's wharf. With that evidence, the trial closed on Thursday evening.

JUDGMENT FRIDAY, FINAL DAY OF COURT

Magistrate Levi March had to sort through the various statements and testimonies, those who willingly gave up goods, those had who admitted guilt, and those who appeared to be still unwilling to admit any wrongdoing. On Friday evening, February 26, he lectured the plunderers, stating how serious the crime of wrecking was. He read out statements coming from officials at Bonne Bay and Trout River, further proving that *Fernwood* had been stripped, looted, and plundered. He then passed judgment.

The case against George Sheppard was dismissed. No evidence had come forth to say or show he was a leader or inciter. Henry Gallant, James Jesso, Peter French, Leonard Perdy, James Drugget, John Sheppard (of Moses), and John Travers were found guilty of appropriating property from *Fernwood* and each fined $50 or three months imprisonment with hard labour. Jonathan Sheppard (of Isaac) and Richard Sheppard were also convicted and were fined $100 each or four months in prison. The fines were paid in each case.

The *New York Times* ran a brief column on February 27, 1904, saying:

> **LOOTED AMERICAN SCHOONER**
> **Newfoundland Fishermen Fined for**
> **Robbing Ice-Crushed *Fernwood***
>
> ST. JOHN'S, N.F. February 26 – The courts today fined nine west coast fishermen from $50 to $100 each, with the alternative of from two to four months in jail, for looting the American schooner *Fernwood*, which hails from Massachusetts, and which was crushed in the ice floes off the seaboard a month ago.
>
> The crew of the *Fernwood* left their vessel and came to land over the ice. The schooner was later driven inshore and the coast people boarded and stripped it.

TRAGEDY AT THE TILTS

TILTON, SPANIARD'S BAY, RIVERHEAD, HARBOUR GRACE

TILTON IS LOCATED ON THE SHORE of a pond just inland from Spaniard's Bay. In the early 1800s, it was a winter house area for the people of Spaniard's Bay and Bishop's Cove. Temporary shelters (or tilts) gave rise to the name the Tilts, or Tilt Town, which was eventually shortened to Tilton. From Tilton a path crossed the barrens of the interior to New Harbour, Trinity Bay, but until a road was constructed between Spaniard's Bay and Harbour Grace in the 1840s, Tilton was considered an isolated community.

On a Sunday morning, May 3, 1873, the general populace of the Tilts and Spaniard's Bay had heard rumours of a violent death, or "a terrible tragedy," as the media of the day termed it. It had happened at the Tilts, about four miles from Riverhead. Head Constable Fallon and two policemen arrived on the scene, where they saw the results of a Saturday night debacle.

As they approached the tilt of a family named Singleton, a man could be seen stretched along the ground with his hands and feet tied, his head and face terribly mutilated, and life almost gone from the body.

After freeing the man from his bonds and trying to alleviate his sufferings somewhat, they entered Singleton's place. There they found more suffering. The father, Richard Singleton, lay on a bench, blood flowing from a wound on his side that had been inflicted by a sharp instrument.

When the police questioned those in the immediate vicinity, it was gathered that on the previous evening, Saturday, the unfortunate man,

James Coffee, found by the police outside the tilt, had returned from Harbour Grace intoxicated.

An argument broke out that turned violent. Who instigated the row was not clear, but Coffee was stabbed with a knife. It seemed as if the disturbance originated in the residence of Singleton, and Coffee, overpowered by a person or persons inside, was unmercifully beaten and thrown outside the door. He remained there until found by police the next morning.

In the evening, Coffee was moved to the police station, where everything possible was done to save his life, but he died a few hours later. A post-mortem examination found the deceased had received several fatal stab wounds about the head and his skull was fractured.

Fallon rounded up six persons connected with the crew, either as perpetrators or witnesses, and took them into custody. In the preliminary examination of the facts, witnesses, and circumstances of the case, a "true bill" was found against Mr. Singleton and his two sons, John and Albert.

The family consisted of the father, two sons, and two daughters, living in the vicinity of Spaniard's Bay. The dead man, James Coffee, not married, lived with the family and courted or was seeing one of the Singleton girls.

On the Saturday evening in question, Coffee was seen by neighbours passing their homes on his way to Singleton's. He was seen to be staggering and assumed to be intoxicated. Coffee was reputed to have a violent temper when drunk and had made use of dire threats against those of the Singleton house.

He arrived at the hut or tilt, and when he entered, he was said to be "surly." When questioned by the girl he knew well as to what was wrong with him, he struck her.

A quarrel arose between him and the Singletons. Some witnesses said Coffee caused the dispute, while others said the Singletons. At any rate, a scuffle broke out, in which the elder Singleton was stabbed. The fight that had started in the tilt continued outside. The elder Singleton knocked Coffee down with one or two blows to the head.

From the depositions given to the court, the brothers Singleton tied Coffee hand and foot where he lay and left him exposed to the cold and frost of a winter's night. He was subsequently covered by the women, but he did not appear to move afterward.

In the morning, the family sent for the police, who arrived and removed Coffee. However, he died that day. The medical evidence at the inquiry showed death resulted from injuries to the head and neck.

The trial of the Singletons lasted one day, May 28, during which the father, Richard Singleton, was found guilty. John Singleton had already been released as there was no proof he had committed any wrongdoing. Albert, found not guilty, was ordered to be discharged.

UNIQUE THEFT OF A BOAT

ROUND HARBOUR, LITTLE BAY ISLAND, BROAD COVE

WITH THOUSANDS OF WATERCRAFT in Newfoundland, the tales or cases of stealing a schooner, a boat, a skiff, or a canoe are probably numerous—enough stories, perhaps, to fill a book in itself. The ubiquitous schooner, rodney, punt, and dory inhabited every cove, harbour, nook, and cranny in Newfoundland and Labrador from the times of early settlement and remained a commonplace mode of travel right up to a generation ago.

Perhaps the only detailed description of a boat theft from the early nineteenth century comes from a man of the cloth, Walter R. Smith. It is not the boat itself or the crime that is of interest, but *who* took it.

In January 1887, Reverend Smith wrote of a parishioner he knew well, Mrs. Elizabeth Mitchell. Elizabeth died that year at the age of ninety-four and was buried in Broad Cove, near Portugal Cove, her place of residence at the time. She was born on St. Patrick's Day, 1793, at Round Harbour, near Tilt Cove, Notre Dame Bay. Her maiden name was King. Elizabeth left Round Harbour when she was about fifteen, living for many years in St. John's and Broad Cove.

One curious part of her life story happened approximately in 1803 when she was ten or eleven years old. She had an excellent memory of events in her early life when Rev. Smith talked to her and she had distinct recollections of the native people of Newfoundland, having seen them in her childhood. She described the Beothuk as a tall and handsome people, both men and women.

She also made reference to the fact Round Harbour is near Indian

Burying Place. Local tradition holds that this name (now an abandoned fishing community) is a reference to the Beothuk, who no doubt had visited the area long before the arrival of European settlers. According to tradition, the first settlers were attacked by natives because the location was, according to *Lovell's Newfoundland Directory*, 1871, "the burying place of the Red Indian tribes and a number of birch coffins having been dug up close by."

A few months before Mrs. Elizabeth Mitchell died, she gave the minister an interesting description of a visit paid to her father and family by the Beothuk. It happened in 1805 when she was twelve years old.

Her father had gone to do his winter's work cutting timber at Little Bay Island. Mr. King was the first temporary or permanent settler there, according to Elizabeth. Just before this, Elizabeth's mother had died, and the girl, even at that young age, was her father's housekeeper. She went with him for the winter to cook and clean at Little Bay Island.

Shortly after their arrival, the natives paid them a visit by night and stole their boat, which contained all their provisions and food for the winter. The father set out to look for his boat and, fortunately, found it, bottom up, on another portion of the island. Otherwise, said Elizabeth, the Kings would have perished from hunger that winter.

Mr. King at once proceeded to Round Harbour and obtained supplies from a Mr. Cole, whose son was the stipendiary magistrate at Trinity, circa 1887. Cole had a business at Round Harbour.

All was well that ended well for that unique theft from one of Newfoundland's pioneer settlers by the first peoples, the Beothuk, who lived in that area around the beginning of the nineteenth century.

ABANDONING A VOYAGE: A TEST CASE

FORTUNE, GRAND BANK

WHEN DISTRICT MAGISTRATE Reuben Sparkes heard evidence in the last week of February 1947, the Grand Bank courthouse was full. The verdict, when it came down, would be of prime importance to the local deep-sea fishery. Everyone knew fishermen were hired for a voyage (the fishing year consisting of the spring trip, the summer trip, and the fall trip) on a "verbal" or spoken basis. There were no written contracts or agreements signed by anyone, often with not even a handshake. Now such verbal contracts were being disputed.

In that era, the greatest concentration of Newfoundland's deep-sea cod fishery vessels was on the south coast, especially the Burin Peninsula, with other centres being Harbour Buffett, Belleoram, English Harbour West, Harbour Breton, and Burgeo. The fish was caught by dory fishermen, by hook and line, and dressed and salted away on a wooden schooner, usually motor-driven.

On the south coast there was still a fairly large fleet: the new banker *Daphne and Phyllis* built at Garnish was to make its maiden fishing voyage to the Grand Banks under owner Harold Dawe of Cupids. He planned to have two other bankers in operation—*Jean and Mona* and *C. A. Anderson*. Eleven schooners were set to sail from Grand Bank—six from Harbour Buffett, three from English Harbour West, and several more from other south coast ports.

Two ships had been purchased from Lunenburg—the *Bessemer* and the *Harriett and Vivian*—and would be operating out of the south coast.

The previous summer, some wooden bankers had been engaged in fresh fishing, then in the winter of 1946–1947, the demand for fresh fish fell off slightly and the owners put them back salt fishing.

In another technological change, Fishery Products in Burin had the *Mustang* fishing all winter, bringing good catches of fresh fish and processing it in their Burin plant. The Burin company also had two new additional draggers. They were steel-constructed ships *Zebu* and *Zebit*, built to replace the wooden vessels in their fleet. They did have a new wooden dragger, the *Dingo*, which was soon expected to operate in the fresh fishing trade.

On the other hand, by 1947, the salt fish trade was dying, destined to be quickly replaced by a fresh fish product—frozen when landed, not salted at sea. As well, by then, some men had been going to Lunenburg, Nova Scotia, for several years. Monies, food, personal life or injury insurance, amenities, and working conditions on the Nova Scotian vessels were better. Men were paid a wage whether they caught fish or not. Yet, in the winter and spring of 1947, there was a fishermen's strike at Lunenburg. Their fleet was tied up, and many Newfoundland fishermen who usually fished in Nova Scotian vessels were seeking berths on local schooners.

Better food! Wages! Steel draggers! Fresh fish! Changes! Innovations! It was almost more than an everyday, hard-working doryman could comprehend. Now in late February 1947, a local magistrate was about to impose another change, bound to have social and economic implications. The decision would have a determining effect upon the future actions of banking crews who had thoughts of abandoning the fishing voyage in midsummer.

Abandon a voyage? In other words, a whole crew could and did say, "We all refuse to sail to the Grand Banks to fish." They would sail out and fish, but if there wasn't enough fish or conditions were not right, they would abandon or give up the voyage. In the summer of 1946, the crew of Lake's *Dorothy P. Sarty* did just that and walked off the vessel, never to return. At the time, the skipper of *Dorothy P.* was George Pauls of Belleoram.

The case before Magistrate Sparkes arose out of the refusal of a prominent Fortune bank fishing firm, Lake and Lake, to pay wages owed to the cook, George Forsey of Fortune, of the fishing schooner *Dorothy P. Sarty*. Why the cook? He was one person who was normally paid a wage, fish or no fish. On most south coast schooners, earnings depended on how much fish was caught, how much a dory brought in to be salted away.

Built in Shelburne, Nova Scotia, in 1915, the ninety-three-foot-long *Dorothy P. Sarty* was registered to Harold Lake of Fortune. It was a ninety-seven-ton schooner that usually carried twelve to fifteen men to the fishing grounds between March and September. Courtesy of Capt. Hubert Hall, Shipsearch Marine, Yarmouth, NS.

The company attempted to convince the crew to continue fishing, but most refused. At that point in the season, Lakes could not find enough men to fill a full crew, and the vessel had to give up its fishing voyage.

Consequently, Lakes did not pay the crew for the fish already caught that spring. The crew was at fault—they didn't finish the season. However, it fell to the lot of Cook Forsey to present the scenario in court to Magistrate Sparkes. George Forsey was right and did the honourable thing to ease the lot of the underpaid and underappreciated schooner fishermen.

According to evidence given in the Magistrate's Court, there was no apparent, legitimate, or logical reason for the crew's actions. Most people understood they were disgruntled with working conditions and low fish catches. In other words, much hard and dangerous work for little pay.

As a result, the cook of *Dorothy P. Sarty* made a "test" case to attempt to secure the money he believed was owed him: $230 for part of a season worked. One person, who described the event when both sides presented their arguments, said, "The courtroom was crowded to capacity with interested spectators."

Lake and Lake, defendants, submitted evidence the complainant had breached a verbal contract to finish the voyage. The action of the complainant was that he refused to equip the vessel with provisions, had walked ashore, and quit working without a legitimate reason.

Because of the importance of the case and the bearing it had on the fishing industry, Magistrate Sparkes adjourned the court for several days to consider the verdict. On February 27, when proceedings resumed, judgment was handed in favour of the defendant. The cook had lost.

Sparkes, however, had words of advice for the merchant operators. It was expected that they would change with the times and draw up written contracts and articles. Up to this point, most operators would have provided the fishermen with a "discharge" book and perhaps a passport in case they entered a "foreign" port, such as Saint Pierre, Sydney, or Halifax. A written contract would set out terms and conditions existing between the merchant owner and the labourer, the fisherman.

But by then, 1947, times had changed. It was an era gone with the waves. The demand for fresh frozen fillets rose higher and higher; the steel draggers replaced the hook-and-line wooden walls; set wages put the piecemeal pay to shame; and the fresh fish plants put the salting technology into obscurity.

DEATH AT SAINT PIERRE

ST. LAWRENCE, SAINT PIERRE

WHEN JUSTICE OF THE PEACE R. R. W. Lilly arrived back in St. John's in the coastal boat *Ariel* on December 6, 1870, he reported a murder, but not one easily investigated and judged in Newfoundland. Lilly had been on the circuit court along Newfoundland's south coast and had made a stop in Saint Pierre. Lilly informed the media of the day that on November 11, two men, Robert Spearing (Spearn) and David Pike, had a quarrel in the streets of Saint Pierre, one which escalated into a knife fight.

William Reeves, a brother-in-law of Pike, tried to separate the two men but was stabbed in the arm by Spearing, cutting a principal artery. Others on the scene tried to stop the flow of blood, but Reeves bled to death in the street.

All three men were married and were termed "planters." That is, they owned land, farmed, as well as fished, and all belonged to Great St. Lawrence. They had been working in Saint Pierre as independent fishermen but were supplied, or given provisions, by Atherton Hughes and Company of Saint Pierre. At the end of Justice Lilly's report, he said that Spearing alone had been brought to trial in Saint Pierre and was confined to jail there.

CASTING AWAY THE VIOLET M.

ENGLEE, BAY OF ISLANDS, BIDE ARM

THE CASE WAS THREE YEARS getting to trial. Back in the early 1900s, this was unusual as most trials began days or weeks after arrest. This nefarious tale of the sea began in November 1901, when the schooner *Violet M.* sank off Englee while on a trading voyage along the French Shore—that coastline extending from Cape St. John to Cape Ray, along which the French had fishing rights.

For nearly three years, the captain and most crewmen on the schooner thought the trouble with the vessel had developed when a plank on the hull worked loose, water flowed in, and *Violet M.* went down quickly. Or maybe it struck a pan of ice that caused a leak that could not be stemmed.

Then the conscience of one deckhand on *Violet M.* bothered him enough, he confessed to wrongdoing. On November 21, 1904, two accused men—William Hopkins and Samuel Moulton—stood before Judge George Henry Emerson in the Supreme Court, St. John's, charged with casting away, or barratry: wilfully causing a vessel to come to harm with the intent to defraud an insurance company.

The case for the Crown was presented by Charles Henry Hutchings, King's Counsel, assisted by Newfoundland's Attorney General, Edward Patrick Morris, KC.

According to the original story from three years previous, *Violet M.*, owned by Samuel Moulton and commanded by Timothy Pike, sank quickly while off Englee. Moulton, a merchant residing in Bay of Islands, owned several trading schooners, *Maggie M.*, *Mary M.*, and this latest casualty, *Violet M.*, all presumably called after members of the Moulton family. With Captain Pike on that final voyage were sailors William Hopkins of Englee, Thomas Aylsworth, G. Aylsworth (sometimes spelled Ellsworth), Aaron Reid, Albert Hancock, and the owner Sam Moulton.

VESSEL LOST

Captain Samuel Moulton lost his vessel, the *Violet M.*, nine miles off the coast, coming up the French Shore last week, by colliding with a small iceberg. The crew had barely enough time to snatch their clothes bags and jump into their small boat when the vessel went down. They were brought up by the SS *Home*.

What was once a luxury is now within the reach of all. Ask your grocer for **Browning's Biscuits.** nov21,tf

VESSEL LOST.

CAPTAIN SAMUEL MOULTON lost his vessel, the *Violet*, nine miles off the coast, coming up the French Shore last week, by colliding with a small iceberg. The crew had barely time to snatch their clothes' bags and jump into their small boat when the vessel went down. They were brought up by the S.S. *Home.*

Among the many attractions on

The news in the *Evening Telegram* of November 23, 1901, of the loss of *Violet M.* was brief and looked like a typical shipping casualty. However, there was nothing commonplace about it when the truth came out three years later.

All the crew left the schooner in its small boat and reached Englee with no harm or injury to any person. On arriving there, the captain and others signed the official protest—the declaration of how, why, and when *Violet M.* sank. The document said the schooner had struck a pan of ice that damaged its bow. It sank within a few minutes, with 240 quintals of fish and much goods aboard. The cargo aboard *Violet M.* was insured with the Union Marine Company for $3,000 and the vessel itself for $900.

Moulton compiled a statement of his losses and was subsequently paid $3,900 by Union Marine. All seemed to be well, except for the deckhand, who knew exactly what had happened that night.

Two years later, William Hopkins talked to his family in Englee of the loss of *Violet M.*, telling the story and saying how the ship had been cast away, sunk intentionally, and he was part of the illegal events. He wished to set the record right. One person of authority near Englee was the local doctor, Wilfred Grenfell, based in St. Anthony. Grenfell convinced the man to do the right thing: Hopkins made a deposition, or statement, witnessed by Dr. Grenfell.

On the strength of that confession, Hopkins and Samuel Moulton were indicted and requested to appear before the St. John's court. Hopkins said that:

> In the fall of 1901, I served with Samuel Moulton, trading, on the schooner *Violet M.* and also on the schooner *Kingfisher*. Captain Pike was master of *Violet M.* and Samuel Moulton was also on board. We transferred fish from the *Kingfisher* to *Violet M.* when both were tied up together at Englee.
>
> I also saw goods moved from *Violet M.* to *Kingfisher*. I saw, afterwards, a small trifle of goods left on board [*Violet M.*], about $40 or $50 worth of boots, homespun, ready-made clothing. The fish on board *Violet M.* when she arrived at Englee was 200 quintals.
>
> *Violet M.* was then sent to Bide Arm for ballast under instruction of Samuel Moulton. Captain Pike took on board seven punt loads of ballast [rock], then came back to Englee.
>
> We sailed for Jackson's Arm. Moulton had a conversation with me, asking me to lose his vessel and promising to give me my winter's board if I did so.
>
> So I got a file and auger and sharpened it. He told me to bore holes in the fore run, partway through the vessel. I did so.
>
> Then we left for Duggan's Arm [south of Englee and near Great Harbour Deep]. We had about eight or nine quintals in the hold when the holes were bored, but before that there was no fish or oil in her, only rocks.
>
> On the way from Duggan's Arm to Englee, Samuel Moulton asked me again to lose the vessel. I demurred or hesitated, but he persuaded me and we went down below. I punched one hole through and Moulton punched four.
>
> He then told me to tie a twenty-eight-pound weight and swing it off to strike the bow of the vessel to drive out the planks. Moulton was alongside me, telling me what to do.
>
> The pumps were tried and water was found in the vessel. We, Moulton and I, worked the pumps to let the captain see we were trying to keep her free of water.
>
> *Violet M.* wouldn't sink fast enough. Moulton told me to cut another hole to let the wind out of her. I made one chop with the

axe and cut a hole at the waterline and she soon sank. We did this as another vessel was coming near.

The Crown brought forward other witnesses: the two Ellsworth men, Reid, Hancock, Fanny Wilcox, and Captain Pike. Pike testified that the goods reported on the deposition as being on the vessel were in fact not on board. Court concluded on November 23, 1904, when owner Samuel Moulton was sentenced to two years in the penitentiary and William Hopkins one year.

UNIQUE NAME, COMMON CRIME

CAPE BROYLE, ST. JOHN'S

CAPTAIN SUTTON IN HIS SCHOONER *X-10-U-8* sailed in through the St. John's Narrows from Trepassey on Tuesday, November 24, 1898. He had stopped along the way at Cape Broyle to take on six passengers, among them an elderly man of eighty-one, W. Devereaux.

Newfoundland's registry of ships shows two vessels with such an odd name: an *X-10-U-8* built in Green Bay whose registry closed in the 1880s, and one built in Random Sound by Nehemiah Frost which sailed in Newfoundland waters right up to the 1920s. This, then, may be the thirty-one-ton schooner on which a common crime happened and was solved by the doggedness of a city policeman.

X-10-U-8 docked at Baine Johnston's wharf and Mr. Devereaux went ashore to do whatever business required. He went back aboard the schooner at 5:00 p.m. and, to his surprise, found the cover of his trunk smashed. A small container in the trunk was broken open and the sock inside it was gone. The sock contained $48 in gold and silver coins.

Normally the crew would have been aboard, but on that afternoon of the theft, all went ashore except one man. Mr. Condon of Cape Broyle, a friend of Devereaux, and another man, Mr. Field of the schooner, walked at once to the police station to report the theft.

At the station they described what had happened to Superintendent John J. Sullivan, who assigned Sergeant Peet to the case. The same morning, District Inspector Grimes and Sergeant Peet brought in the crew of the schooner to the station: Harvey, Carew, Keefe, and Captain Sutton.

All were quite willing to help in any way to help old Mr. Devereaux get his money back and to bring to justice whoever had committed this petty theft. They all agreed to be searched. Various amounts were found on their persons, ranging from $5 to $200. The money could not be identified as stolen cash, and each man could give a good and just cause as to where he had obtained the money.

Upon questioning the crew, the police found three boys had been aboard the schooner around noon that day, selling shoe polish, combs, and other sundry items. Grimes knew who they were and where they lived. Upon questioning, he learned they had left *X-10-U-8* around 1:00 p.m. Devereaux's cache had been rifled between 3:00 and 5:00 p.m.

There was one other man, supposedly a friend to all and not suspected as a thief, aboard the vessel all afternoon. John Hawkins, a fisherman of Cape Broyle, left the vessel when it got dark to sleep at a friend's house.

He was arrested that night and brought into the station. He denied any involvement and nothing of a suspicious nature was found on his body. The only clue to solving the theft would have been in finding a gold or silver coin that had been in the stocking. Suspicions pointed to one of the passengers.

After the crew and Hawkins had been searched, they were free to leave the station. However, one detective, Sergeant Collins, followed the trail with "some admirable detective work."

Collins went to *X-10-U-8*'s forecastle and searched the bunks. In Hawkins's bunk he found one of the missing pieces of silver. Collins then arrested John Hawkins. A portion of the stolen money was found on his body and he later confessed to his guilt. He then took Collins to a place at Riverhead, in St. John's, where the balance of the stolen goods had been concealed.

In court on November 24, Hawkins pled guilty, paid back $36.22, and promised to pay the balance. He was remanded for eight days to await sentencing.

A CRIME MOST FRIGHTENING

PORT SAUNDERS, GRAND BANK, ST. JOHN'S, BURGEO

IN HER BOOK *DON'T LOOK BEHIND YOU* (2011), crime writer Ann Rule, a renowned American author with more than thirty books published on crime and murder, calls rape "the most frightening crime of all." That crime, the forcing of one individual's sexual desires upon a helpless victim, leaves psychological scars that last a lifetime. Rule, like others, believes most victims of rape fear for their lives so much and are so ashamed of the outrage committed upon them that they rarely report the event to authorities.

In the annals of crime in Newfoundland of a generation or two ago, it is rare to find accounts of rape and subsequent conviction. In this story, the victim did seek justice. It happened in the evening of August 30, 1916, when Mrs. R* of Port Saunders answered a knock on her door.

She had been married for four years and had two children, aged three years and thirteen months. Her husband was away fishing on the Labrador, but a neighbour, Mrs. Rumbolt, was visiting. Rumbolt was sitting in the kitchen, or parlour, and would have been unseen by anyone standing in the doorway—especially dark strangers who knocked on Mrs. R's door.

It was just getting dark when the knock came. Two men, strangers, stood by the door and, within a moment, stepped inside. One man asked if Mrs. R had any eggs or milk to sell. Her reply was no. The next question was more ominous: Is your husband away fishing? Mrs. R replied that he was. After ten minutes, the two went away.

Mrs. R knew a south coast schooner was in the harbour. The *Lizzie M. Stanley*, a 125-ton banker, usually carried twenty or more crew. On this occasion it may have been on a coasting or trading mission and had a crew of the captain and four sailors.

About nine o'clock, the woman visitor, Rumbolt, had gone home. The two children were settled away and Mrs. R retired for the night. Shortly after, she was awakened from her sleep by the sound of a strange voice at her door saying, "Hello, let me in."

The woman became frightened, begging the person not to come in, but her pleadings were to no avail. She seemed to recognize the voice as that of the man who had stopped at her door hours before. The door was forced open and, as the *Evening Telegram* described what happened, the man "like a wild beast with all sense of human nature cast aside, violently and feloniously assaulted the woman in the presence of her children."

When he was finished, the man offered her $10, which she refused to accept.

Immediately after he left the house, the helpless and terrified woman gathered up her two children in her arms and ran to the home of her father-in-law, Mr. R*, who lived about 100 yards away.

With tears streaming down her face, she related her story to her husband's parents. It was the same man, a stranger in the small town, who had knocked on her door earlier. Mr. R calmed his distraught daughter-in-law as best he could.

Early the next morning, Mr. R went to the residence of the local Justice of the Peace, Mr. Garland. All the happenings of the previous evening and night were described to him. Garland knew the only strangers unaccounted for in the small community were those men on the schooner *Lizzie M. Stanley*. The description of the perpetrator seemed to fit the captain of that schooner, James Bellman, a resident of Grand Bank.

Garland asked Captain Bellman to step onto the wharf, which he did. He then told him he was a suspect in the rape of Mrs. R, which had occurred on the night previous. Somehow the crew of *Lizzie M. Stanley* knew what was transpiring, let go the mooring ropes, and attempted to sail the schooner out of the harbour.

Garland stopped them; he informed the crew that they would be witnesses if the case went to court. In his own court of inquiry, held right there in Port Saunders, Garland questioned the crew and recorded the names: James Drake, Albert Rose, George Stone, and Stephen Hickey, all south coast mariners. They had knowledge of what had happened, although they all denied being at Mrs. R's residence during the commission of the crime. Stone and Hickey were told they were key or chief witnesses and would have to appear in court to testify.

A little over three months later, December 7, 1916, the accused, Captain James Bellman, stood before the Supreme Court in St. John's, Chief Justice William Horwood presiding. The Honourable Michael P. Gibbs represented the Crown; L. E. Emerson defended the accused. (Later in his life, Lewis Edward Emerson was knighted, becoming Sir Emerson.) A jury (right) had been selected.

William Jackman
Fred Chafe
Michael Wadden
John J. Lawlor
John Savage
Samuel Feaver
Jonas Barter
Ambrose Shaw
George Cook
Raymond Cramm
Frank Connors
Arthur Wood

Statements by Mrs. R were judged by the media of the day, ". . . while not of a publishable nature, was at least pathetic." The first day of trial was taken up with questions from Gibbs for Mrs. R and her cross-examination by Emerson.

The next day, George Stone was the first called to the witness box. He stated he saw Captain Bellman go through the doorway of Mrs. R's house. He further stated that the captain and the four crew, himself included, were drinking rum in a Port Saunders home of a Mr. Rumbolt on the day of the crime. Bellman had supplied the liquor. In the course of the questioning, it was determined that Seaman Hickey had accompanied his captain on his first visit to the home of Mrs. R. Hickey. He was not charged, as the captain had been alone on his second, nocturnal entry.

All witnesses, including the remaining crew and Captain Bellman, had finished by 6:00 p.m. and the court recessed for supper. Then Emerson addressed the jury and "put up an able defence considering the evidence so strongly given against the accused." Gibbs, speaking for the Crown, then reviewed the evidence from various witnesses. After the chief justice's charge, the jury left, returning after fifteen minutes with a verdict. Foreman Raymond Cramm told the court they found the accused guilty.

On the morning of December 9, Captain Bellman was sentenced to two years' imprisonment with hard labour. The judge concluded that, although it was a first offence and Bellman admitted his guilt, the offence was of such a serious nature that giving a lighter sentence was not an option.

As a footnote to this heinous crime, a year later, almost to the day of the conviction of Bellman, *Lizzie M. Stanley*—owned in Burgeo by merchant J. T. Moulton—left Saint Pierre for Catalina. It was last seen on December 10, 1917. None of the crew that had been in Port Saunders a year before was on board. But the *Lizzie M.* was gone, taking with it Captain John Collier, a single man; Joseph Ingraham, aged nineteen and married; Morgan Buffett; Thomas Buffett, aged twenty; Simeon Billard, married; and Harold Knott, aged twenty-two. All were from Burgeo and area.

MANUSING AND OTHER TRANSGRESSIONS

TWILLINGATE, HARBOUR GRACE, BAY ROBERTS, ST. JOHN'S

IN THE SPRING OF 1862, seals were reported in the thousands on ice pans relatively close to shore in Notre Dame Bay. One man from Twillingate reported that the seals had put in an appearance on March 12 and could be seen about eight miles northeast of Gull Island. "I went off for the first time on St. Patrick's Day and about six miles off Gull Island I could stand on a clump of ice and see thousands upon thousands of whitecoats. I could hear nothing but their bawling. I took four [pelts] in tow."

That spring of 1862, the people of Twillingate harvested an unprecedented 40,000 seal pelts. However, the hunt was bittersweet for the correspondent, and his saga of woe appears at the end of this account of sealing misdeeds.

All but one of the sealing vessels of Harbour Grace were doing well that same season. The early April report from Punton and Munn said Captain Neil in the *Curlew* had taken 3,500 pelts. Ridley and Sons had three vessels in the seal hunt: Captain Kennedy's *Superior* had 900, and the *Echo* 1,400. One of Ridley's vessels, the *Mary* in command of Captain Lewis, was reported "clean," returning with not a single pelt or hide.

There was trouble, as it turned out—not with the ship, nor was there anyone sick, but there was a case of "manusing" aboard *Mary*.

Lewis sailed the *Mary* into Harbour Grace on April 19, 1862, with no seals, stating his crew were guilty of "Manus," bringing eleven men before Magistrate J. Peters. The law books said of manus, or manusing, "Any sealer who, by refusing to work, shall wilfully compel any master of a sealing vessel to give up the voyage" and was guilty of the crime of manusing and could be tried in a court of law. The *Standard* of Harbour Grace summed up the crime succinctly: "*Mary*'s sealers had disobeyed orders, obliging Captain Lewis to bring his vessel into port, or in other words, manusing, a word coined to mean a crime akin to mutiny."

On April 23, Stipendiary Magistrate Peters found three of *Mary*'s crew guilty of manusing and sentenced them to twenty-eight days in prison. Eight were given fourteen days' imprisonment. It was a serious offence, especially so that spring of 1862 when seals were plentiful and it was relatively easier to earn some extra income. The sentences, according to the *Royal Gazette*, "will have a most salutary effect, and will hinder others from pursuing the same reckless course in the future."(April 29, 1862)

Mutiny and manusing were not the only infractions with sealers. The men were a hardy and tough lot; the extra dollars the seal hunt represented caused petty and major riots and clashes between rival sealing "gangs." One disturbance broke out on the St. John's waterfront on March 10, 1875. It seemed trifling at first, but the newspapers of the day were quick to point out the bloody battle had "an alarming aspect."

The sealing vessel *Iceland*, Captain Charles Dawe of Bay Roberts, was moored at Stabb's Wharf. A quarrel broke out between *Iceland*'s fireman, who belonged to St. John's, and some of his shipmates who were from Bay Roberts.

Whatever the merits or cause of the fuss, it rapidly grew to a general riot between the St. John's men on one side and the outport men on the other. The battle royal lasted for several hours on the deck of *Iceland* and the finger wharf to which the vessel was tied. It flowed over to the sealer *Greenland* on the other side of the wharf. Each of the major sealing vessels would have carried in excess of 100 men. A violent clash between hundreds of men armed with sculping knives, sticks, poles, and fists was alarming and frightening for the citizens of St. John's.

The conflict spilled onto Water Street and on the ice in the harbour. A contingent of city police, mounted, under Inspector Paul Carty, was called out. These, with the help of Reverend Fathers Forristal, McGrath, and Scott, Chief Justice Hugh William Hoyles, Captains Dawe and Jackman (*Greenland*), and other leading citizens, pleaded for calm and the affray ended some hours later. Several sealers were cut and badly injured. One observer said:

> . . . it was impossible to say to what an extent the disturbance might reach; fortunately, however, though severe bodily injuries were inflicted in several instances, nothing worse resulted. The steamer *Greenland* sustained much damage from the violence from some men who forced their way on board.

In fact, *Greenland*'s repairs were quickly made and it sailed for the ice shortly after. *Iceland* received more severe damage and was unable to sail until it was repaired.

Greenland, left, SS *Vanguard*, right, both bedecked with flags. Scores of men armed with the sealer's gaff line the finger wharf, generally taking two opposing sides—the townsmen and the men from the bay.

In addition to being directly involved in the sealers' riots, the steamer *Greenland* was a hard-luck vessel. It caught fire and sank at its moorings in St. John's harbour in September 1884. It was refloated and repaired. Captain George Barbour put 154 men over the side to hunt seals on March 21, 1898, but a few hours later a sudden storm came up, which took the lives of forty-eight men by exposure or drowning.

Nine years later, on March 23, 1907, Captain Daniel Bragg and crew abandoned *Greenland* when it was crushed in ice while seal hunting off the northeast coast. They were picked up by the SS *Newfoundland*.

One of the first measures taken to prevent any future outbreaks was an order issued by St. John's magistrates forbidding licensed liquor dealers to sell rum and whisky until after the departure of the sealing fleet. Although an investigation began, no personal names of the accused were released.

One relatively obscure strike by sealers became known through a poem, a recitation, "A Crew of Jolly Sealers," describing the event. It was printed by the *Twillingate Sun* in September 1921. The SS *Eagle* sailed for the icefields on March 7 of that year under Captain Sid Hill with his Chief Officer Lewis Kean, both of Wesleyville. Thomas Carrol, Bonavista Bay, was bosun, and Captain Turner the navigator.

On March 9, the barrel man, Wesleyville's Roland Mullett, spotted the first whitecoat, yet four days later the SS *Eagle* had taken only a few pelts, much to the disgust of the fifty-seven sealers aboard. The disgruntled songwriter says:

All though the next day we did not succeed,
With full speed astern and ahead at full speed,
But on the thirteenth, as you understand,
Our little ship *Eagle* she forced through the jam,
A crew of jolly sealers.

The crew was still optimistic of a good trip. However, through the next two weeks, very few seals were seen. "I must say our captain did all that he could / In picking up the whitecoat and shooting the old hood." The captain informed the men they were now into the patch of whitecoats, and he sent them out over the side with flag, gaff, and rope. But few seals were seen or taken.

By March 27, the sealers knew they were into the prime days of harvesting. Perhaps they heard the other vessels were doing relatively well. At any rate, in the evening of that day, forty-six sealers decided to strike, refusing to work, and stayed below when called out. Captain Hill ordered them out on deck, asking why they wanted to quit. Grumbling and muttering, they decided to give it one more day.

"They did not stay long, I am sorry to say / For they gave up their ropes the very next day." Of the fifty-seven men, not one would shovel coal. Officers managed to get SS *Eagle* back to a port, but in truth the voyage was over. The young seals with white fur, the whitecoats, had taken to the water and there was little to hunt. The composer, who says at the end of his story, "A Crew of Jolly Sealers," that he is Captain A. Greenham of Twillingate, concludes:

Just a word or two and then I will end,
But I hope, boys, it will never happen again,
For fifty-seven sealers to heave down and quit,
And fool up a captain in the midst of a trip,
A crew of jolly sealers.

When the season ended, no legal action was taken by the captain or owners of *Eagle*. No charge of manusing, mutiny, or illegal strike was mentioned after the disastrous trip.

In a follow-up to the story of manusing on the sealer *Mary* in 1862, the seals off Twillingate that spring were numerous. Men, women, and young people went off hunting the whitecoats for the saleable pelts. On March 17, a letter writer to *Royal Gazette* says, "I took four pelts in tow, but it was killing work dragging them over the rafted ice. In the afternoon I had a narrow escape from death."

He says another group, George King and his two sons, had "tows" of skins farther out, and the correspondent started for land a few minutes before King and his boys. The ice parted or opened up between him and the Kings. The Kings were stranded.

The wind was veering eastward, so "I dropped two of my pelts and I ran to get in with the crowds who were ahead of me." All got

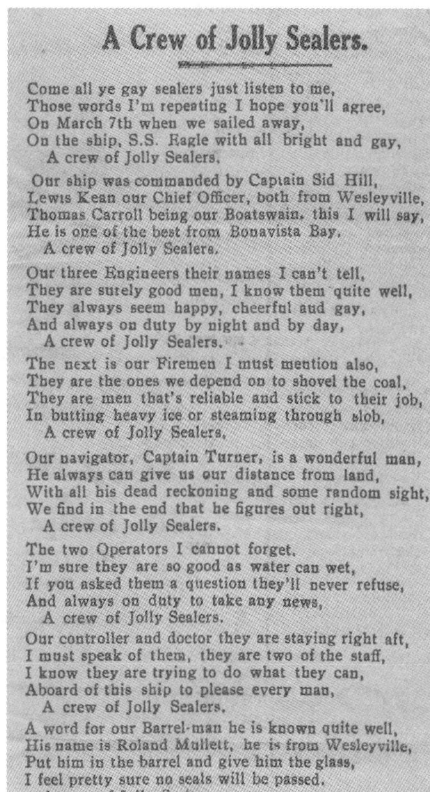

A Crew of Jolly Sealers.

Come all ye gay sealers just listen to me,
Those words I'm repeating I hope you'll agree,
On March 7th when we sailed away,
On the ship, S.S. Eagle with all bright and gay,
A crew of Jolly Sealers.

Our ship was commanded by Captain Sid Hill,
Lewis Kean our Chief Officer, both from Wesleyville,
Thomas Carroll being our Boatswain, this I will say,
He is one of the best from Bonavista Bay.
A crew of Jolly Sealers.

Our three Engineers their names I can't tell,
They are surely good men, I know them quite well,
They always seem happy, cheerful and gay,
And always on duty by night and by day,
A crew of Jolly Sealers.

The next is our Firemen I must mention also,
They are the ones we depend on to shovel the coal,
They are men that's reliable and stick to their job,
In butting heavy ice or steaming through slob,
A crew of Jolly Sealers.

Our navigator, Captain Turner, is a wonderful man,
He always can give us our distance from land,
With all his dead reckoning and some random sight,
We find in the end that he figures out right,
A crew of Jolly Sealers.

The two Operators I cannot forget,
I'm sure they are so good as water can wet,
If you asked them a question they'll never refuse,
And always on duty to take any news,
A crew of Jolly Sealers.

Our controller and doctor they are staying right aft,
I must speak of them, they are two of the staff,
I know they are trying to do what they can,
Aboard of this ship to please every man,
A crew of Jolly Sealers.

A word for our Barrel-man he is known quite well,
His name is Roland Mullett, he is from Wesleyville,
Put him in the barrel and give him the glass,
I feel pretty sure no seals will be passed.
A crew of Jolly Sealers.

Twillingate Sun of September 21, 1921, pokes a bit of fun at the seal hunt and smiles at the time when fifty-seven sealers went on strike, preventing Captain Sid Hill from getting his quota.

their pelts to within a mile of Gull Island, but then the would-be ice hunters dropped their loads and ran for their lives. There was a space of water about 100 yards wide and filled with slob ice and small pans. It was now every person for himself.

"I ran over the slob and got on a pan of ice in the lake. The pan held twenty-one men, one woman, and several dogs. By paddling with our gaffs we, with difficulty, gained the ice connected with Long Point, two miles north of Gull Island, and got safely on shore.

"The people on shore were very anxious for our safety, fearing our being carried off, which would have been if the wind had veered a little more.

"George King and one of his sons were not so fortunate as the rest of us. Two days after, they were found off Western Head, the son quite dead and King nearly gone."

On the other hand, the residents were not perturbed by danger and death: "Men, women, and children of Twillingate have been out day after day." Seal pelts could be seen in every direction, piled in thousands here and there. Older people said the last time that had happened was in 1824.

Thomas Manuel had so many skins aboard his vessel, he and others cut a channel through the ice and off-loaded at Wild Cove, near Twillingate harbour. On calm days when the ice opened, local punts went out and came back, not only loaded, but with fifty or sixty pelts in tow. It was as if it were gifts from God. All this, the correspondent concurs, "is a Providential provision for the people, as many families had been destitute."

THE DEATH RITUAL

SPOON COVE (EPWORTH), GRAND BANK, PORTUGAL

FAMILY TRADITIONS ARE STRONG as the stories of ancestors are passed down through the generations. Families have no need or cause to exaggerate or distort events that had happened in a father's or a grandmother's life. What often appears to be an exaggeration or a distortion of a human event will have a core of truth behind it. And the Welsh descendants of Edwin James Welsh of Grand Bank know their grandfather never returned from a voyage to Portugal. Furthermore, they believe he died unnecessarily and through unusual circumstances.

When his ship arrived back in Grand Bank from a foreign voyage, his shipmates were more than willing to explain why their friend and fellow shipmate didn't return with them. Edwin had died a mysterious death in Oporto, Portugal, in 1906.

Born in Spoon Cove (today Epworth, near Burin) in 1860, Welsh moved to Grand Bank, where his name appears in the town's 1898 census as a fisherman. He had sailed to Oporto on one of Grand Bank's foreign-going schooners.

Enterprising businessmen of Grand Bank began shipping dried codfish overseas to Europe about 1890. Prior to this, local exporters sent fish to Newman's Company in Harbour Breton or to St. John's, but eventually they became independent exporters themselves and bypassed the St. John's merchants.

In the early years, the 8,000-kilometre (4,800-mile) round trip was made in the banking schooners, which averaged between sixty to 120 tons. Between 1910 and 1930s, the tern or three-masted schooners were more economical, had greater carrying capacity, and, with more sail, were speedier.

Bank fishing on the south coast was a spring and summer occupation. In winter, many dory fishermen joined the "foreign-going" fleet for extra work. These ships carried fish to Spain, Portugal, and Greece and brought back salt for the curing of fish. Edwin Welsh sailed to Portugal on a Grand Bank schooner (the name of which and who was in command are lost to time) to discharge dried fish and to load salt for the westward voyage.

While in one of the great ports of Portugal, most likely Oporto, all or some of the crew were subjected to brainwashing or forced into a ritual intended to make them change or mock their religious beliefs. Exactly who the culprits were is not clear. Oral tradition says the Newfoundland seamen had to dance around a fire, chant, sing ritualistic songs, and in general renounce their faith.

Edwin Welsh refused to do so and was made to walk a plank from which he went to his death by drowning. In that era, long-distance investigation of a crime in a foreign country was not feasible, thus the dastardly act was never officially reported to law authorities.

To save their own lives, the other men from the Newfoundland schooner went along with the ritual, but they made their escape and returned home to report the death of their shipmate. Edwin, aged forty-six, was married to Emma Jane (Hickman) of Grand Bank and had eight children: Harriet, James, Amelia, Selena, Charles, Dinah, George Samuel, and Anne Belle.

DARING ACT OF PIRACY IN PLACENTIA BAY

ODERIN, DAVIS COVE

THE MEDIA OF THE DAY, in describing a crime that happened in the summer of 1866, called it "a daring act of piracy" and gave the Attorney General the nudge to bring the case to the attention of Police Inspector Timothy Mitchell. Mitchell, the first person to hold the rank of Inspector in the reorganized Newfoundland Constabulary, left with a group of constables in the St. John's harbour tug *Diamond* for Placentia Bay. His mission: to investigate the story and apprehend any suspected perpetrators.

The tale of crime started in the early morning of July 31, 1866, in Davis Cove, Placentia Bay. A resettled fishing settlement located on the west side of Placentia Bay in a small sheltered inlet, Davis Cove was probably named for an early settler. The village was first reported in the census (1845) with a population of thirty-five, including twelve fishermen engaged in the small-boat inshore fishery. Family names listed in Davis Cove in 1928 were Brewer, Caul, Connors, Davis, Emberly, Greene, Hickey, and Palfrey, familiar names in Placentia Bay.

Robert Hayward of Oderin Island, Placentia Bay, owned a small vessel, the *Fanny*, which he filled with shop goods, common commodities needed by fishing families in smaller isolated villages along the coast. From the travelling salesman, fishermen in the more isolated settlements would buy the goods or exchange fish for Hayward's flour, salt, rope, tools, and other supplies.

But the summer of 1866 was different. The fishery had been a failure, money was scarce, and hunger was rampant. And the winter was coming on.

Robert Hayward wrote up a report of what happened. In the evening of July 30, several Davis Cove fishermen came on board *Fanny* and bought provisions. Others wanted goods on credit. Hayward declined, as they had nothing to trade or give him. The fishermen were "short." There was nothing to be gotten in the cove—firewood, vegetables, dry fish.

Hayward noticed as negotiations went on that about fifteen or twenty punts had anchored near the *Fanny* at the entrance to the cove. He was blocked from exiting Davis Cove. Night was coming on, and Hayward and his one- or two-man crew went below to sleep.

Just after daylight on July 31, the wind came up southwest and Hayward woke his crew to have them get under way. When the men in the punts saw Hayward's intention, two or three punts came in close under his bow. In his report to St. John's police, Hayward said:

> They were not there two minutes before two strokes of the hatchet bespoke their business. I ran forward, but the boats shied off, the men not wishing to be known. I found a good-sized hole had been cut in the bow. I got a large cloth and stopped the leak.
>
> At this time, other boats were lying on their oars a short distance from us. Soon after, they came alongside, fifteen or twenty men coming on deck. When they found out I had the leak stopped, some of them went down forward, not wishing to use the axe at the bow, as I was watching them to take down their names.

While the evildoers were down below, they reopened the leak. But there was only a little water in *Fanny* and it was, at that time, in no danger of going down. Then, to Hayward's further amazement, one man boldly took a hatchet and began cutting down the mainmast.

Hayward tried to stop him, but the man said, "You'll feel the bite of this axe if you try to stop me!"

"You will pay for that mainmast when this is all over," replied Hayward.

At this the man stopped. However, the crowd of pirates had now opened the hatches and began to help themselves. Two men took possession of *Fanny*'s cabin and commenced to plunder it.

Hayward stopped them and asked them to come on deck. He went again to the forecastle, only to find the rag and cloth taken from the hole and *Fanny* leaking again. Again Hayward stopped the leak. Hayward stated:

> A few minutes after, I followed a man on shore and took my shop goods out of his house and put them back on my vessel. By this time everything had been taken out of the hold. Punts were lying alongside. I cast off the boats three or four times, saying, "You now have all. Now let me have my craft."
>
> They would not, but tried all in their power to have her sink at her anchor. I tried to row my craft to the beach. All the boats were in tow and I cast them off several times, but they made fast again.
>
> When at last I got *Fanny* in, the water was within two feet of her hatches.

Robert Hayward finished his report, stating that at 9:00 p.m. that day, July 31, *Fanny* was a total wreck. At that point, the pirates seemed to be satisfied and walked away. By 10:00 p.m., Hayward had the sails off and had put the anchors and chains on board a punt. He went on board a vessel bound for Placentia and left Davis Cove for good—or evil, as the story finally played out.

In his pocket he had a list of names of all those who engaged in the act of piracy and plunder.

On August 4 and back in Oderin, Hayward wrote up his report of piracy to be forwarded to St. John's papers and law-enforcement agencies. Not long after the tug *Diamond* sailed into Placentia Bay, Inspector Mitchell and his force had rounded up the accused men.

In the trial, the Queen versus certain Davis Cove men, held in St. John's on December 11, 1866, seven were found guilty of "plundering Robert Hayward's vessel *Fanny* of a quantity of manufactured goods and scuttling the boat at Davis Cove, Placentia Bay."

Guilty were James Hines, John Hines, John Davis, James Caul, and John Rodgers. Two days later, one of these was sentenced to nine months in prison, the other four to serve six months. Two—James Greene and Thomas Foote—were recommended by the jury for mercy and received no sentence.

TWO WAYS OF TELLING A STORY

NEWFOUNDLAND AND LABRADOR

IN THE ST. JOHN'S NEWSPAPER the *Evening Mercury* many years ago, there appeared a short tale of an exchange in the courtroom between two lawyers and a witness, all unnamed. In a juried trial, the prosecuting lawyer approached the witness:

"Now, Mr. Costello, will you have the goodness to answer me directly and categorically a few plain questions?"

"Certainly, sir," the witness replied.

"Now, Mr. Costello," said the lawyer, "is there a female at present living with you who is known in the neighbourhood as Mrs. Costello?"

"There is," said the witness.

"Is she under your protection?"

"She is."

"Now, on your oath of truthfulness, do you maintain her?"

"I do," said the witness.

"Have you ever been married to her?" asked the lawyer.

"No, sir, I have not!"

At this point, several members of the jury gave a faint scowl or shook their heads in disapproval.

"That's all, Mr. Costello. No more questions."

To which the defence counsel rose and said, "Stop one moment, Mr. Costello. Is the female in question your grandmother?"

"Yes, she is," said the witness.

EXTRA POLICE AND A STANDOFF WITH BAYONETS FIXED AT PLACENTIA

PLACENTIA, WHITBOURNE

WITH RIFLES AND FIXED BAYONETS, a squad of twenty police attempted to restore order at Placentia. But a crowd, estimated to be about 200 disgruntled labourers from Placentia and the surrounding villages, broke through the police line and confiscated the shovels and other tools of imported workers, the so-called scab employees. "A mob," said one of the scabs, "rushed us, snatched our shovels, threw them away, and hustled us out of the railway yard. During this action, the police merely stood by with fixed bayonets, but no orders were given to charge the mob."

The first news that tempers had reached fever pitch at Placentia broke when Captain Thomas Bonia reached St. John's on February 1, 1904. A few weeks earlier, disgruntled workers in the southern Avalon community voiced their opinion on the low wages they received from Reid Newfoundland Company and Job Brothers at the railway coastal boat terminus in Placentia. Some 500 labourers wanted wages equal to those received in St. John's by men doing similar work.

"The chief complaint," said Bonia, the Member of the House of Assembly for Placentia–St. Mary's, "is that they are expected to unload coal steamers at night for the same wages as daytime."

Bonia, perhaps thinking that after a few days and a few delays the fuss would wither on the vine, was in no hurry. He would interview the employers, the Reids and Jobs, and arrange some settlement. Maybe steps could be taken to form a labourers' union at Placentia. By then the so-called strike would be over.

Two weeks later, a scathing letter to the *Daily News* said that Bonia had a meeting, all right, in the Placentia Star Hall, and said that the coal handlers and labourers deserved an extra 25¢ an hour. Bonia failed to say he had convinced the workers some months before to vote down that increase. Bonia and his cohort, identified only as "the jader," were paying a man 75¢ a day to run the ferry at Placentia Gut—a day consisting of twelve hours' work.

"Perhaps if Captain Bonia and Jackman can make the Reids [Robert Reid Sr. and Jr., who owned and managed the Newfoundland Railway Company] pay fifteen and twenty cents per hour it will be all right." The Reids, concluded the letter writer, left quite a few dollars in Placentia and they paid good wages to good men; they could also get all the men they wanted for 10¢ an hour.

Lack of action and continued low wages brought matters to a head by mid-March. On March 14, a large number of would-be labourers turned out in procession, suspending all work in connection with shipping, and laying siege on the coastal steamer *Ethie*, which could not leave Placentia. They had formed a union, a cohesive group, and contended the work being done was not in accordance with their rules.

The angry mob forced the non-union men working at the railway coastal boat facility to stop work. Right in the town the Reids' train was held up: the engineer and firemen weren't allowed to turn the locomotive around and it could not leave for St. John's.

The local policeman was powerless to stop the actions of the gang. Subsequently, on the night of March 14, a squad of armed police from St. John's was sent down by special train to Placentia. In charge of the riot squad was Superintendent John J. Sullivan and with him were Head Constable O'Brien, Sergeant Sparrow, and constables Fitzgerald, Quinlan, Tobin, Manning, March, McFarlane, Keefe, and Martin.

Three days later, word reached St. John's that blood had been shed. Details of this alarming development were published in the *Daily News* on March 18, 1904, saying, "The labourers who took part in this affray were bayoneted by the police. Several of the number were seriously injured."

In St. John's, frantic loved ones and a concerned general public wired the Reid Newfoundland Company at Whitbourne and Placentia for details. Soon the news of bloodshed was declared to be untrue.

The truth was that on March 17-18, eight section railwaymen left Whitbourne for Placentia with the intention of coaling and turning the locomotive. Work had only begun when a mob of local workers forced them to quit and flee by train to Whitbourne. The section foreman, Ferguson, summarized the turn of events:

"When we reached Placentia station, we found the strikers in the yard. The magistrate and thirteen policemen, armed with rifles and bayonets and in charge of Superintendent Sullivan, were also there. The police formed a line in front of us and we commenced to do our work.

"When we began putting the coal aboard, suddenly the mob—about 200 strong—rushed on us almost instantly and took our shovels. We were rushed out of the railway yard. The police stood with fixed bayonets, but no orders were given them to charge the men.

"Less than an hour after our arrival, we were on the train again, returning to Whitbourne."

Ferguson finished, saying, "Placentia took on a grave aspect as it was feared trouble of a more serious nature would follow."

However, trouble had reached a peak. Cooler heads prevailed as leaders of the town spoke out. Monsignor Reardon advised the strikers to cease; he was followed by Captain Bonia, who also appealed for calm. Anger cooled somewhat, though authorities sent for extra police. Reverend Father J. J. St. John and MHA William R. Howley [with MHAs Edward M. Jackman and Bonia, as Placentia–St. Mary's was a three-member district] were asked to come to Placentia with peace-offering speeches. A midnight train to Placentia brought Judge James Gerve Conroy, Police Sergeants Peet and Noseworthy, constables Furlong, Mackay, Byrne, Flynn, O'Farrell, Stamp, Day, Greene, Devereaux, Grouchy, Brown, Churchill, and O'Neill—all police with sidearms. Back in St. John's, Police Inspector General John Roche McCowen kept in contact with his force, exhorting them to avoid violence if at all possible.

Howley's address brought cheers from the strikers and they broke up quietly. When the Reid Company train arrived in Placentia again, Howley spoke to the sixteen men who planned to do their work in the town. Howley boarded the car where they were and explained the mood of the town. If they attempted to get off the train in Placentia, he would not be responsible for the consequences. The strangers, on learning the facts, immediately decided to return to Whitbourne. When Howley again spoke to the strikers, informing them of this turn of events, he was cheered loudly. He then suggested a week's truce between the strikers and the Reids to see if something could be worked out.

The Reid Company, not happy with Howley's message, advised their agent in Placentia to order the MHA off their premises. Accompanied by hundreds of strikers and those who sympathized with them, Howley left quietly, returning to St. John's.

Placentia Strike

TROUBLE IMMINENT

Twenty Armed Police Leave

About 8.30 last night the city was astir with the rumor that blood had been shed at Placentia, over the laborer's strike, and that the victims were two section men of the Reid Newfoundland Company's employ. The report further stated that the laborers who took part in the affray were bayonetted by the police, several of the number being seriously injured. Many other reports were current, but none, we are glad to say, were correct. The facts of the occurrence, as authentically gleaned by a NEWS representative, are:. Yesterday forenoon eight section men, under section foreman Ferguson, left Whitbourne for Placentia, to

NFOUNDLAND MARCH 1

The Strike

AT PLACENTIA.

Seven Hundred Men

Assemble at Station

TO PREVENT STRANGERS WORKING.

HOWLEY THE "LABORERS FRIEND" CONTROLS SITUATION.

(Exclusive to Daily News.)

PLACENTIA, 5 p.m. yesterday.

Intense excitement prevailed her today. At 2 o'clock seven hundred men

Two headlines from the *Daily News*, March 1904, featuring the "armed police" leaving St. John's for Placentia and the estimated size of the crowd who assembled at the train and coastal boat terminal to stop "strangers" from doing local work.

On March 26, the week's impasse was up: Reids sent a special train to Placentia with a group of men to work at the train station and on the SS *Ethie*. They were to work under police protection, recently reinforced by constables Wheeler, Lawlor, and Hillier, and the police from Carbonear and Harbour Grace.

According to the *Daily News* of March 26, 1904, "The total armed force at Placentia numbered over fifty and full protection would be given to the workers, who will be allowed to work at any cost." It also reported the strikers and disgruntled labourers were to be reinforced by men from Fox Harbour and other settlements, all determined to stop the work being done by strangers.

It was the climax to the various wild and unsubstantiated reports, some of which bordered on exaggeration. Within a day or so, it was over: His Lordship Bishop Howley left for Placentia to talk to the residents; the local men went back to work at their former wages; Reids' workers finally performed their work without interruption. There would be no prosecutions, and the charges against some of the strikers were held over.

It was generally believed that the patience and forbearance of the workers of Placentia would help in their future negotiations for a better wage. The final words came from three of the committee for the so-called labourers' union in an April 9 letter to the paper. William Fewer, John Lamb, and Joseph Delaney stated, "Our union is determined and law-abiding. One tenth of the causes of the strike have not been published but are being sworn to before the magistrate today."

It had been a wild and unforgettable month or so in Placentia, a time of trouble never forgotten by the generation who lived through it.

THE PIPER'S HOLE SKIRMISH

SWIFT CURRENT (PIPER'S HOLE)

THE COMMUNITY OF SWIFT CURRENT, located at the head of Placentia Bay, is at the mouth of an inlet called Piper's Hole. The town itself was called Piper's Hole until the name changed to Swift Current around 1920. Piper's Hole River was once the home of a small band of native people, the Mi'kmaq of Conne River, notably the family of John Barrington.

Barrington was said to have settled at Swift Current after he was hired by the English to help with plotting the telegraph line across the south coast of the Island. He later maintained and repaired the overland line between Placentia and Fortune Bay. In time, natives migrated to the area to hunt caribou and to fish.

European contact with the area dates from the time of the French occupation of Placentia Bay, approximately 1660–1713. The French garrison at Placentia regularly sent caribou hunting and salmon fishing expeditions to Piper's Hole. It was during this period when an unsolved murder took place in Piper's Hole.

During the winter in the early 1700s, a hunting group of French soldiers from Placentia camped at Piper's Hole. Included in the group was a piper, or one who plays a tune on a pipe, similar to a flute, often used with drums to lead soldiers into battle.

According to legend, or stories passed down by the Mi'kmaq or the English settlers, a disagreement among the soldiers escalated into violence. The piper was killed. To dispose of the body, a hole was cut in the frozen pond and the piper's body was deposited into the cold water.

When the other soldiers returned to the French fort, they told their superior officers that the piper had become separated from the group. A search turned up no trace of him, and the others had to return to Placentia because they were running short of supplies.

Legend says that English fishermen and woodcutters in the area (mostly from Sound Island, Placentia Bay) could hear the lonely sound of the piper playing his instrument. Other stories say that, in a battle between English soldiers and the French, one man was killed, the French piper.

John Alexander "Jack" White (a Newfoundland magistrate and writer) also wrote of the Piper's Hole tale, saying:

> In the era when the French occupied Placentia and were fighting the English, one day a party of French were at this river, snug in the top of Placentia Bay. According to the legend, one of them never left the river, being killed in a skirmish with the English who suddenly arrived on the scene.
>
> . . . There are other such stories, all telling of the hearing of the piping at the river. Some of the old-timers and elders maintain that . . . [it is] legend which gives one of Newfoundland's salmon rivers its name, the legacy of the French soldier. . . . (*Atlantic Guardian*, July 1952)

Piper's Hole River today. According to local tales, many years ago a violent death occurred at this river—a site with a strange tale of the unexplained.

In every story from Newfoundland and Labrador's past, no matter how strange, far-fetched, or curious, no matter how close it borders on legend, there is always a nugget or kernel of truth behind the tale. Someone, most likely a French piper, died violently at Piper's Hole River.

"THE NEXT TIME WE MAY ACT DIFFERENTLY: ILLEGALLY"

BAY BULLS

"THE NEXT TIME, WE INTEND, if fortune casts another ship on our shore, to treat her in a far different manner," said the men of Bay Bulls. In essence, the salvors were saying, "If we can't salvage a wreck legally, the next time it might be illegally."

In February 1881, the Newfoundland Vice Admiralty Court decided on a salvage settlement for the derelict ship *Alice Lyne*. The men who had submitted a monetary claim under British laws were from Bay Bulls. Although details of ownership, size, or the cause of the stranding of *Alice Lyne* have not been recorded, it is known *Alice Lyne* lived to sail again—not an altogether common phenomenon for ships stranded on the unfriendly rocks along Newfoundland's shores.

The story of its salvage was a curious one. Sometime in late January 1881, *Alice Lyne* grounded five miles north of Bay Bulls. Her crew took to a single lifeboat, rowed into Bay Bulls, and proclaimed the ship an abandoned derelict. The weather that day was terrible. A North Atlantic storm had brought high winds, freezing temperatures, and snow. Combers and white surf pounded the Avalon Peninsula's southern shore.

Had there been a telegraph station in Bay Bulls, the operator would have immediately contacted authorities in St. John's to inform them of the wreck. But a line had not yet been extended to the Avalon southern shore, and for residents along the shore it became a case of act first, ask questions later.

When the Bay Bulls men reached the derelict *Alice Lyne*, they acted legally, declaring their actions and what they salvaged. Thus they were salvors—not "wrackers"—and were entitled to full benefits under marine law.

To reach the abandoned wreck required a feat bordering on heroism. Of the 800 people living near the wreck site, only twenty-one volunteered to brave the elements. After rowing five miles in small open boats, through heavy seas and bailing water constantly, they located the vessel. *Alice Lyne* had drifted off the outermost reef and lay a few hundred feet from breakers near shore.

Not knowing what minute she would strike rocks or become unmanageable in the high winds, the Bay Bulls men boarded *Alice Lyne* and slowly but successfully kept her away from shore. If they had been one hour later, she would have smashed on the jagged rocks. But as it turned out, the ship sailed into St. John's intact. Salvors took great care and delivered her to the Admiralty Court with not even, as they described it, a rope yarn or line injured or broken.

An editorial in the city paper dated February 21, 1881, stated, "While the Bay Bulls men had possession of the vessel, the greatest care was taken of everything about her."

The valiant salvors themselves said, "We destroyed nothing on board of her, but brought her in as we found her. The whole affair was attended with the greatest peril and risk of life."

The men of Bay Bulls knew the sum of the whole was worth more than its parts. Ship and cargo intact were valued at £5,500 (about $15,000 in today's values)—a deal much better than any paltry gains made from "wracking" or destroying the ship and contents. Salvage laws would award them one-quarter value, around £1,300.

In mid-February 1881, the verdict came down. To the chagrin and vocal consternation of the twenty-one claimants, the Court of Vice Admiralty deemed *Alice Lyne* worth £3,500 and awarded the Bay Bulls salvagers the paltry sum of £625 to be shared between them. Subtracted from this sum were towing costs and court expenses. They were forced to settle for a little more than £22 pounds each, or $55.

The Bay Bulls men voiced their disbelief and dismay to the local papers.

> Had we not acted legally in a time when Newfoundland people were branded wrackers by the Whiteway-Shea government?

> Several fishermen (in another case), just for taking a few fathoms of rope for remuneration for services rendered, had been brought to St. John's, tried, and jailed. Would Newfoundlanders, in the future, refuse to lend a willing hand unless paid first?

It is not known if their protestation changed anything or if they carried through with implied threats, but in a harsh letter to the February 25 *Evening Telegram*, the twenty-one Bay Bulls fishermen concluded, "We intend, if fortune may cast another vessel on our shores, to treat her in a far different manner." The letter was appended (with spelling and duplication as the signatures appeared in the paper) with the following:

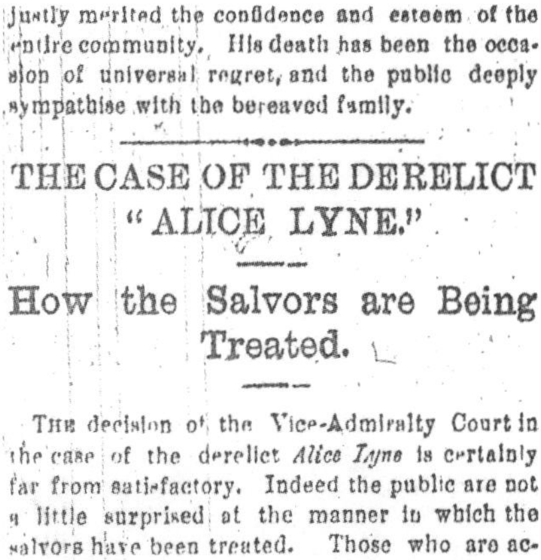

justly merited the confidence and esteem of the entire community. His death has been the occasion of universal regret, and the public deeply sympathise with the bereaved family.

THE CASE OF THE DERELICT "ALICE LYNE."

How the Salvors are Being Treated.

THE decision of the Vice-Admiralty Court in the case of the derelict *Alice Lyne* is certainly far from satisfactory. Indeed the public are not a little surprised at the manner in which the salvors have been treated. Those who are ac-

Alice Lyne lay idle for a while in St. John's until ownership rights were documented and repairs completed. Then John Munn and Company purchased the ship, renamed it *Flora*, and sailed it out of St. John's under Captain Tizzard.

On September 2, 1905, *Flora* was making its way to a south coast port filled with empty casks to be filled with whale oil. It struck a spate of inclement weather near Brunette Island and was forced to run before the gale toward the islands of Saint-Pierre and Miquelon. It struck the sand dunes of the east side of Langlade, near Saint Pierre, in the dark of night.

Tizzard, his crew, and passengers (including his wife, daughter, and granddaughter) put the lifeboat over the side and rowed into Langlade. There the bones of *Flora* remained,

Men [spellings unchanged] of Bay Bulls who Salvaged *Alice Lyne*, February 1881

Richard Mokeler
John Williams
Michael Brien
Patrick Williams
Cornelius Brien
Ambrose Williams
Michael Ryan
Michael Williams
Edward Williams
Joseph Williams
Cornelius Brien
Thos. Getherell
Brien O'Brien
John Getherell
James Glinn
William Gatherell
Martin Brien
Michael Williams
Joseph Williams
William Driscoll
William Getherell

never to be refloated, or, as Tizzard stated to the newspaper the *Standard* (September 8, 1905), "It's a total wreck and its career is closed."

THE DECAPITATION OF JOHN BALL

RENCONTRE WEST, MCCALLUM, FACHEUX BAY

BY THE BEGINNING OF THE twentieth century, the town of Rencontre West was one of the longest settled and most viable communities west of Harbour Breton. Its name, French in origin, literally meant a "meeting place" for the early French fishermen and settlers who had frequented the area prior to the mid-1700s.

The earliest English reference to Rencontre West comes from the diary of William Epps Cormack, a Scottish explorer who walked across Newfoundland from east to west in 1822. On his return journey to St. John's by schooner, he stopped in Rencontre West and noted there were four families.

People lived there to fish the quiet waters of Rencontre Bay, an inlet like many on the south coast, that runs deep—more than 100 fathoms in some places. The inshore fishing areas were once prolific, and the residents of Rencontre West had the best of two grounds at their doorstep, with the shoal grounds fifteen miles out to sea and the waters of Rencontre Bay close at hand. In addition, the hills behind the town were well-forested for fuel and timber. On the inland barrens in those days, deer (or, by today's term, caribou) abounded.

By 1905, the community had a population of more than 200. Older established families in Rencontre West included Durnford, Ball, Buffett, Marsden, Goodridge, Stone, Simms, Cox, Parsons, Green, and Spencer. Some family names indicate their Jersey Island origins: Beauchamp, De-Gruchy, Courtney, Ball, and Clothier.

Indeed, the latter two names, Ball and Clothier, were involved in a mystery and unexplained deaths that occurred to some hunters from Rencontre West. Early in the year 1905, four men from the community—George Ball, John Ball, Thomas Ball, and John Clothier—went deer hunting and never returned. The tale is summarized in the September 6, 1906, edition of the *Western Star*.

The four would have gone by boat to Big Bay, then trekked up to the high country for about a week of hunting. Their base would have been one of the two or three shacks, or "tilts," in the area. After eight or nine days passed, folks back home knew the hunters were in trouble. The first search parties found the body of John Clothier.

According to local lore, two groups had gone to the hills: one group hunted in what was called the "western" country near Prosser's Woods; the second group, comprised of Ball and Clothier men, went to the eastern hills, past Piercey's Pond and around the Nuddick. They all carried a knapsack, or "travelling bag," which contained necessary supplies, food, a change of socks, and mitts.

A blizzard came on with high drifts and low visibility. The four at the eastern country failed to appear, leading to speculation they became lost in the storm and perished. Yet friends and relatives knew they were experienced woodsmen and had traversed the land previously. Clothier's body was found wedged between a cleft or wide crack in a large boulder, as if he were seeking shelter there, leading searchers to think he had become lost in the blizzard.

Weeks of searching for the other three stretched to months, leading relatives and friends to think it doubtful that all four had ever reached a tilt in the high, exposed country. Puzzling, as all four were careful woodmen and hunters. They left well-provisioned and equipped for deer hunting and overnight stays.

Then, in late August 1906, eighteen months after the first body had been located, a man named Ball found a clue. No doubt, although the newspaper story is not clear on this, Ball may have been a relative of one of the other three men. He had never given up searching that general area every time he went to Big Bay.

Ball found clothing and the travelling bag, which he recognized as belonging to one of the missing men. It was near Piercey's Pond, many miles away from the intended hunting area and not a site frequented by hunters of Rencontre West.

Ball, according to the newspaper, went back to Rencontre, notified residents, and several people went back for another search. They found a pocket knife tied to the top of a small, stunted tree.

A closer look in the underbrush near Piercey's Pond revealed the headless body of John Ball. His decomposing remains were identified by his travel bag and clothes. His head rested on the ground ten yards away. In his hands (probably under his body) was a prayer book, showing that death had come while he was in prayer.

Hymnal Board, constructed by William Buffett for St. James Anglican Church in Rencontre West, made from the wood taken from the slides of the four men who were lost in the country. The local word in that area for a slide used for hunting was "train." An altar Cross from St. James showing the names of the four is now located in the Burgeo Anglican Church. Courtesy of Kenneth Ball, Mount Pearl.

Local lore says George Ball's remains were also located, but there was never any sign of the clothes, rifle, or remains of eighteen-year-old Thomas Ball.

Over the years, the stories have persisted of the deaths of the four men. Some in Rencontre believed (in a version of the tale passed down through the generations) John Ball had fallen through the ice in the pond. His body became encased in the ice, but the exposed head was ravaged by an animal. His body may have drifted in to shore after the spring ice melt.

Yet a description of the tragedy written in the newspaper in 1906—a short time after Ball's remains were found—says: "The head was severed from the body. . . ." As well, if he had fallen through the ice, it would not explain the written report that his prayer book was "in his hands."

It became an enduring and unexplained mystery, passed on through the generations.

This was not the only incident of a strange and unexplained death of a hunter on the south coast. Henry Buffett lived in Indian Cove, by Rocky Passage up in Facheux Bay (Faucheaux, or, as pronounced by people of the area, Fushee).

To earn a living, Henry trapped: he was a harvester of furs, and perhaps a fisherman in season as well. His territory to trap was well up the eight or nine miles into Facheux Bay, some of the same watershed and interior general back country as Rencontre West.

According to strong family tradition, in the winter of 1921, Henry had gone up Facheux and inland to trap, carrying with him his dog and slide, plus provisions for several days' stay. After some time, his dog returned to Indian Cove. Curious where Buffett could be, a few men from McCallum, a village near Indian Cove, followed the dog back into the country.

There they found the partial remains of forty-two-year-old Henry Buffett—the torso. The head had been cleanly severed as with a knife, not torn or ripped as might have happened with some wild animal. His slide for transporting furs was intact, the furs still neatly stacked on it. The head was never located, although what remained of his body was brought back to McCallum and interred there.

THE MORE THE MUMMERS, THE MORE THE MISCHIEF

BARENEED, HARBOUR GRACE, BAY ROBERTS

TODAY, WITH INCREASED MEDIA ATTENTION, mummer festivals, and more frequent door-to-door appearances, mummering is making a comeback. However, the old Christmas tradition was at one time viewed as a nuisance and a threat to public safety. Mummering, a custom originating in the Old World, helped Newfoundland people celebrate the Twelve Days of Christmas—December 25 to January 6, Old Christmas Day. It was a time to disguise oneself and to visit the homes of friends and neighbours and to generally carouse. Often, visitors were elaborately costumed and disguised, and in some localities mummers performed a Christmas play in the home.

But a series of crimes in St. John's and in parts of Conception Bay during the early 1860s led Chief Justice Carter to ban mummering in the whole of Newfoundland. One instance of wrongdoing led to murder. On the evening of Friday, December 28, 1860, a group of men was waylaid and attacked by mummers in Bay Roberts. One of the victims, Isaac Mercer, a Protestant and a respectable resident of the town, died the next day. He was thought to have been murdered by a rival religious group. A day or so later, a group of mummers broke into a local school, destroyed papers, and generally made a wreck of the place.

An act, passed by the government of the day to make further provisions for "the Prevention of Nuisances," became law on June 25, 1861, and was subsequently responsible for the repression, and intended extinction, of mummering, "on the pain of a sentence of seven days or twenty shillings."

Yet the tradition continued in the outports, as evidenced by this strange tale of the courts from Harbour Grace. On January 8, 1863, two years after the law was passed, a piece of court work took place arising out of a mummering argument that took place in Bareneed over the Christmas holidays.

A number of people dressed up as mummers attacked a small group of men who were walking on the public road in Bareneed. The men resented the intrusion and, as the *Public Ledger* of January 16, 1863, says, "pitched into the mummers and a general fight took place." The mummers took to their heels and ran.

A Mr. Hennebury, coming out of his house to see what the ruckus was about, was struck by one of the persons in the melee and had to take refuge in a Mr. Hall's house. Hall was spitefully attacked by the drunken or infuriated men, who proceeded to smash out his windows.

Mr. Hall reported the incident to police. Those responsible were brought before the magistrate, and the guilty men were duly fined.

Mr. Hennebury also brought before the magistrate some of the same group who had beaten him, and they were fined.

One of the men who had been accosted by the mummers had his attackers brought before the same magistrate. The Christmas revellers-turned-mummers were also fined.

A mummer (name not given) informed on Mr. Hall. He had supplied liquor to the mummers, but he was selling the liquor without a licence. The magistrate fined Mr. Hall, as well.

When court work was all over, the magistrate had collected £15 in fines for the Crown, yet all groups—the men accosted by mummers, the mummers themselves, Mr. Hall, and Mr. Hennebury—left the Harbour Grace courthouse happy and satisfied that the law had served them well.

THE SAD TALE OF BENJAMIN BRAKE

BRAKE'S COVE, WEST COAST

ON DECEMBER 18, 1875, Benjamin Brake was the cause of someone's death in his home in Brake's Cove, Bay of Islands. Because communications between Newfoundland's west coast and St. John's in this era was slow or non-existent, the story of the tragedy was first published in a Halifax newspaper. After some considerable time, the news reached St. John's. Newspapers claimed Benjamin was a full-blooded native, often referring to him as "Indian," yet he had been raised from childhood by the Brakes, who were of English ancestry. By 1875, Benjamin, his wife, and young daughter lived in Brake's Cove.

THE BACKGROUND

Located in Middle Arm of the Bay of Islands, Brake's Cove, now an abandoned community, was just a short walk from Cox's Cove. Many of the former residents relocated to Cox's Cove.

On that December evening, John Carter came to Benjamin Brake's premises. Carter was a trader from Nova Scotia who worked for his brother, Thomas, who ran a sea-based business via a schooner in Bay of Islands. John Carter knew Brake from previous meetings or business dealings.

The details of what transpired would be revealed in court later, but Carter was shot in the thigh and bled to death within fifteen minutes. By March 24, 1876, Brake was in the custody of the local constable, William Bagg. Bagg held the suspect for months until word came from St. John's that Brake was to go on trial there.

Right from the beginning, there were nuances of the law that cropped up. He would not be tried in the Bay of Islands. Newfoundland's west coast was part of the "French Shore," and France apparently had legal jurisdiction over the villages. Newfoundland, i.e. St. John's, requested that Brake be brought to that city for trial, but said, "We shall have to take a chance for this."

It was generally admitted that no sanctioned British law was present on the west coast, and lawlessness ruled instead of British authority on British soil. "We may point to this case [Brake's] as a new illustration of the utter barbarism which is still the portion of British subjects who live on our western coast."

There was some doubt about the identity of William Bagg. Just what were his duties and status? He was, as far as the long arm of the St. John's law knew, an unpaid and un-pensioned volunteer. "Why it is that he is charged or has charged himself with the functions of peace officer, we don't well know. He does render useful service in this line and that he is the man to hold fast his present prisoner, in needful, with a desperate grip."

The *Newfoundlander* of March 24 said the feeling of the people against Brake "is so strong that fears are entertained of their taking the law into their own hands." In fact, although the newspaper didn't know or state it, just after the death of Carter, Brake's house had been demolished and burned by someone in that locality. Speculation was, although never proven, the deed was done by the dead man's brother, Thomas Carter.

THE TRIAL

During his trial in St. John's, Benjamin Brake already had several strikes against him: he was a native, which carried certain prejudices; and there was much lawlessness on the west coast that had to be curbed. Furthermore, Brake was not able have his witnesses brought across the island—probably due to distance and travel costs. As well, the word was the general populace, especially in the Bay of Islands, viewed the event as particularly heinous and had harsh feelings for the accused. Fearing for their lives, Mrs. Brake and her child had to move out of their home and to Irishtown. Shortly after, the Brakes' house in Brake's Cove was destroyed by someone unknown.

The pretrial inquiry found the "bill" of murder not applicable, and

Brake was arraigned on the charge of manslaughter against John Carter. On December 2, 1876, approximately one year after the crime, defence lawyers Robert John Pinsent, Q.C., and James Gerve Conroy suggested or asked that Brake plead guilty. Newfoundland's Solicitor General represented the Crown before Chief Justice Sir Hugh William Hoyles.

LAWYER PINSENT'S DEFENCE

With a guilty plea, there would be no trial by jury, and no witnesses for the prosecution or defence. Pinsent and Conroy would present their case to the chief justice. Pinsent began his lengthy address saying he advised Brake to plead guilty, feeling he could vindicate the actions of Brake.

Then the plea and his explanation of the circumstances of Carter's death would induce the court to generous clemency or mercy. Protecting one's life and property with a weapon—self-defence—was not an option for Brake's lawyers in that era of justice.

Pinsent produced and summarized statements, or affidavits, which gave particulars of John Carter's acts of violence toward others. He spoke of mob law on the west coast, which had displayed itself immediately after Carter's death. The prisoner's (Brake's) house and property were destroyed and his provisions stolen. That food would have been the main support of Brake's wife and family.

Pinsent then spoke of Benjamin Brake's excellent character as per a written statement from Special Constable Bagg. Brake had willingly surrendered himself. Furthermore, in the months while Brake was in his charge, the prisoner conducted himself in a most creditable manner. Brake, he stated, "had many opportunities to escape from custody, both by land and sea, but made no attempt."

Defence Counsel Pinsent produced written statements from Committing Magistrate George R. Lilly and from the governor of the jail—both gave strong testimony in favour of the prisoner's conduct. Statements from others who knew Brake confirmed what the others had said: Brake had a commendable character and conducted himself with dignity.

Pinsent referred to the demeanour of the deceased, Carter, toward Brake: his violent visit to his house in the dead of night before he was killed. Carter insisted on Brake going to drink with him; his coming to Brake's house the next morning under the pretext of demanding payment for 75¢ for a drink was forced upon Brake.

Carter had said, "Pay up or pay with your life. I can take payment any way I like—in powder and lead." Carter had become violent in the house. Brake then asked him to leave. Finally, as Carter would not leave, he fired his gun at the deceased man's legs as he came toward him in the bedroom. He had no intention of killing him.

Dr. Jacob's statement, produced by Pinsent, said that if the wound had been promptly attended to, Carter's life would have been saved.

"The only direct evidence," said Pinsent, "of prisoner Brake having fired the fatal shot was his own confession."

Under all these circumstances, he would not have advised Brake to plead guilty to manslaughter if there had been any evidence that Carter at the time had had a weapon in his hand. Brake realized that a threatening man in his house could have easily armed himself to take a life, even from among the kitchen utensils and other implements in Brake's house.

The defence then drew a verbal picture of the lawlessness of the west coast. Although it was an area under the protection of the Crown, it was outside the pale of the law and the constitution. Ordinary guards of life, of property, and domestic peace were absent. The only legal code known to the people was self-preservation.

Pinsent concluded with a reference to Mr. Bagg. His prompt and zealous conduct in the midst of lawless men and in absence of the protections of ordinary civil life was very commendable in this case. That Benjamin Brake was there in court at all was a testament to Bagg.

Brake had been in custody nearly a year. Some months of that time, he was with Constable Bagg. That, too, should be favourable toward rendering mercy toward the accused.

When Pinsent finished, the Solicitor General addressed the court, but briefly. He stated that the use of an affidavit from the prisoner's wife should not be accepted. As for asking for mercy or pity because Brake's house had been burned, that matter was still under a rigid investigation. So far (after a year), no one person or persons had been arrested.

THE VERDICT

On December 12, the chief justice addressed the prisoner. Brake had been wise to plead guilty, for there was no doubt he had caused the death of Carter. If Brake had denied it, that is pleaded not guilty, it would have been viewed by the court as an aggravation of the offence.

The chief justice had listened to all the statements presented by the defence and, in summary, said:

> Carter entered your dwelling with violence and threatened you and declined to leave. When you threatened him with a gun if he persisted in remaining, he threatened to take the gun from you. You, Benjamin Brake, have already suffered severely by the violent destruction of your house and property immediately after the death of Mr. Carter.
>
> I realize that for 100 miles the coast you live on has no magistrate, no constable to whom application for redress or protection can be made. If there had been competent authority on the western coast of this Island to maintain law and order, offences like yours would not have occurred.
>
> However, the law does not allow life to be taken with impunity. You had a right to use forcible means to protect your premises. But you should have used means adequate to the offence and not have first fired at the deceased. You cannot use violent and extreme measures. You made no attempt to use more moderate means other than firing a gun.
>
> Under all these circumstances, and considering you have been committed and confined to the penitentiary since July last [1876], you are sentenced to be confined there for twelve months, from July last, with hard labour.

Brake was led away. He had seven more months to serve in the St. John's Penitentiary. When his incarceration was over, Brake returned to the Bay of Islands and opened a small business, which continued even after his death, serving the public right up to the 1960s. All who knew and visited Benjamin loved his hospitality and spoke of his cordial nature.

ACCIDENT, SABOTAGE, MURDER?

LEWISPORTE, PHILIP'S HEAD, BAY OF EXPLOITS

IN THE LATE MORNING of Thursday, June 25, 1942, an explosion ripped through Hann's Point, on the east side of Lewisporte. According to Karen Wells of the *Telegram*, June 23, 2012, 1,800 pounds of dynamite exploded, leaving a crater twenty feet wide and five feet deep. Five Canadian soldiers died, and another eighteen were injured.

"Memorials in Canada," on the Canadian War Museum website, designed to show where important Canadian wartime events are commemorated by monuments, says, "Hann's Point was the location of a lookout that soldiers used who were stationed in Lewisporte during World War II."

In the summer of 1940, Canadian troops came to Newfoundland to protect two strategic sites: the seaplane base in Botwood and the Newfoundland airport at Gander. Lewisporte, situated in the Bay of Exploits in Notre Dame Bay, was part of this base of operations. Aviation fuel for Gander passed through the port, which was considered of sufficient military importance that guns were installed to defend against possible Nazi U-boat attacks.

Three military sites were located there: one called Bowater's Site on the back of the town, another in the town's centre, and one at Hann's Point, overlooking Burnt Bay—the latter considered a high vantage point to observe the waters of the Exploits River.

Although considered accidental at the time, it was first thought a soldier on duty fired a shot that ignited an ordnance, or ammunition, tent. "Memorials in Canada" says thirty-five were injured when dynamite caps exploded. Although Newfoundlanders worked at the site, those killed were Canadians: Gunner George Gordon Bennett of Fairville, New Brunswick; John Fairweather Walker, Meduetie, New Brunswick; Gunner Bernard Harvey Meisner, Bridgewater, Nova Scotia; Gunner Douglas McIntosh, Passchendaele, Nova Scotia; and Private Philip Charles Flamain, Ansonville, Ontario.

HALIFAX HERA

/hat Stands If Freedom Fall? --- Who Dies If England Live?"

HALIFAX, CANADA, MONDAY, JUNE 29, 1942

—FOUR CANADIANS KILLED, 19 INJURED—

Nova Scotians Casualties In Newfoundland Blast

OTTAWA, June 28. — (CP) — Four men were killed, six were seriously injured and 13 slightly injured in last Thursday's explosion at a coast defence station in Newfoundland, National Defence headquarters announced Saturday.

"The reports indicate that the explosion was caused by dynamite being used in construction work by the contractor and which was stored at the camp," a Defence Department statement said.

"There is nothing in the information received so far to indicate that the occurrence was other than accidental, but full investigation is being held.

Definite location of the blast has not been given out but it occurred at an army installation.

—Please Turn to Page 4, Col. 6—

Army Week Edition

Today—on the inauguration of Army Week—Canada salutes the men of this branch of the armed services. And Nova Scotians join with the rest of Canada in paying tribute to these men: overseas, on guard and preparing for their part in carrying the war to the enemy, at home shielding us from danger or fitting themselves to take their places beside their brothers-in-arms across the waters.

Today The Halifax Herald

Sir Charles Ross

Nova Scotian papers carried headlines of an explosion in Lewisporte that killed five men, two of whom were from that province.

Shortly after the explosion, says the *Telegram*, "Major Sinclair and Lieutenant Colonel Mackenzie, in charge of the Hann's Point establishment, were tried in military court for negligence. A court martial later cleared them of all charges."

The cause was later deemed accidental. However, rumours persist there were unexplained facets of the event. Local stories say strangers were seen in the area around Lewisporte before and after that day; certain buildings vital to the war effort caught fire; and German subs may have been near the Bay of Exploits waters. If someone deliberately caused a blast, then the claim of murder is possible.

In 1996, the town of Lewisporte erected a memorial plaque on the site to honour soldiers who gave their lives to protect Newfoundland during World War II.

Author by Hann's Point plaque. Inscription says:"HANN'S POINT MEMORIAM: This plaque is erected in memory of 107th Battery RC Artillery who served at Lewisporte during World War II.

"At this very point, called the observation post, the Canadian military stood watch over Burnt Bay. Nearby, on June 25th, 1942, an explosion occurred in a tent used for the temporary storage of explosives and as a result, five Canadian soldiers died.

"'They Shall Not Grow Old, As We That Are Left Grow Old; Age Shall Not Weary Them, Nor The Years Condemn. At The Going Down Of The Sun, And In The Morning, We Will Remember Them.'" Photo by Sadie Parsons.

Typical fortification found at Philip's Head, also on the Bay of Exploits. Canadian soldiers were garrisoned here during World War II.

When the author taught school in Philip's Head in 1963, there was much evidence that still remained of the soldiers' habitation. Photo of site and Nancy and Dale Parsons taken in summer of 1981 by Sadie Parsons.

RAMPAGE AND MUTINY IN HARBOUR BUFFETT

HARBOUR BUFFETT, SPENCER'S COVE

HARBOUR BUFFETT, once a thriving fishing and shipping port in Placentia Bay, often saw vessels from European ports docking to load salt fish. The flags of Portugal, Spain, and Denmark flew from the topmasts of foreign vessels, and life was good in the busy island town. In December 1922, the ninety-five-ton Danish barquentine *Centaurus* pulled into port. Life aboard this ship had been decidedly unpleasant.

Indeed, the captain and mate were taken to St. John's and held for eight days on suspicion of murder—a deed most foul, brought about by mutiny that arose and was played out in a grim scene in the sea lanes between Harbour Buffett and Spencer's Cove, Placentia Bay. Both towns, situated on Long Island, were a few miles apart by land but several miles by sea.

Captain Kristian Rasmussen, Mate Erik Knudsen, and two members of *Centaurus*'s crew were questioned at His Majesty's Penitentiary, St. John's. The captain and mate were murder suspects, and the two remaining crew of the vessel, Cook A. E. Hansen and Seaman G. Hevrilin, became witnesses.

Centaurus left Wareham's premises at Spencer's Cove on the morning of December 19, bound for Harbour Buffett. There, at Alberto Wareham's business, the barquentine would complete its load. The wind was fair and it sailed toward the northern end of Long Island. While rounding this point of land, the captain and mate, who were unfamiliar with water depth and hidden shoals in that location, had an argument regarding *Centaurus*'s position or route. In order to consult the charts and to discuss the best course, both went into the cabin, where their voices grew louder and louder.

Harbour Buffett in the heyday of the salt fish trade. In December 1922, the quiet, industrious town of Harbour Buffett was shocked by the news of murder and mutiny that accompanied the entrance of the Danish sailing ship *Centaurus* into the Placentia Bay town.

The row attracted one seaman on *Centaurus*, a man named Kristian Lovenssen. Clearly agitated, Lovenssen, a big, strapping man over six foot tall and aged twenty, also went into the cabin, shouting at both captain and mate that neither one of them knew his job. Lovenssen's voice became more agitated and he began to scream and rave. He soon began to bully and threaten the two ship's officers.

Captain Rasmussen and Mate Knudsen ordered Lovenssen to the deck, but the insolent sailor refused to leave the cabin. Instead, he attacked his captain. Mate Knudsen, who attempted to separate them, was also assaulted. The fight lasted for more than half an hour and ended when Lovenssen ran on deck, barred the cabin door, and kept the two men imprisoned below.

This situation lasted several hours despite repeated attempts by the captain and mate to gain the deck. Lovenssen would meet them at the doorway and kick them in the face if their heads appeared in the companionway.

Finally, Rasmussen and Knudsen reached the deck. The captain was armed with a gun in order to frighten or to calm the distraught sailor. This had little effect and only served to enrage Lovenssen more—he grappled with the captain and, in the scuffle, the gun went off. No damage was done, for the shot went into the sea. Seeing the captain armed and ready to shoot, Lovenssen turned his attention to the unarmed mate and tried to push him overboard.

The ship's chief officers then stopped, for the battle with the enraged bull of a man had worn them down. Both men went below, and again Lovenssen barred the companionway door. By now it was nearing four o'clock in the evening. The weather had turned into a typical December snowstorm and *Centaurus* drifted dangerously close to land.

Lovenssen realized this, too, and practically took charge of the vessel. Grabbing the wheel, he ran *Centaurus* out into Placentia Bay some three or four miles. As the captain made another attempt to break out of his confinement, the man saw him and ran down to slam shut the companionway door.

This time, Captain Rasmussen had his gun and, just as the sliding hatch of the entrance was closing, he shot to frighten or to warn Lovenssen. The mutinous sailor received the shot in the left arm near the elbow, breaking bones and severing an artery. He immediately went forward, where another crewman dressed the wound to stop the gush of blood.

A few minutes later, Lovenssen came on deck and, of his own accord, stripped the bandages off and ranted around deck like a madman. The crew managed to calm him down, enabling Rasmussen to take charge of his well-being and to replace the bandages. Taken to the cabin, he lay in the captain's berth, white and weak. Within two hours, he had bled to death.

By the time the scuffle was over, the wind had changed. *Centaurus* beat back into a cove near Harbour Buffett. There, the crew made anchorage five hours after the sailor died. Mr. Wareham, the consignee for the cargo, sent Mr. Collett out in search of the vessel to pilot it into port but was unable to find it. Collett was harbourmaster at the time.

Not long after, Rasmussen rowed into Harbour Buffett and reported the matter immediately to the Sub-Collector of Customs. The town customs officer wired this message to the Deputy Minister of Customs, Henry W. LeMessurier, in St. John's:

> "Mutiny on board Danish vessel Centaurus, entering harbour at 5 p.m. yesterday. One sailor shot."

Constables Lee and Bennett left St. John's for Argentia by train to connect with the government vessel *Sevastopol*, steaming on to Harbour Buffett. The arrest of the captain and mate followed.

Within a few days, they, with *Centaurus*'s two other seamen as witnesses, were transported to St. John's. The coffined remains were also sent to St. John's, where Doctors Anderson and Templeman conducted an autopsy. No one from Harbour Buffett was called as witness, as the vessel had been moored off in the stream and it had received no visitors from the town.

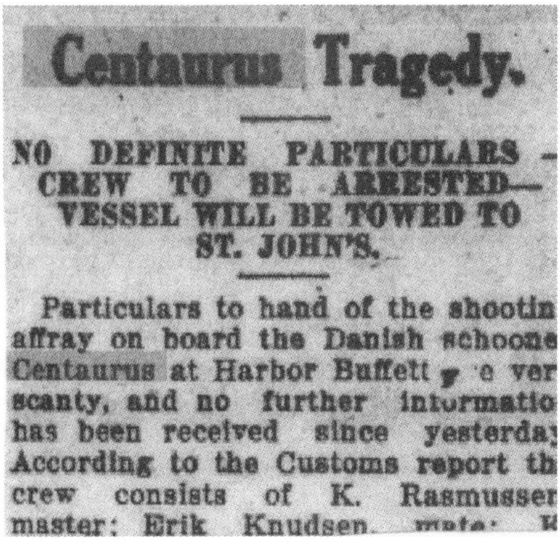

Centaurus Tragedy.

NO DEFINITE PARTICULARS - CREW TO BE ARRESTED— VESSEL WILL BE TOWED TO ST. JOHN'S.

Particulars to hand of the shootin affray on board the Danish schoone Centaurus at Harbor Buffett . . e ver scanty, and no further informatio has been received since yesterda According to the Customs report th crew consists of K. Rasmusser master; Erik Knudsen, mate; K

On December 26, 1922—that day typically part of the Christmas festive season, Boxing Day—newspaper headlines claimed in bold: **CENTAURUS TRAGEDY: Crew to be Arrested.**

Following the investigation by the Department of Justice, headed by Judge Morris, the two accused were released, for no evidence could be found for murder. It was an act of self-defence in the face of a mutiny by Lovenssen. On January 3, 1923, all four took the train to Placentia, then joined a small passenger boat, joining *Centaurus* awaiting in Harbour Buffett. Harbour Buffett at this time had a population of about 400, and no doubt the whole town was abuzz with news of *Centaurus* and the story of murder and self-defence. The Danish Consul in St. John's, the Honourable Tasker Cook, sent a full report to the Danish authorities. *Centaurus*, now freed to sail again, was short-handed with the death of one crewman. To fill his crew, the captain hired a young man, Jimmy Brennan, from Merasheen Island.

On February 7, *Centaurus* slipped out of Harbour Buffett and headed for Malaga, Spain, with a load of fish. But the Danish ship never arrived there, nor, as far as could be determined, at any port. By early April, it was sixty-six days overdue. On July 16, 1923, after inquiries that spring and early summer from Denmark on its whereabouts, *Centaurus* was posted as "Missing with Crew." Presumably it had gone down, taking Captain Kristian Rasmussen, Mate Erik Knudsen, its two Danish sailors, and one Newfoundland man with it.

The *Evening Telegram* of April 17, 1923, stated the Newfoundland sailor was probably "a Viscount" belonging to Marystown or Merasheen. However, John Lou Ennis of Merasheen in his book *Adapting to A Changing Situation in Placentia Bay, Newfoundland* (ESP Press, 1999) relates the story of Jimmy Brennan. Jimmy, hearing a foreign vessel needed a man, walked across Merasheen Island to Indian Harbour on the eastern side of the island, then took a small boat for Harbour Buffett.

Captain Rasmussen was only too delighted to have this young, hard-working man and signed Jimmy on for the trip. As Ennis says, "That was the last I heard of Jimmy Brennan, except for the story that spread around Placentia Bay."

Various mutations and translations of the "murder" ship circulated. Many locals thought it was a Spanish vessel that afterwards sailed for South America. In fact, Jimmy drowned on *Centaurus* not long after he and his Danish shipmates left Harbour Buffett.

In time, whether through an accidental discovery or a subsequent search by Placentia Bay fishermen, someone reported the tops of three masts of a sunken sailing ship not far from Long Island. They only became visible at low tide. Most likely, they said, since no other vessel, especially a tern or three-masted schooner, had been reported missing in Placentia Bay at that time, it was the *Centaurus*. Certain markings on the topmast seemed to confirm it, as well.

THE SIGNAL HILL PRISON BREAK

SIGNAL HILL, ST. JOHN'S

IN THE BEGINNING, the Signal Hill prison was constructed as a soldiers' barracks. It was converted into a prison in 1846 after the stone structure was deemed unfit as a military quarters and after the old courthouse jail burned down. It remained in operation for twenty years.

It was a two-storey building, but it lacked proper ventilation, windows, and sanitation—that is, adequate toilet facilities. Capable of housing twenty prisoners of both sexes, those incarcerated there were more than anxious to get out, resorting to prison breaks whenever possible.

One unusual escape happened on a Friday night, January 26, 1855, between 9:00 and 10:00 p.m. A prisoner in the Signal Hill jail who had been convicted for stealing a cow gained his freedom by "using more ingenuity on his part than prudence on that of his keepers," according to the January 13, 1908, edition of the *Evening Telegram*.

The jailor on duty that night, accompanied by the jail servant or assistant, went upstairs to secure the cells for the night. Having unbolted the outer door leading into the room where the cells were, both entered together. The prisoner, who was hiding behind the door of his cell nearest the outer door, darted out, closing the door with the same bolt the keepers had used to open the door. The keepers were locked in upstairs.

He was nearly free. There was still a bolted trap door on the stairs at the top landing that prevented him from getting out of the building. He rang the bell, the usual signal for those below to draw back the bolt and open the trap door. When it was opened, the prisoner walked out of the building, free.

At that time, Mr. McGill was in charge of the prison. Such was the consternation of certain wags about St. John's that a song was made up about him and the Signal Hill jail. The first verse says:

There's old McGill, the Governor, and Jimmy Brien the cook;
I can't forget Peg Cullen, whose nose is like a hook.
I was there last summer, but I won't go there no more;
I must not forget Jonathan, the porter on the door.

It is not stated if the prisoner who bolted was ever captured, but by 1866, prisoners from Signal Hill were transferred to a new facility on Forest Road. For a while, both prisons were in use.

Perhaps one of the most unusual songs composed about a prison break came to be after a famous (in his day) escapee was recaptured. The escapee's story was so entertaining, to the Newfoundland public, at least, that local poets competed with each other to publish the most amusing verse.

The composing of songs, poems, doggerel, a " verse or two," was a popular form of entertainment, a diversion, a generation or two ago. Newfoundlanders could and frequently did make up a song or poem about any event of significance. Much of Newfoundland and Labrador's oral history was preserved in songs, poems, and yarns. Many were and are preserved in newspapers, while others were memorized and sung at concerts, kitchens, and informal gatherings. Many are, unfortunately, lost today.

The following piece about a prison break is annotated, that is, certain terms and names are expanded upon for the benefit of readers who need more background information on what's mentioned in the verses.

Brady's Recapture[1]

You all have heard about young Phil Brady;[2]
He who escaped from out our city Pen.[3]
We were inclined to think that he had left us;
And yet we find he's rambled back again.[4]

Chorus:
He's rambled back again;
He's rambled back again.[5]

Of course the police had to use persuasion;
To make Phil Brady ramble back again.[6]

His holidays, alas; they all are ended;
And now he'll in his Home Sweet Home remain.[7]
Where he will have to don the regulation;
And never more will wear Pat's pants again.[8]

And so, with many keen regrets we leave him;[9]
His notoriety will never wane.
And when his present term it has expired;
We hope he'll never ramble back again.[10]

(Signed) G. W. R.[11]

1. The songwriter says this piece is sung to the tune of "They Called Me Back Again," a rather obscure song, perhaps, with a Newfoundland flavour.

2. Young Philip Brady, an English seaman living in St. John's, was eighteen years old. On September 5, 1906, he had been sentenced to serve eighteen months after being found guilty of stealing $40 from a "poor box" in Holyrood. He was five foot, four inches, with blue eyes, blond hair, and light complexion—hardly distinguishable features.

3. In early November, six weeks after incarceration, he escaped from Her Majesty's (Queen Victoria was the reigning monarch) Penitentiary, situated between Forest Road and the shore of Quidi Vidi Lake, St. John's. The original stone structure, built in 1859, was in Brady's day on the outskirts of the city.

4. Brady, with cellmate John Farrell, stole a rope from a workroom and hid it in a slop barrel. Later, he and other prisoners took the barrel outside and dumped it, making sure the rope was out of sight. That evening, he and Farrell asked to go the toilet and slipped away from the escorting guard, across a roof and down to the garbage dump. When the coast was clear, they used the rope to get up the prison wall. Brady went over first, but Farrell was scared off by pursuing prison dogs and was captured by the guards.

5. Within hours after he ran, a $50 reward was posted for Brady's recapture. One instance of his sighting came from Patrick Coughlan of Heavy Tree Road. He claimed Brady had broken into his house, taking clothing and food and leaving behind his prison garb before he ran. Brady had also been arrested a few months previously for stealing a shirt from Coughlan.

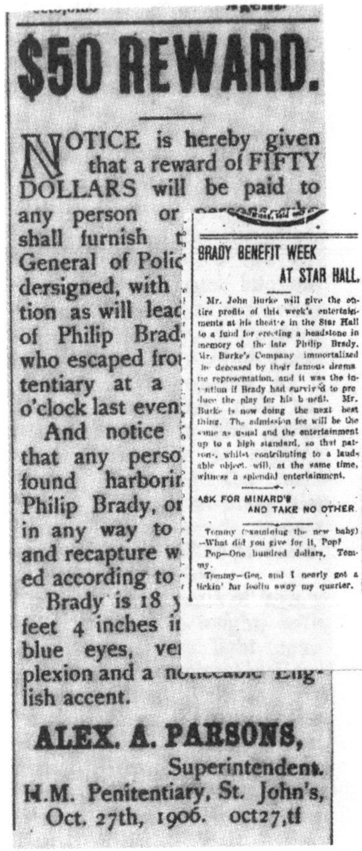

$50 REWARD.

NOTICE is hereby given that a reward of FIFTY DOLLARS will be paid to any person or
shall furnish t
General of Polic
dersigned, with
tion as will leac
of Philip Brad
who escaped fro
tentiary at a
o'clock last even
And notice
that any perso
found harborir
Philip Brady, or
in any way to
and recapture w
ed according to
Brady is 18
feet 4 inches i
blue eyes, ve
plexion and a
lish accent.

ALEX. A. PARSONS,
Superintendent.
H.M. Penitentiary, St. John's,
Oct. 27th, 1906. oct27,tf

BRADY BENEFIT WEEK AT STAR HALL.

Mr. John Burke will give the entire profits of this week's entertainments at his theatre in the Star Hall to a fund for erecting a headstone in memory of the late Philip Brady. Mr. Burke's Company immortalized the deceased by their famous drama tic representation, and it was the intention if Brady had survived to produce the play for his benefit. Mr. Burke is now doing the next best thing. The admission fee will be the same as usual and the entertainment up to a high standard, so that patrons, whilst contributing to a laudable object, will, at the same time, witness a splendid entertainment.

ASK FOR MINARD'S AND TAKE NO OTHER.

Tommy (examining the new baby) —What did you give for it, Pop?

Pop—One hundred dollars, Tommy.

Tommy—Gee, and I nearly got a lickin' for foolin away my quarter.

6. Searches there and elsewhere by the Constabulary intensified, but so did public criticism in the local papers in letters, songs, jokes, and general laughter. Two policemen in Manuels arrested the wrong man; Police Inspector McCowan and other officers caught a short, blond-haired man in a hotel at Pleasantville. He looked like Brady, but was, in fact, not him. That same lookalike was caught again a few days later. Two policemen searched schooners at the waterfront; two others combed the White Hills. Crowds gathered at the train station as false reports had Brady coming in under police escort from Brigus.

A humorous letter-poem appeared in the *Evening Telegram* (October 31, 1906) while another letter two days later poked fun at authorities. Another letter suggested Superintendent Sullivan sing "Phil Brady (Bill Bailey), Won't You Please Come Home."

Ironically, the police did use "persuasion" when constables Mackey and Savage found him in a potato cellar on Mr. Brennan's property in Kilbride. Brady, armed with a pitchfork, was subdued and escorted to St. John's in a police wagon.

7. Brady was free a mere eighteen days, indeed "eighteen" seemed to be an ill-omen number for the boy. Brady told Sullivan he read the papers while on the run, finding the blunders by police amusing. He also said the first night he hid near the high Cross in Mount Carmel Cemetery.

"Home, Sweet Home" is in reference to Her Majesty's Penitentiary (HMP). It was also called Hotel Mr. Parsons, in reference to Alex M. Parsons, Superintendent of the Pen.

8. Prisoners wore the black-and-white striped garb. When caught on November 14, Brady wore stolen clothes belonging to Pat Coughlan. These few lines indicate people felt sorry for and sided with "the little English lad."

9. With keen regrets, the people of St. John's lost a great diversion in the days before popular entertainment as exists in today's world. Local poets vied with each other during the event. In a way, Philip Brady became a Newfoundland folk hero.

Even a year later, sarcastic poems appeared as with "Fifty Dollars Reward for Brady's Re-Capture" to the air of "The Wearing of the Green"—*Evening Telegram*, September 19, 1907. The song suggests Pat Coughlan knew Brady prior to his escape. As well, Brady was fed by a sweetheart, Mary Barnes. Perhaps jealousy led to a tip to police to the whereabouts of Brady. Mary was later taken into custody for abetting Brady's escape. However, her conviction is unclear.

10. In February the next year, Brady's charges of theft (of stealing clothes from Coughlan) were dismissed, but he was sentenced to serve twelve months for jailbreaking. According to the *Daily News* of December 24, 1956, "Christmas in St. John's: Yuletide in 1906," Brady contracted tuberculosis due to his exposure during his escape in cold November. Still a prisoner, he died on June 19, 1908, in the Signal Hill hospital.

His funeral was attended by hundreds of citizens when he was buried in Mount Carmel Cemetery, not far from the Cross where he hid on his first night of ill-gotten freedom.

11. There is no indication of who "G. W. R." is. However, it is known that the comedian, poet, and playwright Johnny Burke staged his play "Brady's Escape" about the event, with a local actor taking the part of the little English lad.

CLOSE TO HOME: THE STRANGE DEMISE OF REVEREND MERCER

FOGO, SELDOM-COME-BY, BAY ROBERTS

HE WAS A MIDDLE-AGED MAN, thoughtful of his own health and well-being, in good physical shape, and knowledgeable of and experienced in winter conditions in Newfoundland. Reverend William Seeley Mercer had already spent seven years on the Labrador Coast, and he claimed he had weathered many a storm there.

The son of Edward and Rebecca (Seeley) Mercer, William was born in Bay Roberts, went to school in Griquet, and graduated from Mount Allison University in New Brunswick. After teaching school for two years in Newfoundland, he studied for the Methodist ministry and was ordained in 1913. He married Mary Langley of Nova Scotia.

Mercer Memorial Drive. The signpost on the main road into and out of Fogo is dedicated to the clergyman who died near that area. Author photo.

In 1922, Mercer was posted to the Fogo Island mission, and it was there, somewhere between Fogo and Seldom-Come-By, he died, prematurely in a snowstorm. Why he undertook a nine-mile walk in the face of a raging blizzard became the talk, the speculation, and the unexplained on the island of Fogo for many years.

Even though people shook their heads in wonder, his life and death are commemorated in the town of Fogo. On the stretch of road leading into Fogo from Seldom-Come-By, there is a prominent signpost, "Mercer Memorial Drive." Mercer had died relatively near that marker under questionable circumstances.

In those years, it was customary for clergy to walk, or in winter to use a dog team and slide, if available, from community to community on Fogo. On February 3, 1924, Reverend Mercer had done just that. He walked from Fogo to Seldom-Come-By to hold Sunday evening service.

A church meeting in Seldom had been planned for Monday evening, so the reverend stayed the night at the home of Moses Holmes. But come Monday morning, high winds and driving snow pounded the island of Fogo. The storm was so bad, the church meeting was cancelled. Around 10:00 a.m., Mercer decided to return to his wife and young child in the town of Fogo.

Families in Seldom-Come-By implored the clergyman not to venture out in such a storm, but for some strange reason, Mercer left to walk the nine miles of trail and road. Well, he reasoned to those concerned for his well-being, he was used to much more severe Labrador storms. He was physically fit, and he figured the storm would taper off.

Conditions didn't improve. In fact, the storm became worse. Somewhere on that road on Monday, February 4, Reverend William Mercer fell. Monday passed with no break in the weather. Somehow, the people of Fogo learned he had left Seldom-Come-By. Telegraph operators between the two towns each communicated, awaiting word he had made it back to Seldom or had eventually reached Fogo.

Between both towns, there once existed a rough shack or shed used as a temporary shelter or rest spot in summer or in winter. This was commonly called a halfway house. Quite possibly the minister had found this and would be there, cold but alive.

Later on Monday, John Gill and his son Fred went on a mission to find the reverend. After several hours out, wind and ice conditions forced them to give up the search. Early Tuesday, the blizzard had still not abated. Although there was less snow, the winds were very strong with temperatures well below freezing.

That evening, several men got together in the Fogo Fishermen's

Lodge. Volunteers divided into two search groups. One would plow through the snow over the hills behind the Methodist parsonage. Perhaps the missing clergyman had buckled down behind a rock or in some low shrubs or tuckamore. The other group followed the regular trail between Seldom and Fogo.

Both groups decided to wait for the other at the halfway house. According to the book *Tales of Fogo Island* (Fogo Island Literacy Association, 1999), the search party beating its way over the icy trail included Arthur Gill, Javis Hart, Matthew Bennett, and Matthew Mehaney. They carried two dogs and a sled with them.

Not too far from the parsonage, the dogs stopped, barked, and refused to move ahead. The men saw a black coat or boot in a snowdrift. It was part of Reverend Mercer's clothes. He had covered most of the walk to his home and was within a mile of his home when he perished. Unofficial sources say a bunch of raisins, sustenance he never used, was clutched in his hand.

The body was brought to Fogo for burial preparations while the local magistrate and the Anglican clergyman went to relate the terrible news to Mrs. Mary Mercer. Their child was eight months old.

William Mercer's gravestone is in the Fogo Methodist (today's United Church) Cemetery. His wife and child left the island the next spring. In time, a church in Joe Batt's Arm and a school in Fogo were named in his memory. Today, the signpost bears witness to the strange and untimely passing of Reverend William Mercer.

DELLECNAC SPELLS "CANCELLED" BACKWARDS: COINCIDENCE OR NOT?

HARBOUR GRACE, THE ATLANTIC OCEAN

THE LARGEST SCHOONER ever constructed in Newfoundland was the 613-ton *Dellecnac*, the only one over 600 tons. It was built by the Newfoundland Shipbuilding Company, which began constructing ships at Harbour Grace in 1917 and launched six terns, or three-masted schooners, in its short existence.

Beginning with the 379-ton *Armoreal*, launched in 1917, the company lasted a little over two years, for in 1919, the yard burned down and the company went out of business. The chief financiers and owners were the Hannevig brothers of Norway, one of whom was millionaire Christoffer Hannevig.

Dellecnac was built in the winter of 1918-1919 by Jacob Evans for the Hannevigs. The company also had a subsidiary branch in Norris Arm, Notre Dame Bay, called the Norris Arm Shipbuilding Company. This was sometimes referred to as the Martin Shipbuilding Company (named for Michael E. Martin, the supervising contractor).

Dellecnac, however, had less than an auspicious maiden voyage and a controversial demise. Even the word *Dellecnac* is odd and totally unlike most names put on Newfoundland vessels. Newfoundland schooners usually commemorated landmarks or community references or family names.

Although this oddity may have had nothing to do with its quick and suspicious exit, and it may just be a quirky coincidence, but the ship's name is "cancelled" spelled backwards. Its existence was nullified within a few weeks after it went in the water.

Dellecnac was equipped with engines as well as sails, making it, in effect, an auxiliary vessel capable of steaming under engine power or canvas when the wind was fair. It went to the bottom three months after its May 1919 launch.

Its crew on that maiden voyage consisted of twelve men. The names of a few are recorded: Captain Rangvald Hannevig of the Shipbuilding Company; First Mate J. W. Grey; Chief Engineer Arthur Wells; Second Engineer Pynn; and Third Engineer Noseworthy.

Dellecnac went but a short distance on its initial voyage when it was discovered the wrong kind of oil had been supplied for the engines, and the ship was forced to return to Harbour Grace for the proper oil. This problem was corrected, and the crew changed somewhat.

It left port again on Wednesday, July 16, and was put on an east-by-south course. Two days later, the starboard engine became disabled. The ship was discovered to be leaking badly, plus the deck beams on the starboard and port sides of the engine rooms had been scorched, probably from the engines.

The crew put *Dellecnac* back to St. John's, slowing the speed down to between two and four knots. The engine was not going regularly and the ship was leaking, but the pumps worked fine. *Dellecnac* reached St. John's at 9:00 a.m. on Tuesday, July 22. On July 26, the ship went on dry dock, where it was discovered the pintles (bolts) on the rudder were broken, the seacocks were damaged, and the pipe leading to the circulating pumps was also damaged.

When this litany of problems, breakdowns, and general disrepair was corrected, a new master and some new crew were shipped, and at 10:00 a.m. on August 25, 1919, *Dellecnac* left again to try to steam to Norway. By noon, Cape Spear bore west five miles distant, and five hours later, the port engine stopped and the ship began to leak.

From that Monday until Sunday, *Dellecnac* drifted as the crew tried to repair the engine and to slow the inflow of water. On Sunday, when *Dellecnac* was eighty-five miles off Newfoundland, the schooner *Carrie Hirtle* picked up the crew. The log of *Dellecnac* for August 31 records an account of how and when the crew finally abandoned the ship (see chart opposite).

The Marine Court of Inquiry looked into the loss of the ship on April 17 and 19, 1920. The court found that, although *Dellecnac* was in a seaworthy condition and passed as fit by the Lloyds of London agent when it left dry dock at St. John's on August 24, the real cause of the leak was not determined.

As well, the new captain and first mate taken on at that date were not certified. The first mate was totally unfit for his position, and the engineering staff was not competent. The chief engineer had considerable experience on stationary shore engines, but had little experience on a ship. At the inquiry, it was also determined there were defects in the engine.

Although there was no evidence of misconduct or neglect on the part of the master, mate, or crew, the master was severely criticized for not having kept a proper log. It was not written up until days had elapsed, and by then it was incomplete and inaccurate.

The chair of the inquiry, Judge Francis J. Morris, and Cyril D. Fenn, Lieutenant Commander, RN both quoted the "Merchant Shipping Act of 1894," saying that no ship registered in Newfoundland over 100 tons shall go to sea out of Newfoundland unless the master and first mate possess certificates of competency or service.

Morris concluded, "The Owners of such vessels and any person going therein as Master or Mate are each liable on conviction to a penalty, under the Merchant Shipping Act, of two hundred dollars."

The court of inquiry had no choice but to administer the letter of the law to the master, mate, and owners of *Dellecnac*. Usually, officers had to forfeit their certificates of competency for a period of time, typically six to twelve months. In this case, however, neither Captain Hannevig nor Mate Grey had to give their certificates of qualifications, as they were not qualified and did not possess the documents.

Final Logbook Entries for *Dellecnac*, August 31, 1919

4 a.m., engineers and engine room staff gave up the engines. Engine room flooded and five feet of water in hold.
8 a.m. similar conditions.
10:30 a.m. sighted a schooner and signalled her. She bore down on us and all came aft and refused to remain longer on the ship as she is totally unmanageable and making a large quantity of water and drifting helplessly.
12:30 launched boat and dory alongside, took off four men and remainder in lifeboat and boarded the fishing schooner *Carrie Hirtle* of Lunenburg in approximately latitude 47.54 and longitude 50.40 West. The schooner was bound for St. John's or Cape Broyle.
Set *Dellecnac* on fire before leaving her.

MURDER OR WARFARE AT TURPIN'S ROCK

TILTING, FOGO ISLAND, EXPLOITS RIVER

MURDER ISN'T SIMPLY THE ACT OF KILLING someone. It's a legal term that defines an unlawful killing. The adjective "unlawful" makes all the difference. One person shooting another on the streets may be murder, but on the battlefield, taking the enemy's life is condoned.

In a war, in which the involved parties have all openly declared hostilities, killing opposing soldiers on the battlefield is legal. Since murder is illegal by definition, killing a person on the battlefield in a war cannot be murder. A soldier who kills an enemy under the rules of war isn't a murderer.

The white settlers of Newfoundland had informally declared war on the native Indians, the Beothuk. The Beothuk retaliated, although outnumbered and with inferior weapons, by making war on the whites, who were seen as the enemy who took their lands and blockaded food sources.

A part of that war was played out at Turpin's Rock on Fogo Island. Michael Turpin and his companion, Patrick Murray, were tending their potato gardens. It was June 13, 1809. Potato sprouts had appeared above ground and both men were "trenching" potatoes, that is, spading more earth to the mounds.

They were residents of Tilting and the garden was in Sandy Cove, about half a mile from Tilting (then called Tilton Harbour). Tilting, one of few Roman Catholic communities on Newfoundland's northeast coast and one of the most "Irish" of Newfoundland outports, was used by migratory fishermen in the early 1700s. One of the first settlers was Thomas Burke of Ireland, who was joined over the next few decades by such families as the Keefes, Foleys, Lanes, and McGraths. Turpin was probably an employee of the Burkes and worked in his master's gardens in the spring.

Sometime on that June day, Turpin and Murray saw a band of Beothuk creeping up on them. Another source says they noticed someone throwing small stones at them, as if to lure the men into the woods. One of the men looked over an embankment and saw hostile natives.

In those times, it was more common for settlers to carry guns when going any distance from their homes, but neither man had one and they decided to run for their lives. Turpin knew there was a small schooner at anchor in the cove and, being a good swimmer, decided to swim to it. Murray ran toward Tilting to escape and to raise an alarm with the residents.

Murray, although slightly lame, was strong and energetic. One story, in the *Evening Telegram* of December 12, 1894, says of him:

> Some of the Indians followed and "forelaid" him before he reached the path in such a manner that he had to pass between two. Gathering his utmost strength, he dashed between them with such force as to bring both of them to the ground.
>
> They discharged their arrows at him. In all, three took effect. There is a hill two-thirds of the way from Sandy Cove to Tilting, near which were several more gardens. A woman named Mrs. Foley was also tending potato gardens in one of them.

Mrs. Foley (one source has her name as Fowlow) saw the Indians in pursuit of Murray, and she raised the handle of her spade to her shoulder. The Beothuk, some distance away, mistook it for a gun and gave up the chase. Murray, with an arrow in his back, ran on to Tilting to tell others of the raid. In addition, he had lost one of his boots along the path at the Muddy Bridge, near Reardon's Rocks.

Meanwhile, poor Turpin swam for his life toward the schooner. Alas, there was no one aboard. Others of the band of Indians launched a canoe they had secreted in the woods and soon caught him.

He was dragged ashore and killed on a rock. As was their custom, the victim was beheaded, and they took his head with them as they fled.

After Murray gave the alarm in Tilting, men with guns ran to Sandy Cove. Others tended to the wounded Murray, extracting the arrow from this back and stemming the flow of blood. Patrick Murray lived to tell the tale.

A search party found Turpin's body on or near the rock, but the natives had gone. According to local tradition (and as posted on an informational board at Sandy Cove), in the spring of 1810, Turpin's head was found on a pole near High Point on the Exploits River. Apparently the Beothuk had used it for ritualistic purposes, as was their custom. It was sixty miles or more from the spot where he was killed.

The rock is still called Turpin's Rock today, and local tradition says it still bears the stain of blood, shed by a settler engaged in an informal war with the native people.

The scene at Sandy Cove, Tilting, today with an interpretative signboard telling of the clash between the white man and the native people more than 200 years ago. Author photo.

A CELEBRATED CASE

FOGO, SOUND ISLAND, PLACENTIA BAY

IT WAS THE TALK OF THE TOWN. Anyone with the time and inclination, especially those who loved a bit of scandal, wanted to attend the trial. The November 3, 1881, *St. John's Times* said, "owing to the novelty of the case, very many citizens attended the Court" to hear the love story and to the listen to the contents of letters from a enamoured young man to his fair Juliet.

Petty Jury for Supreme Court Trial, November 1881

James Wear
Joseph Moyst
William Mitchell
Henry Watkins
John Wiseman
Richard Martin
John McGrath
George Thompson
Edward Warren

In the midst of Supreme Court trials of murder, arson, manslaughter, shipwrecking, and theft, here was a case of love, or unrequited love. The trial of "Breach of Promise of Marriage" began November 30, 1881. Appearing before the petty jury (see box, left) and Mr. Justice Robert John Pinsent, a highly regarded lawyer who had recently been appointed Supreme Court Judge, was plaintiff Marianne Hollett and the defendant, John Haddon.

Ms. Hollett, who belonged to Sound Island, Placentia Bay, had lawyers George Henry Emerson and John Hoyles Boone to represent her. Haddon was defended by Alexander James Whiteford McNeily and I. R. McNeily. The plaintiff wished to recover damages for an alleged breach of promise from Mr. Haddon to marry her.

Ms. Hollett was a milliner, a hat maker, who left Sound Island to further her career in St. John's. In early 1878, she went to Fogo to work at her trade for merchant Robert Scott at an annual salary of £25 (about $38 in today's value). She worked in Scott's business for nearly three years.

Marianne Hollett took the witness stand, reviewing the background of her relationship with John Haddon. About three weeks after she arrived in Fogo, Ms. Hollett met John Haddon, who was a bookkeeper employed by another Fogo merchant, Edwin Duder. The *Times* said of their relationship, "She met what she fondly but not wisely believed to be her destiny in the person of John Haddon," the latter now the defendant in a trial.

Many of his verbal and written promises of love, commitment, and marriage would now, as they were read in court, be revealed to the world, much to the delight of those spectators who loved a titillating tale of scandal.

In the courtship, Marianne and John conformed to the routine of outport life and to the proprieties and decorum of the times. Despite the cautions of Hollett's employer, the young couple became engaged to be married. John Haddon was nineteen and would, according to custom, become "of age" when he was twenty-one years old. Then both would take the vows.

Haddon knew she was to be going back to St. John's, so he wrote Marianne (whom he affectionately called "Polly") a letter:

> March 26, 1878.
> My Dear Polly,
>
> You need not be afraid to trust me. . . . You think that when I arrived in St. John's and see other girls I will forget you, but I shall never cease to think of the girl who has led me toward my duty to God. . . . From your ever dear and loving,
>
> John

While in Fogo, John would meet Polly every night, and eventually he gave her a ring and a gold watch. The watch was to make sure she knew when 10:00 p.m. came, as that was the time they parted nightly. The court presented another letter John wrote to Polly two weeks later, April 8:

> My Darling Pet,
>
> You cannot think what impressions of happiness I feel at finding that

my love is reciprocated. I could die for you, but I feel now that I must live and work for you. If I saw you walk with any other fellow it would kill me on the spot. You know that I love you. . . .

Yours, forever, John

Then on May 12, 1880, this letter was sent to St. John's, as Ms. Hollett was then in that place:

My Own Polly,

I hope it will be all right for me or I will die. I rely on your promise. No Scott, or any other man, will go between you and me. If I am allowed to walk with you when I return [to St. John's] I shall be able to give up smoking and chewing; otherwise I shall again fall into my old habit. . . .

Yours forever.

Several love letters of a similar bent flew from Fogo to St. John's, each one promising undying love and the grand prospect of marriage, and each read in Supreme Court. As soon as Haddon finished his work in Fogo, he would return to St. John's, saying: "I am almost wild at the thought of spending a winter in St. John's. Tell your mother that I hope to see her before you change your name from Hollett to Haddon."

The promises flew, right up to mid-December 1880, when John Haddon turned twenty-one. Ms. Hollett, when asked by her lawyer, explained what happened next.

I left Fogo in May 1880 to come to St. John's and left for Sound Island around June 22, 1880. Because of a letter sent by the defendant, I left Sound Island and came on to St. John's again. This letter, which contained £2 to pay for my passage, was sent August 20.

. . . We were to be married in the fall of 1881. He told me so the day I was leaving Fogo. . . .

Alas, when Haddon arrived in St. John's, he continued his promises, but took another girl to a Wesleyan Tea Meeting. Ms. Hollett wrote a note of complaint to Haddon, and from that point on, "I noticed a coolness in his manner. . . . He began not to fulfill his appointments and his visits fell off." Haddon said he was tired of her and wanted a change and that she might have suited him in Fogo, but not in St. John's. The final goodbye note to Hollett from Haddon simply stated:

> May 11, 1881
>
> I will have nothing more to do with you. If you write me again I will return your letter, unopened.
>
> John Haddon

Before Ms. Hollett left the witness box, her counsel, Emerson, asked her one final question: her age now. To which she replied, twenty-seven.

Defendant Haddon was not called as a witness. His counsel, Mr. McNeily, addressed the jury, saying that although there was a promise to marry while the defendant was underage, there was no confirmation of the promise after that.

Judge Pinsent, in his address to the jury, said the actions of the two were of a rare and unusual occurrence and that there was no impropriety or reflection on the plaintiff's conduct to bring this case before the public in a court of justice. Without the court, Pinsent would not know of any other means to redress grieved parties.

Evidence, in Pinsent's opinion, supported a fresh promise to marry, and the only consideration for the jury was one of damages—how much to award Ms. Hollett.

The jury should be guided by the fact that the defendant was a bookkeeper employed by Mr. Duder. Also, they should consider the youthfulness of the defendant, twenty-two, as compared to the more mature plaintiff. Her maturity must have exercised an influence on the youthful Haddon. It would have been better for all if she had left him alone and not encouraged his actions.

The jury retired for a few minutes, returning with a verdict to award the plaintiff $400. So ended the love story of "Polly" and John Haddon, bookkeeper.

Almost.

There was much public chatter and smiles as St. John's discussed the couple's affairs, the testimony, the verdict, and the contents of seven love letters and one goodbye note.

The final media say in the matter came from the *Patriot and Terra-Nova Herald* of December 5, 1881, critical of a rival paper, the *Times*. "The papers last week gratified a morbid appetite for gossip by publishing skeleton reports and brief notices of the recent extraordinary case in the Supreme Court of Hollett vs Haddon for a breach of promise to marry." In their article **THE BREACH OF PROMISE CASE**, the *Patriot* concluded:

> We don't know how much the lady sued for in damages, but the jury awarded her with £100 ($400) for the loss of a potential husband, Mr. Haddon. But there was manifest injustice inflicted upon the man when everything was suppressed on his behalf. But by publishing his *gushing* love notes, it was ridiculous and unprincipled. We [the *Patriot*] think it was unfair toward the character of the defendant. It would have been better for him if he had been advised to settle the matter outside the court.

"YOU CUT A BIG HOLE IN HER BOTTOM"

ST. JOHN'S, HARE BAY

JABEZ NURSE FINLAY, a St. John's merchant, owned several fishing schooners, including the *Sparkler*, *Dove*, *Water Lily*, and *Somerset*, which he sent to the Labrador each spring. Only the last named caused him any trouble, and that trouble was not of Finlay's making. The *Somerset*, built in Gambo, Freshwater Bay, in 1877, sank under curious and suspicious circumstances in the spring of 1880.

Somerset, not a large vessel at twenty-eight tons and fifty feet long, had only six or seven crew. It probably operated out of the western side of Bonavista Bay.

Many of crew names seem to indicate that: Edmund Vater and his son, Stephen Vater; James Lane; William Lush; Cornelius Goulding; and a man named Petten, although the latter was probably from Conception Bay. Petten alone was not present when *Somerset* ran into trouble. Vater, who gave most orders and made decisions during *Somerset*'s final run, must have been skipper or captain.

There were rumours, speculations, and loose talk about how and why the vessel sank. The head rumour was that the crew had intentionally caused *Somerset* to go down. Owner Jabez N. Finlay appealed to the law, and four crew—the two Vaters, Lane, and Lush—were brought to trial under judge and jury in St. John's in late November 1880.

The charge against them was "barratry," or fraud by a crew at the expense of the owner of a ship or its cargo for the purpose of collecting ship or cargo insurance monies. Word had leaked *Somerset* was scuttled some miles off Hare Bay, approaching Freshwater Bay. Further hearsay claimed two or three of the crew had spoken quite openly about it.

For the Crown in the courthouse in St. John's on December 2 and 3, 1880, were Newfoundland's Attorney General and Alexander James W. McNeily, Q.C. Defending was John Hoyles Boone, assisted by George T. Carty. There were a number of witnesses for the Crown and the defence.

The Crown's chief witness was Cornelius Goulding, one of the crew of *Somerset*. After establishing that *Somerset* was supplied by J. N. Finlay, Goulding stated they left Triangle, a Labrador fishing station located on the north side of St. Michael's Bay, in early October 1880. *Somerset* and crew had taken about 230 quintals.

At Triangle, the fish was put aboard Mr. James Johnson Rogerson's vessel *Flying Mist* (but misunderstood as *Flying Fish* by the court reporter). Goulding, under questioning, stated:

> I heard the mate of *Flying Fish* ask Edmund Vater his name, and Vater replied, "John Lane." He [Vater] said he shipped off the fish of Lane as he was going to lose the craft. All the crew was present at the time he said this, with the exception of one, Petten.
>
> We then went to Hare Bay, where we headed up in a hogshead our caplin seine, herring net, and fishing gear and put this in Mr. Snow's store. They all went ashore with the gear, except me. Edmund Vater said he hid away the fishing gear, as he was going to lose the craft.
>
> From Hare Bay we went to Stag Harbour Run. Five days later, we left Stag Harbour Run for home. We got within ten miles of Freshwater Bay and then began to lose the vessel.
>
> Vater told me to haul the boat alongside, and everything useful was removed into the boat. I went into the cabin and saw Stephen Vater with a hatchet tearing up the locker. William Lush was standing by at the time. I did not see Stephen chopping the timbers, but after I turned in [went to bed or bunk] with one, Petten.
>
> At the request of Vater, Petten was to be kept in ignorance of what was going on. I later heard more cutting with a hatchet. I heard the anchor chain run.
>
> Petten and I ran on deck. Edmund Vater said she had struck a rock. We left *Somerset*, and in about five minutes, she sank. Skipper told me never to say how she was lost.

> He said, "She went down shocking quick."
> I said, "Yes. You must have cut a large hole in her."
> He said, "Yes, I cut a big hole."

Goulding then came under intense cross-examination by defence lawyer Boone. Under questioning, he admitted he was as much in the know of the plot as any one of the crew. At first, Goulding didn't intend to say anything about it. Goulding estimated *Somerset* went down in about twenty fathoms of water.

Owner Finlay, upon cross-examination, said he was the owner of the vessel and that he had not told Vater it was all right to try to collect insurance on *Somerset*.

The Crown closed its case, whereupon lawyer Boone made a long and eloquent address to the jury to discredit the statements given by Crown witnesses. He attempted to find discredit in Goulding's testimony, saying that the man himself was guilty.

On December 3, the jury, after a long deliberation, came back with the verdict:

> "We find the prisoners Edmund Vater and Stephen, his son, guilty, and we find Lush and Lane not guilty."

The judge thanked the jury, saying that, in his opinion, it was a proper verdict. While the record is silent on the punishment for the son, the father, Edmund Vater, was sentenced to six months' imprisonment.

POLITICS AND MURDER

HARBOUR MAIN, CONCEPTION HARBOUR, AVONDALE

AROUND THE MIDDLE of the nineteenth century, the people of Harbour Main and Cat's Cove (today's Conception Harbour) took their politics seriously, to the point of murderous riot.

The community of Harbour Main–Chapel Cove–Lakeview is an amalgamation of three formerly separate communities situated at the head of Conception Bay. Cat's Cove, today's Conception Harbour, is also in the southwestern part of Conception Bay, relatively near Harbour Main. By 1836, the population was around 250 people.

Historically, as well as being somewhat of a religious and educational centre, Harbour Main also became an election centre. At Harbour Main, the district's nominations for candidates to the House of Assembly were made. Electoral stations were also established there during each election. More often than not, elections proceeded relatively trouble-free in Harbour Main and the district.

In 1861, however, the pre-election campaign became quite violent. That spring, four candidates for the two Harbour Main district seats were nominated, all of them Liberal.

Two candidates, George James Hogsett and Charles Furey, who were openly supported in church and on the streets by Father Kyran Walsh of Harbour Main, ran against the other two candidates, Patrick Nowlan and Thomas Byrne. The latter were apparently supported by another priest of a neighbouring parish.

On election day, Father Walsh led a group of 300 men from Harbour Main and nearby Salmon Cove (today's Avondale) to Cat's Cove, where a few dozen men in the group were going to vote.

The residents of Cat's Cove, who, it is said, supported Nowlan and Byrne, assumed that the Harbour Main group had malevolent intentions and prepared for a battle. What ensued on May 2, 1861, was a brawl that resulted in one death and many injuries.

The day previous, a message was hand-delivered to Rev. Walsh from the people of Cat's Cove. It read:

> The people of Cat's Cove have been told that you intend to bring a mob to this place on polling day for the purpose of beating and intimidating the voters here.
>
> If this be your intention, we fear something bad may take place. We intend to defend ourselves and will do so fearlessly.
>
> . . . At the same time, we wish you to understand that we want to carry out the election peaceably. . . . We wish an answer to this note by the bearer.
>
> (Signed) Maurice Mahoney, Thomas St. John
> James Buck, Thomas Connell
> Thomas Trikey, Edward Bryan

The answer was verbal: "I will, with a party of men, accompany the Salmon Cove voters to Cat's Cove."

On May 2, voting day, Father Walsh advanced along the road to Cat's Cove with the body of men and with flags and "colours flying." Along the way, they were joined by men from Chapel Cove, about seventy or eighty from Salmon Cove and a few from Gasters. At the head of the group was one of the political candidates, Charles Furey.

At the crossroads where it turns down into Cat's Cove harbour, the throng was met by Captain Thomas St. John. St. John begged Walsh and the rabble not to go farther, as they would be fired upon. Father Walsh's only reply was, "Surely the men are not mad enough to fire their guns upon us."

Farther along, two other men from Cat's Cove, Maurice Wade and John Keating, also met the group and told them, "If you proceed to Cat's Cove, there will be violence!"

On they went. Farther up the road was a high and wide barricade put up by the Cat's Cove people. In a hilly meadow not far from it were some men loading and preparing their sealing guns and several women collecting large rocks to throw. Again, Father Walsh and his angry contingent, estimated to be about 300, were asked to go back.

The forty to fifty Cat's Cove people looked at the mob of hostile men in alarm and fear. They had no idea what damage a violent mob would do in their little community.

Charles Devereux from the Harbour Main group shouted, "We will pull down this fence and take the hill of the enemy!"

The barricade fence was savagely ripped down and the hill surrounded. At that moment, the women hurled their stones and the Cat's Cove guns erupted.

The would-be politician Furey was hit by stones, but not injured. Michael St. John actually rested his gun on a fencepost, aiming at Furey. One piece of shot hit his cap. Richard Baker and Michael Gorman were struck by shot, but not seriously injured. William Hicks and Richard Moores were hit, but not fatally. George Furey met his cousin, Charles (the politician), saying his brother William had been hit in the thigh. A few minutes later, George was fatally wounded and died there on the road between Harbour Main and Cat's Cove.

Charles Furey, accompanied by William and Daniel Fling and John Meaney, slipped away from the violence by going down to the seaside and following a little-used path back to Salmon Cove. (As spellings are given as presented in publication documents, Fling may actually be Flynn.)

By May 12, the police had rounded up twenty suspects at Cat's Cove and brought them to the Penitentiary in St. John's. Between late November and early December that year, the trial for the murder of George Furey proceeded. The charge was eventually reduced to manslaughter. Those who had been identified as "gun-carrying" were arraigned before Justice Bryan Robinson. (See box, next page)

After hearing witnesses and evidence, on December 6, Robinson gave his charge to the jury. The accused were not justified in shooting and killing unless their homes or property were directly threatened. Although it was not determined which gun wielder killed Furey, all who were present were equally guilty as the man who actually fired the gun.

On December 26, nine were found guilty and sentenced: James and Michael St. John, Edward Brien, and Michael Dunn were sentenced to twelve months in jail; Edward, John, and Patrick St. John, Patrick Brien, and Thomas Dunn nine months. Time of incarceration began from May previous, thus they had five more months to serve. The nine were then, by order of the court, removed and taken to the Penitentiary.

Cat's Cove Men Accused of Manslaughter in the Harbour Main Skirmish, May 2, 1861

Edward Brien
Patrick Brien
Michael Dunn
Thomas Dunn
Edward St. John
James St. John
John St. John
Michael St. John
Patrick St. John

Several Accused Were Released for Lack of Evidence or Found Not Guilty

Aaron Cullen
William Dalton
John Harman
James Keefe
James Mahoney
John Mansfield
Patrick Nowlan
John St. John Jr.
Thomas St. John
Michael Walsh
William Walsh

After some political blunders and mishandling of returns, Hogsett and Furey were assumed to be winners after the May 2 election. When they tried to take their seats in the House of Assembly at the opening of the session, they were forced to leave. Political wrangling gave Nowlan and Byrne the seats.

This resulted in further violence among partisans, and within a few days, many gathered outside the Colonial Building, St. John's. The mob destroyed property, much of it belonging to friends and relatives of Nowlan and Byrne.

Before peace was restored, three people were killed by garrison soldiers called in to contain the violence. Sporadic violence continued to occur for years after in Harbour Main and the surrounding area.

LOOTERS IN A KILLER STORM

ENGLEE, VARIOUS COASTS OF NEWFOUNDLAND

AS IF THE DEVASTATING and demoralizing effects of a killer storm were not bad enough, then news came of wrackers—thieves and plunderers—who used the cover of the hurricane to do their dirty work. Along with the trauma, sadness, and heartbreak of missing ships, the case of shipwreckers became an outrage to the people and the law. More than enough lawmen made sure the pillagers of Englee would be brought to justice.

The storm! In Newfoundland and Labrador, it had no name. However, the hurricane of September 1900 caused so much damage and hardship in Texas that it was later labelled "Isaac's Storm," after the American meteorologist Isaac Cline, who erroneously predicted it was of no consequence.

When the 135-mile-per-hour winds hit Galveston Island, Texas (where Cline lived), on September 8, the storm surge and waves destroyed half—roughly 3,600—of the homes and buildings in Galveston and killed more than 8,000 people. Some years later, the flattened Galveston was rebuilt and a sixteen-kilometre seawall was constructed to protect the low-lying city from storm surges.

Before the death-dealing calamity hit New Brunswick and PEI two or three days later, it brought hurricane-force winds to Chicago and Buffalo, killing several loggers and riverboat men in the area. Winds downed so many telegraph lines that communication throughout America's Midwest came to a standstill.

It also ravaged Saint-Pierre and Miquelon, the French islands near

Newfoundland. According to J. P. Andrieux's book *Shipwreck at St. Pierre: Tragedy and Heroism in Sail and Steam* (W.F. Rannie, 1982):

> Today, with modern navigation and weather reporting, there is time for warning of these fierce storms, but at the turn of the century, no such warnings were given. On September 13, 1900, such a hurricane struck St. Pierre.

No lives were lost on the ships sunk in Saint Pierre harbour, but nine fishing schooners at the offshore banks had nowhere to seek shelter. They failed to return to port, and approximately 120 French fishermen were drowned.

With its last slap at North America, the storm crossed Newfoundland from the southwest corner to Notre Dame Bay in a side swath, from the Great Northern Peninsula to the Straight Shore and along the south coast.

In its wake, eighty-two schooners had been driven ashore or sunk and another hundred seriously damaged. This damage was the first reported. Exactly how many Newfoundland ships were missing would not be known until weeks after the storm. It was only then that bank fishing and coastal schooners and those returning from the Labrador fishery should have reached home.

They didn't. Reports trickled in through the latter part of September and early October 1900 of the ships that would never report: eleven, with an aggregate total of ninety crew aboard.

Squeezed in among the "anxiety reports" of missing vessels came a news clip from Englee, south of St. Anthony. First reports said the small trading schooner *Annie* ran in there to escape the storm. It wasn't there long before men from that shore boarded the vessel and commenced to plunder and loot the schooner's stores.

An older man aboard *Annie* was knocked down and ill-treated. Some of the other crew were verbally and physically abused.

Although it was nearly a month after the terrible storm, by the first week in October the long arm of the law reached from St. John's to the tip of the Great Northern Peninsula. Several lawmen from St. John's, termed at the time "a posse of police," led by Sergeant O'Brien, brought back the alleged perpetrators.

Eight men were charged with plundering the schooner *Annie* at Englee. They arrived in St. John's on October 16, but before their trial began, the Englee men were remanded at the St. John's Penitentiary for a week.

Meanwhile, the talk in St. John's and generally around Newfoundland was of ships missing in the September 13 hurricane. On the same day the Englee plunderers were remanded, October 31, word in local papers said the schooner *Lilydale* with Captain William Edgecombe of Catalina was missing. It was last seen on the Grand Banks fishing. Eight Saint Pierre fishing vessels never reported, carrying a total of 118 men—not including the losses of French vessels from Saint-Malo, Bordeaux, and Granville.

After those terrifying September days, the Gale of 1900, or "Isaac's Storm," a deadly force of nature, slipped away from the Atlantic maritime regions and headed north, arcing across the colder seas and finally disappearing from human knowledge.

The effects of the storm that nearly annihilated Galveston became the subject of Erik Larsen's book *Isaac's Storm*, published in 1999.

The trial of the plunderers got under way November 2 with Judge James Gerve Conroy presiding. Martin Williams Furlong represented the Crown. Lawyer Alexander James W. McNeily spoke for the prisoners: J. Wilcox, J. Handcock, Mark Hiscock, R. Johnson, John Compton, Levi Canning, William Canning, and George Canning.

First prosecution witnesses were W. Burton and Moses Waterman, the latter the mate of *Annie*. Both spoke of how the Englee men boarded the vessel and used rough words and physically manhandled *Annie*'s crew. Evidence came from Mr. Howell, master of the schooner *Ajax*, owned by Josiah Manuel of Exploits. Howell had made an agreement with the captain of *Annie* to secure what was left of its cargo and take it to St. John's.

Two men, Edgar Barbour and Levi Gill, from

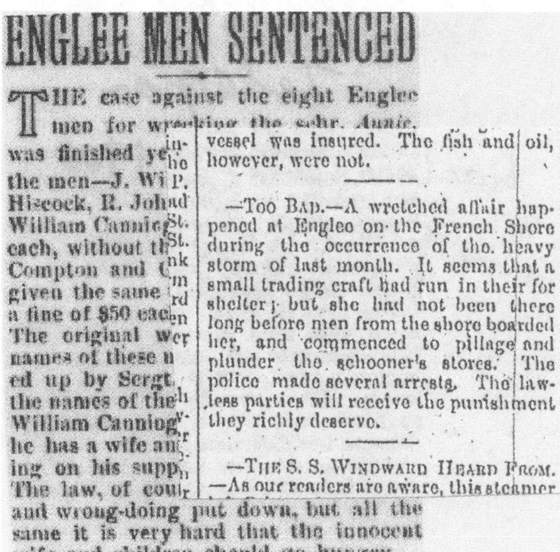

ENGLEE MEN SENTENCED

THE case against the eight Englee men for wrecking the schr. Annie, was finished ye
the men—J. Wi
Hiscock, R. Joh
William Canning
each, without th
Compton and C
given the same
a fine of $50 eac
The original wer
names of these n
ed up by Sergt.
the names of the
William Canning
he has a wife an
ing on his supp
The law, of cou
and wrong-doing put down, but all the same it is very hard that the innocent wife and children should go hungry.

vessel was insured. The fish and oil, however, were not.

—Too Bad.—A wretched affair happened at Englee on the French Shore during the occurrence of the heavy storm of last month. It seems that a small trading craft had run in their for shelter; but she had not been there long before men from the shore boarded her, and commenced to pillage and plunder the schooner's stores. The police made several arrests. The lawless parties will receive the punishment they richly deserve.

—The S. S. Windward Heard From.—As our readers are aware, this steamer

Too Bad: The *Harbour Grace Standard* of October 19, 1900, with its heading **TOO BAD** is followed by comments on the ". . . wretched affair at Englee . . . during the heavy storm of last month. . . ." and another from a St. John's paper that says there was a case against the eight for wrecking the schooner *Annie*.

another schooner, which had taken shelter in Englee from the storm, testified. However, their statements were given reluctantly. The town of Englee had given them shelter from the storm. Plus, perhaps they might have to harbour there sometime again in a future storm. Perhaps the next time, Barbour and Gill might not be so welcome. At this point, the trial was delayed for a week to bring in other witnesses.

On November 13, testimony from George Howell and the owner of *Annie*, Mr. MaCauley, was given. MaCauley proved he was the owner and that there was no insurance carried on the vessel or cargo.

McNeily put up a strong defence for the eight, especially for Levi and William Canning, who were recalled to the witness stand a second time.

Englee, taken from Barr'd Island Hill, overlooking the town. Author photo.

The trial ended on November 15. Judge Conroy sentenced Wilcox, Handcock, Hiscock, Johnson, Levi Canning, and William Canning to six months in prison, without the option of a fine. John Compton and George Canning, who had been found somewhat less culpable, were given the same time, but with an option: they could pay a fine of $50 each.

Those who viewed the trial and who had listened to McNeily's plea for mercy were particularly touched by the case of William Canning. He had a wife and nine children who were depending on his support for the coming winter. Thus ended the trial of the plunderers of *Annie*, almost two months to the day after the great September 13 hurricane of 1900.

THE BRIEFLESS BARRISTER

NEWFOUNDLAND

IN THE 1880S, one of Newfoundland's most notable makers of verse, poems, doggerel, comedy skits, and plays was Johnny Burke. He is best known as a poet, actor, singer, and playwright who immortalized in satire and song many local events and people. Much of his work was parody with pointed allusions to political happenings, court appearances, and the questionable actions of contemporary bigwigs and lawyers.

Often, his poems were published in local newspapers. In late January 1881, this piece of comedy appeared in the *Evening Telegram*. Johnny Burke (1851–1930), often referred to as the Bard of Prescott Street, was in his poetic prime in 1881 and is believed to have written this masterpiece.

The Briefless Barrister

An attorney was taking a turn;
In shabby habiliments drest.
His coat was shockingly worn;
And the dust had invested his vest.

His breeches had suffered a breach;
His linen and worsted were worse.
He had scarce a whole crown in his hat;
And not a half crown in his purse.

And thus as he wandered along;
A cheerless and comfortless elf.
He sought for relief in a song;
Or complainingly talking to himself:

"Unfortunate man that I am!
I've never a client but grief:
The case is, I've no case at all;
And in brief, I've never had a brief!

"I've waited and waited in vain,
Expecting an 'opening' to find.
Where an honest young lawyer might gain;
Some reward for the toll of his mind.

"'Tis not that I'm wanting in law;
Or lack an intelligent face.
That others have cases to plead;
While I have to plead for a case.

"O, how can a modest young man;
E'er hope for the smallest progression.
The profession's already so full;
Of lawyers so full of profession!"

While thus he was strolling around;
His eye accidentally fell.
On a very deep hole in the ground;
And he sighed to himself, "It is well!"

To curb his emotions, he sat;
On the curbstone the space of minute.
Then cried, "Here's an opening at last!"
And in less than a jiffy was in it!

Next morning twelve citizens came;
('Twas the coroner bade them attend).
To the end it might be determined;

How the man had determined his end!
"The man was a lawyer, I hear,"
Quoth the foreman who sat on the corse.
"A lawyer? Alas!" said another;
"Undoubtedly died of remorse!"

A third said "I knew the deceased;
An attorney well versed in the laws.
And as to the cause of his death;
'Twas no doubt the want of a cause."

The jury decided at length;
After solemnly weighing the matter.
That the lawyer was drowned, because;
He could not keep his head above water!

NEWFOUNDLANDER'S WRONGFUL DEATH, HALIFAX

NEWFOUNDLAND AND HALIFAX

A PATIENT, PATRICK FOLEY from Newfoundland, fifty years old and a lodger at Youngs Boarding House on Upper Water Street, Halifax, checked in at the Halifax Victoria General Hospital on November 20, 1889. He could give no information as to exactly how he was hurt, but complained of a pain in his chest. His breast was swollen, skin bruised, indicating to the attending Doctor Farrell that his pain came from a hard kick or blow to the chest.

From Foley's incoherent mumblings, he had apparently gotten the blow during a drunken quarrel. On the morning of November 21, he died, under what the doctor and subsequently the undertaker and the coroner all said were suspicious circumstances. The autopsy performed the next day revealed Foley had suffered a violent death, and Coroner Almon found witnesses to question.

The first was Abram Young, owner of the boarding house. Foley had been there a month ago, for a week, after which he went to sea on the SS *Alpha*. He returned from the sea a few days prior and, on a Sunday morning, asked for a drink of liquor. He didn't eat much, saying he didn't feel well. On Monday, he was taken to the hospital.

Mrs. Young said she had no idea where Foley was Saturday night, but thought he had fallen on the wharf at Halifax's deepwater terminus. Foley had not complained of being struck by anyone.

Halifax policeman Andrew Sullivan testified he was on foot patrol in that area and saw the deceased on Lower Water Street near Cunard's wharf. Foley complained of being cold. Sullivan guided him to Youngs. The next day, Sullivan checked on Foley, but while talking to Mr. Young, he heard a terrible noise and moaning from upstairs. It was Foley on a sofa, apparently in terrible pain. There was a mark on his right hand, and the man was able to blurt out that he was from Newfoundland and had been drinking. Sullivan thought Foley suffered from DT's—delirium tremens—uncontrollable shaking stemming from alcohol withdrawal.

Charles Putner, a druggist at the hospital, testified that he saw the man when he checked in. Foley had left the SS *Delta* the day before. Foley said he had been drinking on Saturday night and that someone had beaten him, but didn't know who.

Dr. Pearman, the admitting doctor for Mr. Foley at the Victoria on November 18, said the man complained of severe pains in the neck and chest. He said he had been kicked in the chest, had taken a beating, and had vomited blood, but had no idea who struck him. Pearman's examination showed a bruise on the collarbone and fractures on some ribs.

Coroner Almon, in summing up, said he did not think the injuries received by the deceased were the result of a fall, but were received at the hands of persons, at present unknown. The murder of Patrick Foley, Newfoundland, remained unsolved.

Seventeen years after Foley's curious death, another Newfoundlander died under strange circumstances in Halifax. On Christmas Eve night, 1906, William Snow (from Newfoundland, but place of birth undetermined) was found floating at Cunard's wharf—the same place where Foley had been.

Detective Hanrahan, in his investigation of the suspicious death, learned there had been a fight in an Upper Water Street bar. Snow had fought with Michael Collins. Collins, a Newfoundland seaman on the SS *Harlaw*, had gotten the best of Snow inside the bar, then the fight spilled out into the street.

William Snow received several more blows and ran toward Cunard's wharf and dock, followed by Collins, who was chasing after him. Two other men in the bar who had witnessed the fight followed the men to the wharf, but Collins was nowhere to be seen.

A few minutes later, Snow was seen struggling in the water near the dock. The quartermaster of the cable steamer *Minna* threw a rope to the floundering man, but he did not seem to have the strength to hold on and sank to the bottom shortly after.

Owing to a bend or right angle on the wharf, the two men following the combatants lost sight of Collins and Snow for a few moments. Just what happened in those moments they could not say. It may have been Snow, while trying to escape, fell off the end of the wharf, as the night was very dark. It may have been possible Collins knocked or pushed Snow over.

Halifax Chief of Police Power believed Collins was the direct or indirect cause of Snow being in the water and, subsequently, drowning. Medical Examiner Finn ordered an autopsy on the remains and requested the police to investigate. On December 30, Nova Scotia's Attorney General ordered the apprehension and arrest of Michael Collins.

Detective Hanrahan went to Mulgrave, Nova Scotia, where Collins and the *Harlaw* had gone, and came back to Halifax with Collins in cuffs. Collins, twenty-three years old and a resident of the West End of St. John's, had arrived in Halifax in mid-December 1906 to join the SS *Cape Breton*. When he found *Cape Breton* had sailed without him, he signed on the *Harlaw*.

On January 8, 1907, Collins was arraigned before a stipendiary magistrate at Halifax, who ordered him to jail and thence to appear before the Supreme Court of Nova Scotia on a charge of manslaughter.

THE FISHERMEN'S ROW: FOURTEEN AGAINST THREE

THE FRENCH SHORE, OR TREATY SHORE, on Newfoundland's northern coasts came about as a result of the centuries of war, rumours of war, peace agreements, treaties, and battles between England and France. The treaties, while blocking the settlement of hundreds of miles of coastline by English Newfoundland fishermen during most of the eighteenth and nineteenth centuries, gave the French full access to the coast and its cod.

By 1783, the French Shore limits were marked as between Cape Bonavista to Point Riche on the northwest side of the Great Northern Peninsula. Later, an international compromise relocated the boundary from Cape St. John to Cape Ray.

For generations, resident Newfoundland fisher families and the migrant French managed to get along fairly well. However, from time to time there arose smouldering animosity that often broke out into sharp disagreements.

Ports and sheltered harbours like St. Julien's, Croque, Conche, Quirpon, and Cape Rouge were traditional fishing grounds and home bases for many Newfoundland fishermen. Sometimes they became a scene of conflict between the French and the Bonavista Bay and Conception Bay fishermen. In 1904, the French agreed to give up their rights to the French Shore, and the English were free to settle there.

However, even two or three years later, a few French fishermen lingered, leading to conflicts on the former "French Shore," or, as the French called it, "Le Petit Nord."

In late August 1906, at Cape Rouge—located at the southeast extremity of a small peninsula on the east coast of the Great Northern Peninsula, between Conche and Croque—one of the final "rows" broke out between the French and English.

Thomas Russell of Bay Roberts, with the help of two other men, set fishing trawls at Cape Rouge. Not far away was the Saint-Malo schooner *President* under Captain Paul Revert. Legally the French were allowed to be there, and so they proceeded to set their fishing gear not far from Russell's.

One morning, Russell went out to his trawls only to find them tangled up, and then learned the French had actually hauled them and thrown the gear back overboard.

In retaliation and anger, Russell pulled up 150 fathoms of the Frenchmen's trawls and, along with buoys and grapnels, dumped it all overboard in one big tangled mess—such a tangle that the French gear was practically destroyed.

While Russell was in the act, fourteen French fishermen in their boat accosted the three Newfoundlanders. The three defended themselves with oars and boathooks, and one Frenchman suffered a deep gash from an oar. However, the odds were too great. Russell was struck with an oar, and his two crewmen were badly battered.

The foreign fishermen jumped in Russell's boat, taking him forcibly to the side of the French schooner *President*. The captain asked him his name, then let him go.

Not finished yet, Captain Revert wrote to the French Consul in St. John's, Mr. Rigoreau,

THE

14 FRENCHMEN

Against 3 Englishmen.

Insp. O'Riel
Rouge in the F
had gone to
trouble betwee
ing French fis
Sunday night,
day morning,
examined 18
by fining Tho
erts, one dollar

Fishermen's Row.

INSPECTOR O'REILLY supplies us with the following particulars regarding the row between the French fishermen and the Newfoundlanders at Cape Rouge: The French and Newfoundland fishermen had trawls set near each other, and Mr. Russell, a Bay Roberts man, on going to his trawls one morning found them tangled up and discovered that they had been hauled up by the Frenchmen and thrown out in a ball. Russell then retaliated by hauling up the Frenchman's trawls. While he was in the act of doing this the French crew came up. There were 14 men in the French boat, and they boarded Russell's boat

And Took Him Forcibly On Board

Two local papers, the *Evening Telegram* and the *Evening Herald*, comment on the fishermen's row.

complaining in alarming terms about the treatment he was getting from certain Englishmen, especially Thomas Russell.

As an outreach of Newfoundland's Circuit Court, Inspector O'Rielly was sent up to the French Shore in the SS *Fiona*. His mandate was to investigate reports of trouble between the livyers along the coast and the French fishermen. O'Rielly examined eighteen witnesses in three days.

In conclusion, he ruled against Russell, saying the French still had fishing rights along the shore and Russell was wrong to interfere with their activities. He gave the Conception Bay fisherman a token punishment: a fine of $1.

Back in St. John's, O'Rielly reported, perhaps with tongue in cheek, that, "Quiet reigns again and an international episode has been avoided."

CAPTAIN COURAGEOUS

CATALINA, ST. JOHN'S, FLORIDA

HE HAD THE ADVENTURES from which movies are made. By the time he reached his late twenties, Edward Murphy, born in Catalina in 1863 and schooled in navigation in Saint Pierre, became master of the Newfoundland Government coastal steamers *Falcon* and *Curlew*.

Later in his life, he captained the American vessels *Commodore*, *Bermuda*, and *Laurada*, all of which illegally carried arms to Cuban rebels. Murphy was shipwrecked off a Florida beach (in that disaster, eleven others perished), he was arrested, tried in Delaware, and died of malaria in New York. His remains were shipped home on the SS *Portia* to be buried in Belvedere Cemetery, St. John's.

The James Ryan diaries, written by Nicholas Ryan of the Ryan premises, Bonavista, says of Murphy that on August 16, 1891, "The *Falcon*, with Captain Edward Murphy of Catalina in command, came into Bonavista with the lighthouse inspector aboard." Murphy had a master mariner's certificate from Newfoundland and later acquired this certification from Britain and the United States.

Seven years later, Nicholas wrote another diary note, this one a little sadder. "On September 1, 1898, Captain Murphy died at New York. The deceased was engaged in carrying ammunition and guns to Cuban rebels during the late war. Murphy and the writer [Nicholas Ryan] were schoolmates at Saint-Pierre and Miquelon."

It is not clear why Edward Murphy left high-profile work in Newfoundland and migrated to the United States to seek employment. Perhaps Captain Murphy's life would have been more obscure, only for the fact that the novelist and short story writer Stephen Crane became Murphy's shipmate on the American steamer *Commodore*. Because of Crane's popularity, Captain Murphy became immortalized and somewhat of an American hero. Crane himself went on to become a well-known and beloved author.

Crane wrote several great pieces of literature, including *The Red Badge of Courage* and a book of short stories *The Open Boat*. When *The Open Boat* was published in 1898, Stephen Crane dedicated it to "the memory of Captain Edward Murphy . . . of the ill-fated steamer *Commodore*."

LOSS OF THE COMMODORE

EIGHT OF HER CREW ARE STILL UNACCOUNTED FOR.

Evidence that the Boat Was Sunk Through the Treachery of a Spanish Agent—The Three Frie Going to Search for the Missing.

JACKSONVILLE, Fla., Jan. 3.—
lowing dispatch, giving an accoun
sinking of the filibuster steame
modore, was received from Dator
o'clock to-night:

"About 10 o'clock Friday night,
picious leak was discovered in the f
something definite has been learn
them, a signal has been arranged
the Captain of the Three Friends.

ONLY NINE LOST.

Others On the "Commodore" Reach Shore in Safety—Second Boat From Sunken Steamer Arrives—Conflicting Stories as to Cause of Disaster—One Survivor Thinks the Engineer Was Drunk—Another Claims It Was the Result of Treachery.

JACKSONVILLE, Fla., Jan. 4, 1897.—The second boat from the lost filibustering steamer *Commodore*, containing Cubans, has reached shore in safety. The only persons lost are the eight Americans in the crushed lifeboat and Higgins, who was killed on the beach here after saving Capt. Murphy, Stephen Crane and C. B. Montgomery.

Conflicting stories are told as to

Media of the day tells of Captain Edward Murphy: "Only Nine Lost" from the *Evening Telegram*, January 18, 1897; the other, "Loss of the Commodore" from *New York Times*, January 4, 1897.

For a few years prior to the Spanish-American war, Murphy, who by then was living in the United States, had been running guns and ammunition to Cuban rebels, trying to shake off Spain's dominance. On at least two occasions, Murphy, in SS *Commodore* and SS *Bermuda* out of Jacksonville, Florida, had reached Cuba's shores with arms.

Although the United States sided with Cuba, Murphy's actions were actually against American law. He was gun-running, smuggling arms, which came under the illegal activity "filibustering" or supplying arms to a foreign country to support a revolution. But he hadn't been caught—yet!

In December 1896, the SS *Commodore* was ready to go on another filibustering expedition out of Jacksonville. Newspaper correspondent Stephen Crane became friends with Murphy, who signed him on the *Commodore* at $20 a month. *Commodore* left Florida for Cuba on January 1, 1897. The steamer's cargo manifest showed "200,000 cartridges, 1,000 pounds of gunpowder, forty bundles of rifles, two electric batteries, 500 machetes, fourteen cases of drugs, and four bundles of clothing."

Crane, also looking for adventure and a tale to write about, got his story when *Commodore* exploded and sank in a storm off the coast of

Florida the next day while en route to Cuba. It was never clear or proven if it was a case of sabotage or a faulty engine that caused the explosion. The two lifeboats launched in choppy seas overturned, drowning ten Americans and six Cubans.

Captain Murphy, Crane, Cook Montgomery, Oiler Billy Higgins, and an unidentified sailor got into the vessel's ten-foot dinghy. Within a few minutes, *Commodore* had gone to the bottom. Those in the dinghy, under the command of Murphy, who had sustained a broken arm while leaving the wreck, pulled away in heavy seas and high winds for the shore.

The near-death experience in the dinghy was immortalized when Stephen Crane later wrote the classic short story "The Open Boat," about his thirty-hour experience off Mosquito Inlet Lighthouse—today's Ponce de Leon Inlet Light—at Daytona Beach, Florida. In the beaching of the boat, it capsized. All except Higgins, who drowned in the breakers, were able to reach shore. Murphy saved Stephen Crane by helping him out of the water when Crane was seized by a cramp.

A year later, Stephen Crane included his gripping story in a critically acclaimed book of tales entitled *The Open Boat*, although in it he doesn't specifically use Murphy's name. In another publication, Crane did praise the Catalina-born sailor and captain, saying:

> . . . From [the story] would shine the splendid manhood of Capt. Edward Murphy and William Higgins, oiler. But let it suffice to say that when we were swamped in the surf and making the best of our way toward the shore the captain gave orders amid the wilderness of the breakers as clearly as if he had been on the quarterdeck of a battleship.

After the disaster aboard *Commodore*, Murphy and Crane parted ways—the captain filibustering in another ship, and Crane off to write stories and to correspond via newspaper articles from Cuba and Greece.

Murphy's new ship was SS *Laurada*, which he soon loaded with arms and headed for Cuba. He and his crew were apprehended by the US Coast Guard and taken to Delaware to the USA District Court in late 1897. However, it was a period in the United States when Americans felt much sympathy toward Cuban insurrectionists and anyone trying to help them get rid of Spanish rule. In a sense, Captain Edward Murphy was a champion. A jury soon found him not guilty.

In a later visit to Cuba, Murphy, as a war correspondent, caught malaria and was brought back to the United States. He died in a New York hospital in early September 1898 at age thirty-five.

Relatives in Newfoundland arranged to have his body brought back. The remains arrived on the SS *Portia* on September 29. When *Portia*, with its flags half-mast, arrived in St. John's, undertaker Myrick took charge of the body.

A crowd of people had assembled at Harvey and Company's wharf to show their respect for the late Captain Murphy, and followed the hearse from Water Street to Belvedere Cemetery. Rev. Charles H. O'Neill conducted the service.

Captain Murphy, a hero in the eyes of Cubans and Americans in that era, died just two years prior to the death of Stephen Crane, the man who praised him in a New York newspaper article and lauded him in the dedication to the book *The Open Boat*. Crane, age twenty-nine, succumbed to tuberculosis in June 1900 in Germany.

There's a saying often repeated of adventurers: "It was the life and stuff movies are made of." In fact, there was a movie made of Murphy's and Crane's ventures and misadventures. The twenty-nine-minute black-and-white film *The Open Boat* was produced in 1965 at the University of Michigan and is available from the US-based Film Video Library.

Reproduction of headstone of Captain Edward Murphy, located in Belvedere Cemetery, Section One. He was a man of international fame in his day, helping establish the country of Cuba. Not long after his trial in the United States, he died in New York City. Edward was brother to the Hon. John J. Murphy, Newfoundland MHA.

ELEANOR POWER:
THE FIRST WOMAN HANGED

ST. JOHN'S, HARBOUR GRACE, GREENSPOND

ELEANOR POWER MAY HAVE BEEN SAVED from execution had she had an adequate, knowledgeable lawyer at her trial. Indeed, if she had any lawyer at all. Eleanor herself was not even present when the man she was accused of killing was murdered. Nevertheless, on October 11, 1754, she and her husband were tried, convicted, and swung together in death in downtown St. John's.

Incredibly, the victim, Keen, was the first and sole Justice of the Peace in Newfoundland, when he was burglarized and brutally attacked. Keen, born in Boston in 1704, had moved to St. John's as a young man to act as an agent for New England merchants operating in Newfoundland. He became a successful trader himself, accumulating wealth and property in St. John's, Harbour Grace, and Greenspond.

In that era, Newfoundland justice consisted solely of "Fishing Admirals," who came to the island from England during the summers with the fishing fleets. The admirals, or captains, ruled whichever harbour they fished out of. Certain capital offences, like murder and other heinous crimes, were tried in England. However, no judicial officers were present on the island during the winters.

This situation led to a high crime rate in St. John's and the British Government—Governor Henry Osborn—appointed William Keen as the first Justice of the Peace during the winter when the fishing admirals were away.

Fishing admirals in court. Many of these early "justices" were crude, rough fishermen, many of whom could neither read nor write, using their power mainly for the benefit of family and friends. Courtesy of Francis Briffett's *The Story of Newfoundland and Labrador.*

On September 9, 1754, Keen was attacked in his bed at his summer home. He awoke to what was a burglary and, as witnesses said after, was beaten unconscious. He died of his injuries in St. John's three weeks later. Eight men and one woman were brought to justice before the court that Keen had presided over. Four, including Eleanor Power, were executed for the crime.

Eleanor and her husband, Robert Power, and eight other men—all Irish fishermen and soldiers—initially broke into Keen's house and stole a chest that was thought to contain some silver spoons. When the chest was opened, it had only alcohol in it. Eleanor and one of the male accomplices left the scene.

Eight returned to Keen's residence to make another attempt to steal some valuables. Eleanor Power was not among them.

Keen awoke in his bed during the second robbery and attempted to get up, only to be beaten with a scythe and the butt of a musket by two of the thieves. He died of his injuries on September 29, 1754. Nine days later, nine of the gang, including Eleanor Power and her husband, were brought to trial for murder before the "new" court that Keen himself had helped set up.

The tenth burglar, Nicholas Tobin, became the sole witness against the nine defendants. With no lawyers to defend them, all nine were convicted of murder by a jury after thirty minutes of deliberation. The sentence was death by hanging.

Two were executed on October 10, 1754. Eleanor and Robert Power followed them the next day, becoming the first married couple to hang together in Newfoundland, indeed in the whole of what is present-day Canada. As well, Eleanor was the first non-native woman to be executed by British authorities in present-day Canada. The five remaining defendants spent years in prison, but were eventually pardoned on the condition that they leave Newfoundland and never return.

In those days, there were no lawyers, barristers, or solicitors of any stripe or calibre in Britain's colonial outpost. An attorney may have convinced a judge that Eleanor was guilty of burglary, but as for murder, no, as she had left the scene after the first break-in. She had played no part in the planning or execution of that crime.

Keen's murder greatly alarmed St. John's residents, as they feared it was a sign of trouble from the Irish immigrants—some of whom were termed "masterless men"—who were flocking to Newfoundland in large numbers at this time. Keen's son, William, inherited his property and his position as a justice official, but moved to England in 1760. The Keen family retained property in St. John's and Harbour Grace until the 1830s.

Some years after this dramatic event, the St. John's newspaper *Evening Telegram* published a short article, **DEFYING THE HANGMAN: Amazing Escapes from Death**. It illustrated cases where hanged persons revived, unlike the final minutes of Eleanor Power. However, since this aside is not central to the story of Power's execution, it is presented in Appendix C.

THE UNTIMELY DEATH OF JOHN YETMAN: NEWFOUNDLAND WITNESSES AT A MURDERER'S TRIAL

CAPE BROYLE AND SEVERAL OTHER NEWFOUNDLAND VILLAGES

THE NEWFOUNDLAND CREW on *Helen F. Whitten* knew their vessel had problems. Trouble haunted the schooner, not of seaworthiness, leaks, or shipwreck, but just about any other difficulty a bank fisherman could have: the crew had problems finding fish; there was a lack of bait; poor weather; men adrift; and arguments and personality clashes. Just about anything that could happen did happen, including murder.

Under Captain Wollard, married, forty-eight years old and with three sons, the Gloucester banker left that US port on March 13, 1903. Short some dorymen, Wollard put into Yarmouth and stayed there for nine days, then sailed for Louisbourg and Sydney, finally hiring five Newfoundlanders: John Yetman; Celestine Power; Daniel Rose; Joseph Hartson; and a Jessup.

Yetman, a good worker with experience in bank fishing, worked in Sydney but belonged to St. Mary's on the southern Avalon Peninsula. The young single man had no way of knowing the trauma and hardship that would befall him on "the *Whitten*"—personnel problems and conflict that ended with his violent death three months later.

In a previous book, *Born Down by the Water* (Flanker Press, 2004), I told the story of the actions aboard the vessel that led to murder and the arrest just after the dire deed. This story, which I believe to be different and unique, describes the court work, revealing the names and testimony of the Newfoundland dory fishermen who were called as witnesses.

When Captain Wollard reached Port aux Basques, he put ashore one man, Conrad, who was lame, and hired two replacements, John Woundy and John Brown. Both were from Burin and were in Port aux Basques after becoming shipwrecked on their previous vessel.

The *Whitten* then had a full crew of nineteen: sixteen dorymen for the eight dories; one cook; a bosun or second hand; and Captain Wollard. While fishing on Scaterie Bank, two men named McLeod went astray in a dory. Wollard went to Sydney to see if they had been picked up and maybe carried there. The McLeods did eventually arrive at Sydney but, fed up with discipline and work conditions on the *Whitten*, took their clothes bags and deserted.

While in Sydney, three more disgruntled men left *Helen F. Whitten*, joining the banker *Madonna*. Wollard was again short four or five men, but he found four replacements. He and his crew then went to fish off the Magdalene Islands. On May 27, one of his dories capsized, drowning two men: Edwin Goodwin of Argyle, Nova Scotia, and William Strickland, a Newfoundlander.

Another dory, with Jessup and Roberts aboard, went astray, but were found by the vessel *Lake Champlain* and carried to Quebec. Again without a full crew, the *Whitten* went to Port aux Basques and hired four more men.

By now, the *Whitten* was short of bait and ice and sailed to Burin. Lack of bait and poor weather delayed the schooner and Captain Wollard from fishing for fifteen days. The *Whitten* then went to Cape St. Mary's, from there to Placentia, and then on to the Grand Banks. It was now late June, but fishing was relatively good.

On the banks, John Yetman and John Penney became lost in the fog and were picked up by a French vessel. They were transferred to a Newfoundland schooner under Captain Dan Ryder and carried to Bay Bulls.

Through news exchanged on the fishing grounds, Wollard learned the two men had been carried into Bay Bulls. Wollard sailed to Cape Broyle, a highly frequented port a little south of Bay Bulls, to get more bait and ice. While there, he telegraphed Bay Bulls, asking Yetman and Penney to rejoin the ship. It was the first day of July.

Wollard intended to take more bait and ice at Cape Broyle, but heavy rain delayed the work. In their idle time, the captain and several crew gathered at "Careys," a well-known drinking establishment in or near Cape Broyle. Here, the alcohol flowed freely, as did the arguments, personal vendettas, power struggles with other crew, and faulty and good advice for Captain Wollard. But Captain Wollard welcomed Penney and Yetman back, shaking their hands, congratulating both on a safe return, and paying for their drinks at Careys.

In the course of conversation with other crewmen, John Yetman, probably fed up with trouble, arguments, and delays, said he wanted to leave *Helen F. Whitten*. On July 4, as the schooner prepared to leave Shore's Cove, near Cape Broyle, Yetman readied the dory to row ashore. Wollard, agitated again by the loss of one of his best workers, had told others when he first learned of Yetman's intentions, "If Yetman leaves this ship, he leaves a dead man."

True to his word, he fired his revolver at Yetman in the dory and killed him with a shot through the heart. The captain was arrested at Cape Broyle by Constable Greene, taken to the Ferryland jail, and thence transported to St. John's to await trial.

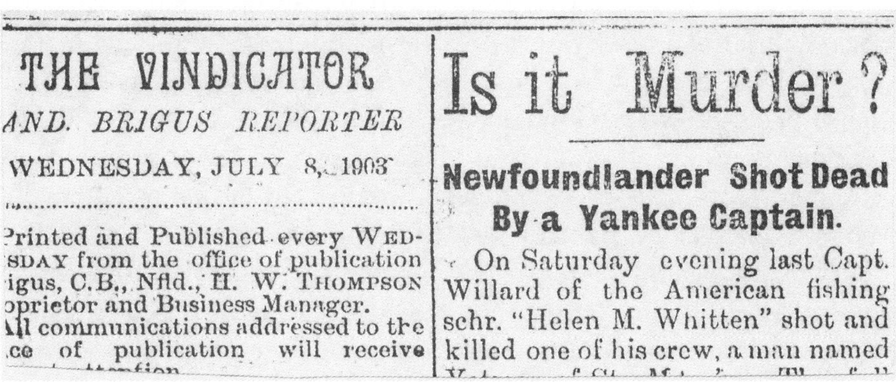

THE VINDICATOR
AND BRIGUS REPORTER
WEDNESDAY, JULY 8, 1903

Printed and Published every WEDSDAY from the office of publication igus, C.B., Nfld., H. W. THOMPSON oprietor and Business Manager.
All communications addressed to the ce of publication will receive

Is it Murder?

Newfoundlander Shot Dead By a Yankee Captain.

On Saturday evening last Capt. Willard of the American fishing schr. "Helen M. Whitten" shot and killed one of his crew, a man named

Newspapers in Newfoundland, including Brigus's *Vindicator* of July 8, 1903, covered the trial of Captain Francis Wollard, accused of killing John Yetman of St. Mary's.

On August 13, 1903, Wollard's judge-and-jury trial for "having feloniously and with malice aforethought shot and killed John Yetman" began in St. John's. By the morning of the next day, a twelve-man jury was selected from a pool of seventy-eight.

Crown Prosecutor Edward Patrick Morris presented the case before Chief Justice William Henry Horwood, the latter assisted by Judge George Henry Emerson and George M. Johnson. Captain Wollard was defended by Martin Williams Furlong and James Mary Kent. Kent informed the court they would call up just five witnesses.

The Crown would bring forward twenty-four to testify, including nearly the whole crew of *Helen F. Whitten*—many of them Newfoundland fishermen from outlying communities.

The first witness sworn was an argumentative and troublesome drinker, Joseph Walsh, born in Placentia, but at that time a resident of Gloucester. His statement as a dory fisherman on the *Whitten* was long and detailed, taking up much of the first day of trial. He described ports visited, voyages, fishing, obtaining crew, troubles, and events leading up to the shooting—as did most of *Whitten*'s crew in their time on the witness stand, but for the purposes of this tale, will not be repeated hereafter.

Walsh admitted he was "in liquor" on July 4 and that after the shooting he tried to hide and then keep Wollard's revolver from the arresting policeman, Greene. His resistance and assault landed him in jail for a few days. He was still in jail when the trial began. After cross-examination by Furlong, Walsh stepped down.

The next witness gave his name as Joseph Gosling—other witnesses called him John; probably his name was John Joseph—testifying that he resided at Burin. On June 2, he joined *Whitten* at Port aux Basques after he had been shipwrecked in a schooner belonging to Burin. He was on deck that evening and saw Wollard lean over the rail and fire four shots at Yetman. Gosling described physically to the court how it was done. He said to Wollard after, "Captain, look what you have done!"

On cross-examination by Kent, Gosling said he saw Walsh take the gun from the captain after the shots and also later saw Constable Greene tussle with Walsh to get the same gun from him as evidence.

Harbour Main resident John Penney, who had worked at the Sydney Steel Works and joined the schooner from Sydney, said he was Yetman's dory mate. Both of them had gone astray in thick fog on the *Whitten*'s voyage. He spent much time in the box describing the various vessels that gave them transportation to Bay Bulls. He said how, on the evening of July 4, Gosling went ashore in a dory to get liquor for the captain. Upon return, Yetman had gotten into the same dory to leave the *Whitten*.

Joining the schooner at North Sydney, but not stating his hometown, John Dominy said that between 2:00 and 3:00 p.m., the anchor was hauled up and sails set in preparation to leave Shore's Cove, Cape Broyle.

He was at the wheel when he saw the captain fire the shots. Yetman had said he wanted to go ashore to get a pair of pants.

On cross-examination, Dominy stated that while Gosling was ashore, he heard the captain say, "If Yetman goes ashore, he will go dead." As well, Dominy said that *Helen F. Whitten* was anchored about 200 yards from Cashin's wharf and had moved away, about 200 yards, when the shooting occurred.

Joseph Hyde, born in Bay Bulls, but a resident of Gloucester, had made three trips in the *Whitten*. After the captain fired, he said, Yetman's dory drifted aft. After the shooting, the schooner was brought to, stopped. Furlong's cross-examination revealed that Hyde had seen and heard a quarrel between Captain Wollard and Joseph Walsh. After that, he saw that the captain's jaw was cut. Hyde had only one glass of liquor that day.

The first witness on Friday, August 14, Cook George Hipson, had little to testify. He was below in the galley during the scene on deck. He added on cross-examination that Yetman left his clothes aboard, taking only his oil clothes.

Sworn and examined by prosecutor Morris, Burin-born John Brown said he worked with Yetman on the windlass, heaving up the anchor that fateful evening. After the captain fired, he saw Yetman fall over in the dory, his head near the water with the dory listed out on one side.

Celestine Power of English Harbour, Fortune Bay, joined the schooner at Louisbourg on April 1. He gave the same details as the others, but added that the dory, with the body of Yetman in it, was towed into Shore's Cove by two men from the shore, Ernest and Augustus Carew.

A crewman from Gloucester, John Rippendale, testified, adding upon cross-examination by Furlong that Yetman said he was going to leave the *Whitten*, not saying why.

James Buffett of Rose Blanche said Joseph Walsh took the revolver from the captain; Constable Greene then took it from Walsh. To Judge Johnson he said he did not see Walsh strike the captain when he took the revolver. He did not see a knife in John Yetman's hand to cut the dory painter.

Not asked his hometown, Doryman Daniel Rose, who joined the schooner at Louisbourg, testified he saw Yetman cutting the painter with a knife when shots were fired. Upon cross-examination, Rose said he was nineteen and this was his first season to the fishing banks. Juryman W. H. Maddock asked Rose where he was standing when the captain fired.

Joining the *Whitten* at Port aux Basques and belonging to Burin,

John Woundy added that he was five or six feet away from the scene and had heard no conversation between Yetman and Wollard moments before the shots.

The parade of witnesses changed to men other than *Whitten*'s crew for a session: Augustus Carew, Shore's Cove, was with his brother when he saw, from a distance, what happened. He rowed out and recognized Yetman, whom he knew. Taking the dory in tow, he brought the body and dory to shore and sent for Constable Greene. Carew said the constable asked him to watch the body while Greene went aboard the schooner. Augustus stated he was talking to Yetman about an hour before this and testified Yetman was sober.

In his lengthy testimony, Constable Greene stated that he asked Thomas and Ernest Carew to assist him in the King's name. When he and Thomas Carew tried to board the schooner, two men—Joseph Walsh and Thomas Hogan—tried to prevent him from going to the cabin to see the captain. Greene called to Captain Wollard, who came up to the deck. Walsh then swore that the constable would not take the captain. When another crewman signalled Walsh had a revolver, Constable Greene had Walsh arrested, confiscating the weapon.

On the row to shore, Captain Wollard was put under arrest and handcuffed. Wollard then asked if Yetman was dead—the answer was yes. Greene warned Wollard that anything he said could be brought against him in a trial. But Wollard continued, saying, "Yes, I shot him. I put four bullets in him. I calculated on doing it and told you [Greene] yesterday I would do it."

"No, Captain Wollard," testified Greene. "Yesterday you said you would shoot Walsh and that Yetman was your best man."

"At Cashin's wharf, when we arrived, I called on schoolteacher John Hussey to take care of Yetman's remains. I took the prisoner to the Ferryland jail."

Sergeant Cleary took the witness stand, describing his role in the examination of the body, along with Dr. Freebairn and Constable Greene. He also explained his theory of bullet trajectory, entry and exit wounds, and that he found a bullet in the clothing of the deceased.

Superintendent John J. Sullivan, sworn and examined by Morris, briefly testified that he was part of the magisterial investigation held at Ferryland, identifying the victim's clothes, the revolver, and the bullet.

Crewman Thomas Hogan admitted on the stand he was drunk on July 4 and recalled nothing.

Identifying himself as one of the *Whitten*'s crew and belonging to Burin, Joseph Hartson said he joined the *Whitten* in Sydney. After describing the events of July 4 evening, Hartson stated he and Gosling rowed Sergeant Greene and Wollard ashore afterward. Hartson said that when Greene put the handcuffs on Wollard, the captain said, "I know I shot the man and I am not sorry for it."

A physician at Ferryland, Dr. Freebairn described at length to the court his role in the post-mortem. He found two wounds, one on the left shoulder and the fatal wound in the chest. A bullet had passed through the heart, causing almost instant death.

On Saturday morning, August 16, the three men who lived in Cape Broyle—Ernest Carew, Louis Williams, and James Keefe—took the witness stand, all describing events after the shooting and the transporting of the body to shore.

The last witness for the Crown was Edward Brien, who was from St. John's, but was in Cape Broyle that day with Dr. Rissmuller. The constable hired him and his buggy to carry Captain Wollard to the Ferryland jail. Brien said that, on the way up Long Hill, Wollard asked him if he had ever driven a murderer before. "I said, 'no' and Wollard said, 'You're driving one now and I don't give a damn.'"

For the defence, lawyer Furlong asked Captain Francis Wollard to take the stand. His was a long testimony of his experiences as captain, the troubles on *Helen F. Whitten*, winding down to a detailed version of the events of the evening of July 4, 1903. Furlong attempted to make a point that Wollard was, in fact, trying to stop a mutiny, led by Yetman, and was under the threats of a troublesome giant, Walsh. This contention was ruled out.

His statement was followed by character witnesses, firstly from a Mr. Wicks, who did business at Bay Bulls and who knew Wollard for fifteen years. Then, John Power of Tor's Cove, who fished with Wollard in 1895 and 1896, found him to be a good man and good to his crew. James Byrne of Brigus South knew an even-tempered and sociable Wollard for twelve years.

Michael Peter Cashin, a politician—who later went on to become Prime Minister of Newfoundland—was born in and did business at Cape Broyle, including business transactions with American schooners. He had known the captain for ten years. He recounted the troubles Wollard was having controlling his crew that summer. Cashin remarked to another person that he would not wish to be captain of an American vessel like the *Helen F. Whitten*, as all the members of the crew were captains telling Wollard what to do. (Appendix D shows the complete list of witnesses called during Wollard's trial.)

Monday morning, August 17, court resumed with Mr. Furlong's address to the jury, followed by Morris's summary of the Crown's case. At 2:30 p.m., Chief Justice Horwood gave his instructions to the jury. Clear distinction was made between what constituted manslaughter and what was murder.

The jury retired at 4:40 and at 5:50 came back with a verdict of "guilty of manslaughter." Two days later, Captain Wollard was sentenced to sixteen years hard labour at the St. John's Penitentiary.

In the sheriff's office, he was permitted to speak a few words to certain members of his crew before he was taken to the penitentiary. Captain Wollard, suffering from remorse and struggling to contain his emotions, broke down as the crew shook his hand and wished him goodbye. Both the prisoner and crew exchanged kind greetings and, as the crew filed out of the room, their eyes were wet with tears of sorrow and sympathy. Despite all that had happened for six weeks, the crew all said Wollard had treated them well at all times.

Due in part to intense and voluminous letters and correspondence initiated by Wollard's family back in Gloucester, and numerous appeals from the American Government to Newfoundland justice authorities, Wollard did not serve his complete sentence. He was released, with the local agencies citing ill health as the reason, on May 24, 1909.

The Jury of St. John's Citizens in the Trial of Captain Wollard, August 14, 1903

H. J. Jardine
John E. Furneaux
N. J. Collier
Albert Wood
James G. Hunt
Richard Purcell
J. F. Canning
S. J. Feaver
W. H. Maddick
Robert Cousens
W. J. Ford
W. Chancey

SUPPLEMENTAL TO COURTING DISASTER, PUBLISHED 2009

In 2009, Flanker Press published my first crime book, *Courting Disaster: True Crime and Mischief on Land and Sea*. In the five years following its release, I located additional information related to five stories published in it. These were found in archival newspapers or records or in information someone sent to me. Again I thought the tidbits would be interesting or unique to readers.

The story "Who Was To Blame?" in *Courting Disaster*, page 16, tells the story of the schooner *Fanny W. Freedom*. In July 1921, it ran over a fishing craft from Flatrock, causing the death of Thomas Hickey of Flatrock. The three occupants of *Fanny Freedom* were brought before the courts sometime after.

Oddly, the court absolved Captain Wallace Batstone, saying he was not to blame, although in marine law and lore he was ultimately responsible for the ship and the conduct and actions of his crew. The man at the wheel, John Rideout, was found blameless, although he directed the course of the schooner right into the path of the fishing craft. Then, the only one left—who was on deck at the time as two other crew were asleep below—to try in a court was the young man who was lookout, Stephen Wells.

That initial story in *Courting Disaster* did not report on the actual trial of Wells, hereby presented in this supplement. The trial got under way on October 21, 1921, with Wells accused of manslaughter due to negligence. Justice Kent presided, with F. A. Mews acting for the Crown and W. K. Higgins defending Stephen Wells. Mews stated that there was culpable negligence if a vessel sailing north on a straight line and on a fine clear day could not see the motorboat. Therefore, Wells was standing on trial for manslaughter.

First witness for the Crown was Michael Hickey, brother of the victim, and who was in a second fishing boat located not far from the victim. He described the accident and was cross-examined by Higgins. Another brother, Patrick Hickey, also in the other motorboat, was called, and his evidence was practically the same as his brother's.

Captain Batstone, owner and captain of *Fanny W. Freeman*, testified John Rideout was at the wheel and Stephen Wells was on watch. He was supposed to be on lookout, but was in fact employed and instructed by the captain to be a general man on the schooner, expected to do any kind of work about the deck. Batstone said his vessel was going about eight knots with a fair wind, and that he had been sailing over the same course for twenty-seven years and knew the location of the fishing grounds off Flatrock.

The other two crew, Mate Leslie Batstone and Seaman King, were asleep below at the time, and their testimony was brief.

Stephen Wells, twenty-one years old at the time, was the only witness called for the defence. He told his story in a straightforward manner. He explained all the circumstances leading to the accident and did not depart in the slightest from his original story, despite being under stiff cross-examination. That evening, his position on the schooner was at a low level relative to sea level, although there was little wind and waves were high and choppy. The colour of the fishing craft blended with the waves.

Just before cross-examination, the jury went to James Baird's wharf to view the *Fanny W. Freeman*. There they saw the relative layout of the vessel and where Rideout and Wells would have been positioned at the time of the collision.

Higgins, after an hour in an eloquent and forceful address as he reviewed the case, said there

Principals in the Wrongful Death of a Flatrock Man

Crew of *Fanny W. Freeman*: Captain Wallace Batstone, Mate Leslie Batstone, Seaman King, Seaman John Rideout, Seaman and Lookout Stephen Wells. Most of this crew belonged to Silverdale, Harry's Harbour.

Fishermen from Flatrock: Brothers Michael, Patrick, and Thomas Hickey (victim).

Members of Jury: Ronald Knight, Richard Kenny, James Bowden, Fred Noseworthy, William Oliver, Rupert Morris, Thomas Thistle, Michael Tobin, Donald Willard, George Reid, Michael Healey, and Henry J. Burnell.

was no evidence of negligence on Wells's part. Lawyer Mews addressed the jury, after which Justice Kent explained the various points of law. At 9:00 p.m. on October 22, the jury retired, and forty-five minutes later, they came back with the verdict of not guilty and Wells was released.

As for the schooner *Fanny W. Freeman*, it was lost on August 18, 1926, when it struck the rocks off the Penguin Islands. Captain Wallace Batstone and his crew survived.

Beginning on page 149 of *Courting Disaster* is the story "Law Enforcement and Time in Jail, 1936," which summarizes the loss of four seamen from the Placentia Bay schooner *Ada and Maude*. The actual story was not centred around the untimely deaths, but details the month spent in prison by a man accused of taking rope from the wrecked schooner.

The empty derelict *Ada and Maude* drifted into Lear's Cove, Placentia Bay, in late December 1935. There were rumours the four crewmen had met with foul play: the schooner had been lured into Lear's Cove and the crew murdered. Whispers said the crimes were committed by the Youngs, the only family name associated with Lear's Cove at that time. However, there was never any proof or any investigation by the police or by the families of the missing men.

Sometime after *Courting Disaster* was published, I received communication from Dan Porter, born in Hibbs Cove, Conception Bay. Apparently, about a century prior to the loss of *Ada and Maude*, the cove into which the schooner had drifted did have other occupants in addition to the "Youngs." Lear's Cove was named for and occupied by two Lear brothers from Hibbs Cove. Indeed, the name Lear is a Conception Bay surname and not associated with Placentia Bay, thus the tiny community (now a resettled town) could have been so named after those Lear boys who first lived there.

Family tradition says the two brothers were murdered by the Youngs. At some point during a summer fishery, dispute arose regarding the Lears' fishing activities in the cove or the wrecking of their vessel, which the Youngs had proceeded to salvage.

Stories handed down also say the two, likely named William and Henry, were found on the beach—one was dead, and the other remained conscious and lucid long enough to tell of foul play before he, too, died.

Thus, Lear's Cove to this day is shrouded in mystery, mayhem, and most likely murder, not once, but twice.

Since the publication of "Isaac Mercer and the Mummers" in *Courting Disaster*, page 166, the Newfoundland and Labrador newspaper the *Telegram* carried an article about Mercer and the Mummers. The *Telegram*'s December 6, 2012, issue says: **MURDERED BY MUMMERS: New facts uncovered in the unsolved case of a man killed by Christmas visitors in 1860.**

While a recent researcher didn't find out who killed Mercer, certain new facts about the curious death were discovered—for example, the coroner's report of Mercer's autopsy and witness statements. On the subject of police interviews regarding Mercer's death, one person said regarding a visit by mummers (*Telegram*, December 6, 2012):

> I opened the door an inch or two, and one fellow who was dressed up asked me to let the mummers in. . . . I said what did you let this fellow in for; with that they pushed open the door and five of them rushed in, they caught hold of Josiah Calpin and poked [him] with a stick, very much like pickets.

Another testament says: "I carried my knife for my own protection in case I should be attacked by jannies."

The article indicates some people were afraid of mummers, or jannies, as they were called in some localities, and armed themselves. Oddly, the research gives the date when mummering in Newfoundland was banned—two years after Mercer's death—but not the exact date when the legislative ban was repealed, except to say it was 100 years later.

It is known mummering was still alive and well by December 1907. During that Christmas season, a group of mummers went visiting a household in Adam's Cove, Conception Bay. Late at night, when they approached a house, the woman who answered the door was so frightened she fainted, and, after coming to, became hysterical. Her husband became alarmed at her condition and, without a hat for the cold winter's night, travelled to Western Bay for the doctor.

The story "It Was A Graveyard Clash," page 282, relates a verbal dispute between two clergymen who had different ideas about who should be buried in a certain graveyard in Hart's Cove, Notre Dame Bay. Today, Hart's Cove is part of the town of Durrell on Twillingate Island.

The problem between the men of the cloth was resolved in court.

However, after the publication of *Courting Disaster*, the author happened to visit Twillingate Island and went to Hart's Cove. There is a beautiful large sign in front of the Hart's Cove "Undenominational" cemetery that lists all those buried within the enclosure. It is the only cemetery—the only one this author has seen—that identifies on an informative and inspiring signboard those interred within the consecrated ground.

Signboard for the Hart's Cove cemetery. Author photo.

One of the greatest thefts of jewellery in Newfoundland's nineteenth century occurred in St. John's in 1845. Commentators at the time said, "It was a great haul of valuables. Lucrative."

Some person or persons broke into Snooks Jewelry Store on Water Street and stole watches and jewels valued at £500. The brief story, found on page 263 of *Courting Disaster*, says no one was ever arrested for the theft. The story makes no mention if the valuables ever showed up in pawnshops or if they were hidden somewhere.

However, while I was looking for other information in archival newspapers, I found this article in the St. John's paper the *Chronicle* of September 10, 1867:

> **JEWELRY FOUND:** About the year 1844 [sic], the shop of Mr. Robert Snooks was burglarized and robbed of a number of watches, rings and etc. Twenty-two years later some boys who were trouting at

> Beaver Pond on the South Side Hill near Blackhead Road stumbled upon a cache. They had found a variety of jewellery among which was 22 silver watches.

Yet, as of that date, twenty-two years later, the perpetrators of the crime were not identified. As far as it being "a lucrative haul of jewellery," that was debatable, since a group of boys found the stolen loot and returned it to authorities.

APPENDIX A

Other Wreckers Fined in the "*Bessie Williams* Case"

Sidney Bixby, $5
Jonathan Blundon, $25
Thomas Blundon, $25
Charles Boone, $8
Kenneth Boone, $3.75
W. Budden, $5
Art Burden, $2
Elijah Carnell, $1
Richard Carnell, $50
Alex Coish, $5
Ambrose Coish, $5
Samuel Coish, $5
Thomas Coish, $5
Moses Collins, $5
Richard Collins, $3
Walter Collins, $5
Fred Cullin, $8
Theophelus Dawe, $5
George Day, $5
Jonathan Frampton, $20
Samuel Gale, $34
Benjamin Hodnott, $2
Percy Hodnott, $5
Samuel Hodnott, $10

Moses Holmes, $2
Nathaniel Howell, $5
George Hynes, $7
Richard Hynes, $20
Ernest Kendon, $5
Daniel Kendon, $5
George Nicco (Nichol?), $12
John Nicco, $12
Ernest Penny, $1
Garland Penny, $20
George Penny, $8
J. Penny, $1
Jordan Penny, $12
Mark Penny, $7
Noah Penny, $1
Samson Penny, $5
Walter Penny, $20
George Perry, $20
W. Perry, $20
Arch Power, $5
Elijah Power, $5
Lemuel Power, $10
Charles Sheppard, $8
Eli Sheppard, $8
George Vincent, $5
Jonathan Vincent, $2

APPENDIX B

Missing Newfoundland Vessels
After the September 13–15, 1900, Hurricane

Vessel	Number of Crew	Home Port
Amelia Corkum	6	Harbour Grace-Carbonear
**Angler*	6?	Owned by Grieve, fished off Cape Pine
Barbara Heck	9	Burin and area
Fiona	14?	Saint Pierre (owned by Frecker's NL business)
Goodwill	5	Musgrave Harbour
Lillydale	8-10?	Catalina and area
Lizzie	8	Burgeo
Omega	10	St. Bernard's, Fox Harbour, Fortune Bay
P. K. Jacobs	10	St. Lawrence
Rosebud	6	???
William Burton	7	Bay de L'Eau, Placentia Bay
	Total 90 approx.	

* The newspaper the *New York Times* of October 17, 1900, wrote of four missing Newfoundland ships, carrying a total of thirty-eight men: the

Fiona, with its entire crew; *Rosebud*; *Angler*; and *Amelia* (*Amelia Corkum*, possibly the same ship, was also reported in Newfoundland papers). The *Times* also stated the schooner *Huntress* was wrecked on the Labrador shore and five of its crew drowned.

Author's Additional Note: Although my hometown, Grand Bank, had an extensive fishing fleet at this time, it had no ship losses or deaths resulting from the gale. Approximately twenty schooners were at sea, plus others were coasting or moving fish and supplies.

However, a report on the hurricane from Grand Bank says a one-year-old building, the "Rope Walk," where rope was manufactured, was blown down. It was located on what is now Marine Drive, Grand Bank.

As well, an ironic tale of the gale: the schooner *William Henry Jane,* owned by George Pope of Stone's Cove, rode out the gale. One month later, on October 17, 1900, James Elms and his son, Albert, landed George Pope at Barasway de Plate, a few miles from Stone's Cove, to cut firewood. The Elmses loaded wood on *William Henry Jane* to take to Stone's Cove, but a freak cut of wind capsized the schooner. The schooner was seen floating bottom-up, but the two men were never found again. Albert, aged twenty-six, was married to Rosie Riggs; his father, James, fifty-two, was survived by his wife, Charlotte.

The *Evening Telegram* of November 14, 1900, says, "To make matters worse, both of the men were out in the gale of September 15, and had a narrow escape and to say, after all, they should come home to be drowned alongside their own doors."

APPENDIX C

Defying the Hangman

Perhaps in light of the tales and media attention given to historic hangings in St. John's, the *Evening Telegram* (March 1921) published an article, **DEFYING THE HANGMAN: Amazing Escapes from Death**, saying: "There is no person living today who has actually been hanged, but here are some records of resuscitation after hanging," then gave these illustrations of those who have escaped death despite the noose.

- Back in history to the year 1264, Madame de Balsham was condemned to death for harbouring thieves. She was hanged and left suspended on the gallows from Monday morning until sunrise Thursday. Yet, on being taken down, she revived. Henry III granted her a pardon.

- In 1650, an Oxford servant girl was hanged for the murder of her child. When handed over to the doctors for autopsy, she revived. The doctors asked her about her sensations and feelings during suspension, but she remembered nothing, saying only that her revival was like awakening from a deep sleep.

- A house thief named Smith was hanged at Tyburn in 1705, and a reprieve arrived after he had been suspended for fifteen minutes. When he was taken down, he revived.

- William Dell had a hard fate. He was hanged in London in 1740 and was carried to Surgeons' Hall for autopsy. Before the doctors began, he came to life again. This ought to have won him another chance, but it did not. He was transported (banished), a fate not always preferable.

- At Cork, Ireland, a man was hanged in 1767 for street robbery. On being taken down, he was hurried to a surgery, where an incision was made in his windpipe to allow him to breathe. He recovered so quickly that he went to the theatre the same evening.

- After the banker-turned-forger Fauntleroy was executed in 1824, a rumour circulated that he had escaped death because, some days before hanging, he had a silver tube inserted in his throat. This prevented strangulation, and he was restored to consciousness. However, there is no confirmation of this story.

- A prisoner was taken from Cardiff Prison and placed in the dock (court) in London on a charge of murdering his wife. Until then, he had not heard of her death, but before he could realize his position, he was convicted and sentenced to death.

Then he implored the wardens and governor to tell him the date of his wife's death.

"My good man," said the governor, "you have only a short time to live. Don't worry about such a detail."

Day after day, however, the prisoner asked this question until he got an answer.

"But," he exclaimed, "I was in prison on that date!"

"Then why didn't you say so at your trial?"

"Because I was neither asked nor allowed to say anything."

He was released.

APPENDIX D

Witnesses at Captain Wollard's Trial: For the Murder of John Yetman, July 4, 1903

Helen F. Whitten's crew of nineteen men was typical for an eight-dory banker: Captain Wollard, sixteen dorymen, one cook, and one mate (or second hand, as it was termed in Newfoundland).

Testifying for the Prosecution

First witness: Joseph Walsh, born in Placentia, lives at Gloucester, bully.
Second: Joseph Gosling, belongs to Burin, joined Whitten at Port aux Basques, after being shipwrecked in a Burin vessel; friend of Captain Wollard.
Third: John Penney, belongs to Harbour Main, joins sch. at North Sydney; Yetman's dory mate.
Fourth: John Dominy, permanent address not given; joins sch. at North Sydney.
Fifth: Joseph Hyde, born in Bay Bulls, lives in Gloucester.
Sixth: John Quinn, joins sch. at North Sydney.
Seventh: George Hipson, cook, Nova Scotia.
Eighth: John Brown, belongs to Burin, joins sch. at Port aux Basques.
Ninth: Celestine Power, belongs to English Harbour, Fortune Bay, joins sch. at Louisbourg.
Tenth: John Rippendale, crewman, belongs to Gloucester.
Eleventh: James Buffett, belongs to Rose Blanche, joins at Rose Blanche.

Twelfth: Daniel Rose, joins at Louisbourg, age nineteen, dory mate Patrick Farrell leaves, new mate is Penney.
Thirteenth: John Woundy, belongs to Burin, joins at Port aux Basques.
Fourteenth: Augustus Carew, of Shore's Cove, sends for Const. Greene, watches body while Greene goes to sch.
Fifteenth: Const. Greene, stationed in Cape Broyle, called on the Carews to help him.
Sixteenth: Sergeant Cleary, stationed at Ferryland.
Seventeenth: Superintendent Sullivan, part of magisterial investigation held at Ferryland.
Eighteenth: Thomas Hogan, crew of schooner.
Nineteenth: Joseph Hartson, belongs to Burin, joined sch. at Sydney.
Twentieth: Dr. Freebairn, physician at Ferryland, did post-mortem at Ferryland on July 5.
Twenty-first: Ernest Carew, belongs to Cape Broyle, went to vessel with Const. Greene.
Twenty-second: Louis Williams, belongs to Cape Broyle, on Cape Broyle wharf when crime occurred.
Twenty-third: James Keefe, lives in Cape Broyle, saw body after it was brought to shore.
Twenty-fourth: Edward Brien, belongs to St. John's, was in Cape Broyle with Dr. Rissmuller, drives accused to Ferryland.

Testifying for the Defence

Twenty-fifth: Capt. Wollard, born in Exeter, Eng., fishing out of Gloucester for twenty-seven years, forty-eight, married with sons.
Twenty-sixth: Mr. Wicks, Newfoundland businessman who had known Wollard for fifteen years.
Twenty-seventh: John Power, belongs to Tors Cove, fished with Wollard for two years.
Twenty-eighth: James Byrne, belongs to Brigus South, fished with Wollard for twelve years.
Twenty-ninth: Michael Cashin, business at Cape Broyle, deals with Am. bankers, knew Wollard for ten yrs.

Two crew, including Fred Nooyros, a Russian-Finn, and Paddy Farrell, did not testify.

Other Events

Two men named McLeod who left the schooner previous to the murder.
Two men, Goodwin and Strickland, had drowned on a previous voyage.
Roberts and Jessup had gone astray in a dory but were found and taken to Sydney.
John Yetman, the deceased, and John Penney, had also gone astray in fog, but were found and carried to Bay Bulls.

SOME LEGAL TERMS

Arson: The malicious burning of another's house or property, or, in some statutes, the burning of one's own house or property, to collect insurance.

Barratry: Fraud by a master or crew at the expense of the owners of the ship or its cargo for the purpose of collecting ship insurance monies.

Bootleg: To make, transport, or sell something, especially liquor, illegally or without registration or payment of taxes.

Casting Away: Setting a ship adrift, thereby causing it to be wrecked.

Common Law: The system of law originating in England, as distinct from the civil or Roman law and the canon or ecclesiastical (Biblical) law.

Court (or Board) of Marine Enquiry: Tribunals established in common law to investigate matters relating to shipwrecks, ship disappearances or collisions, casualties affecting ships, or into charges of incompetency or misconduct on the part of the masters, mates, or engineers of ships.

Filibustering: Acting as an irregular military adventurer, especially one engaging in an unauthorized military expedition into a foreign country to foment or support a revolution.

Fraud: Deceit, trickery, sharp practice, or breach of confidence, perpetrated for profit or to gain some unfair or dishonest advantage.

Graft: The acquisition of money, gain, or advantage by dishonest, unfair, or illegal means, especially through the abuse of one's position or influence in politics, business, etc.

Grand Jury: A jury, in common law, of twelve to twenty-three persons, designated to inquire into alleged violations of the law in order to ascertain whether the evidence is sufficient to warrant trial.

Grand Larceny: Larceny in which the value of the goods taken is above a certain legally specified amount.

Homicide: The killing of one human being by another. Not all homicide is unlawful; killing in self-defence, for example, is not a crime.

Larceny: The unlawful taking and removing of another's personal property with the intent of permanently depriving the owner; theft.

Libel: Defamation by written or printed words, pictures, or in any form other than by spoken words or gestures.

Manslaughter: The unlawful killing of a human being without malice aforethought.

Murder: The unlawful killing of another human being under conditions specifically covered in law. **First-degree Murder** is committed with malice aforethought, characterized by deliberation or premeditation or occurring during the commission of another serious crime, such as robbery or arson. **Second-degree Murder** is murder by intent but without deliberation or premeditation.

Mutiny: Revolt or rebellion against constituted authority, especially by sailors against their officers.

Negligence: Failure to exercise the degree of care considered reasonable under the circumstances, resulting in an unintended injury to another party.

Petit (or Petty) Larceny: Larceny of property having a value less than some amount (the amount varies by locale).

Petty Jury: In a civil or criminal proceeding, a jury, usually of twelve persons, empanelled to determine the facts and to render a verdict pursuant to the court's instructions on the law.

Piracy: Practice of a pirate; robbery or illegal violence at sea.

Plunder: To rob of goods or valuables by open force, as in war, hostile raids.

Privateering: Actions of a ship privately owned and crewed but authorized by a government during wartime to attack and capture enemy vessels.

Public Mischief: Direct misguided attempts at troublemaking for the sole purpose of destruction.

Rum-runner: A person or ship engaged in smuggling liquor.

Slander: Defamation by oral utterance rather than by writing, pictures, etc.

Smuggle: To import or export goods secretly, in violation of the law, especially without payment of legal duty.

Swindle: To put forward plausible schemes or use unscrupulous trickery to defraud others; cheat.

Trespass: A wrongful entry upon the lands of another; or an unlawful act causing injury to the person, property, or rights of another, committed with force or violence, actual or implied.

Wrecker (or Wracker): A person who plunders shipwrecks.

AUTHOR'S POSTSCRIPT

At book signings, readings, and craft shows, I'm often asked, "What is the step, or process, or means, that *you* take when you want to write a book—or have one partly done—whereby you contact or get a publisher to take what you are offering, or read or look at what you are doing to see if it is fit for publishing?"

My background as thirty years an educator forced my inner conscience to try to help others or to answer the question above. I felt, rightly or wrongly, I could do this by example, using this book and consulting the notes in my log. I have always kept a daily journal or log of work, e.g. writing. As well, I usually keep a record of the contacts and communications made as my book moves through the publishing process. I looked back at what evolved for this book from the time of concept to the day of acceptance (not publication).

To begin, in the fall of 2011, I had an idea for another book of crime and began to research, write, edit, revise, and shape it into something I thought the general Newfoundland and Labrador populace might like to read. I felt the format of short stories would be the way to go. I might add at this point, if an idea enters into a writer's head, something has to happen to shake it loose—it sort of commands you to write it down.

Actual words from a keyboard to a monitor to a storage unit began on December 29, 2011, when I scoured through my file of crime stories I had gathered from research in archival sources. The writing of those progressed sporadically, or piece by piece, until March 2012, when I had about fifteen stories written. Summer, travel, and holidays bumped me down to the fall, when I wrote two or three more.

At that point, I decided on a working, or tentative, title: *Mischief, Mayhem and Murder in Newfoundland*. Since I was running short of research or potential tales, in the interim, when I might gather more material, I decided to contact a publishing company to see if they were interested. Flanker Press, publisher of my first crime book, was an obvious and first choice.

In my daily log of work done is the following notation:

October 14-16 Formatted page numbering and story headings in anticipation for presentation of M/S (partial) to Flanker Press for analysis. At this point of presenting to Flanker, it runs about 120 pages, double-spaced.

With that much done, I considered the work to be at a stage where it could be evaluated. It was time to slow down to see what a publisher thought of my idea. I felt any initial approach should be brief and in point form, for publishers don't need a long, wordy letter of inquiry. The exact letter, accompanied by a hard copy of the partial manuscript, which I sent to Flanker Press, was:

October 28, 2012

To: Jerry Cranford, Flanker Press

Enclosed is partial M/S of crime and mischief in Newfoundland and Labrador and tentatively entitled *Mischief, Mayhem and Murder in Newfoundland*.

- It is about 1/3 to 1/2 done and I'm working on other stories;

- I don't anticipate publication until 2014;

- I submit, before proceeding further, as I would wish to know if this type of work i.e. this M/S is going in the right direction or if it is something Flanker Press is interested in;

- It is not being submitted to any other publisher and is exclusively written for Flanker Press, based on the relative success of *Courting Disaster*, 2009.

A reply at your earliest convenience would be appreciated.

Respectfully submitted, Robert C. Parsons

Within a month, Flanker Press, via Jerry Cranford, the production manager, replied with an update—not a formal contract of publication. That would come later. The reply said, in essence, "Your new manuscript has been read and it is fine. Would you be open to a different title suggestion?"

With that impetus from a publisher, I continued to research and write in November and December 2012, adding four or five new stories. Also, at this point, armed with added confidence, I formatted the chapter headings, arranged the table of contents, added bits and pieces of the foreword, began my appendices and the index, continued editing and revising, and so on.

The project began, at this point with approximately 40,000 words, to look more like a book, now with a slightly revised working title: *Mischief, Mystery and Murder in Outport Newfoundland*. The work, the fully completed manuscript with fifty-nine stories, nearly 67,000 words, went to mill on April 1, 2013, for further revising, editing, and preparation for eventual publication.

On May 14, I received the final page proofs. When these were again checked and some corrections made, the "work" was sent to the printers for a June 2015 publication. The title was changed to *Murder on the Rock: True Crime in Newfoundland and Labrador*.

Robert C. Parsons has been called one of the most popular and prolific writers on the subject of Atlantic Canada's ships and ship disasters. He is the author of more than twenty-five non-fiction books. His work has also appeared in a number of newspapers and magazines such as *Downhome*, the *Telegram*, the *Newfoundland Quarterly*, and *Newfoundland Lifestyles*.

In May 2009, Robert's non-fiction prose was judged an award winner in the annual Arts and Letters Competition.

In December that same year, he was presented with the Polaris Award from the Canadian Coast Guard Alumni Association, Newfoundland and Labrador division, in recognition of his outstanding contribution to the preservation and public awareness of the marine heritage and history in the province of Newfoundland and Labrador. This award was only given out two previous times in the years of the Alumni Association's existence.

Robert's book *Courting Disaster: True Crime and Mischief on Land and Sea* was a *Globe and Mail* bestseller.

A former fish plant worker and educator and a present-day researcher and devotee of all items marine-related, Robert lives in Grand Bank, Newfoundland.

INDEX